Formatting Toolbar

Y0-DDP-685

Style Box   Font Name Box   Font Size Box

AutoFormat

Currency Style

Light Shading

Justify Align

Decrease Decimal

Strikeout

Increase Decimal

Underline

Comma Style

Italic

Percent Style

Bold

Macro Toolbar

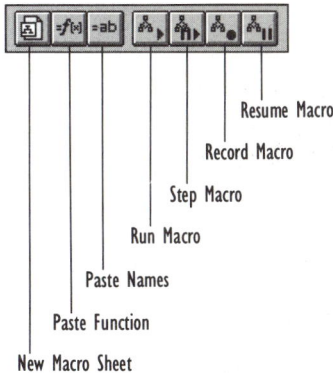

Resume Macro

Record Macro

Step Macro

Run Macro

Paste Names

Paste Function

New Macro Sheet

Books that Work Just Like Your Mac

As a Macintosh user, you enjoy unique advantages. You enjoy a dynamic user environment. You enjoy the successful integration of graphics, sound, and text. Above all, you enjoy a computer that's fun and easy to use.

When your computer gives you all this, why accept less in your computer books?

At SYBEX, we don't believe you should. That's why we've committed ourselves to publishing the highest quality computer books for Macintosh users. Externally, our books emulate the Mac "look and feel," with powerful, appealing illustrations and easy-to-read pages. Internally, our books stress "why" over "how," so you'll learn concepts, not sequences of steps. Philosophically, our books are designed to help you get work done, not to teach you about computers.

In short, our books are fun and easy to use—just like the Mac. We hope you find them just as enjoyable.

For a complete catalog of our publications:

SYBEX Inc.
2021 Challenger Drive, Alameda, CA 94501
Tel: (510) 523-8233/(800) 227-2346 Telex: 336311
Fax: (510) 523-2373

SYBEX is committed to using natural resources wisely to preserve and improve our environment. As a leader in the computer book publishing industry, we are aware that over 40% of America's solid waste is paper. This is why we have been printing the text of books like this one on recycled paper since 1982.

This year our use of recycled paper will result in the saving of more than 15,300 trees. We will lower air pollution effluents by 54,000 pounds, save 6,300,000 gallons of water, and reduce landfill by 2,700 cubic yards.

In choosing a SYBEX book you are not only making a choice for the best in skills and information, you are also choosing to enhance the quality of life for all of us.

EXCEL 4 FOR THE MAC
—— at Your Fingertips

EXCEL 4 FOR THE MAC®
—— at Your Fingertips

DOUGLAS HERGERT

SYBEX®

San Francisco

Paris

Düsseldorf

Soest

Acquisitions Editor: David Clark
Developmental Editor: Kenyon Brown
Copy Editor: Peter Weverka
Project Editor: Brenda Kienan
Technical Editor: Celia Stevenson
Word Processors: Ann Dunn, Scott Campbell
Book Design and Chapter Art: Claudia Smelser
Screen Graphics: John Corrigan
Typesetter: Dina F Quan
Proofreader: Rhonda Holmes
Indexer: Nancy Guenther
Cover Designer: Ingalls + Associates
Cover Illustrator: Hank Osuna

Library of Congress Card Number: 92-82603
ISBN: 0-7821-1157-2

Manufactured in the United States of America
10 9 8 7 6 5 4 3 2 1

To Mom, with love

ACKNOWLEDGMENTS

I want to thank Dianne King, Kenyon Brown, Peter Weverka, Celia Stevenson, and Brenda Kienan for their work on this book. Also sincere thanks to Claudette Moore.

TABLE OF CONTENTS

INTRODUCTION

Microsoft Excel is the popular Macintosh spreadsheet program that provides worksheets, charts, database capabilities, and macro programming all in one software environment. In Version 4, Excel takes many steps forward in both the simplicity of its operations and the sophistication of its features. On the one hand, Microsoft has added a variety of tools designed to make your work more efficient, including toolbars, shortcut menus, the ChartWizard, and special worksheet operations such as drag-and-drop, AutoFill, Auto-Format, and AutoSum. On the other hand, you will find many new high-end features that extend Excel's power and flexibility for calculating, organizing, and analyzing data.

Excel 4 for the Mac at Your Fingertips gives you succinct, accessible instructions for all the important tasks that you'll want to accomplish in Excel. In over a hundred alphabetically arranged entries, you'll find the information you need to complete your work with accuracy and understanding. The entries provide step-by-step procedures, shortcuts, examples, notes on usage, and cross references to related tasks. In addition, you'll find five *SnapGuides*—short tutorials designed to introduce you to Excel's major components. The goal is to help you work more efficiently and effectively with worksheets, charts, databases, and macros.

Add-In Macros

Creating and installing an add-in macro sheet is a convenient way to incorporate macros into the Excel environment. Using the File ➤ Save As command, you can save any macro sheet in the special add-in file format. When you subsequently open an add-in macro sheet, the sheet itself remains hidden but all the macros on the sheet are available for use. If you want Excel to open an add-in macro sheet automatically at the beginning of each session, you can use the Options ➤ Add-ins command to add the sheet's name to the add-in macro startup list.

To Create an Add-In Macro Sheet

1. Choose File ➤ New, select Macro Sheet, and click OK to open a new macro sheet. Then enter or record any number of macros on the new sheet. Alternatively, choose the File ➤ Open command and open a macro sheet you have previously created.

2. Choose File ➤ Save As. Type a name for the macro sheet into the File Name box, and select the folder where you want to save the file.

3. Click the Options button. In the Save Options dialog box, pull down the File Format list and select the Add-In option. Click OK.

4. Click Save. Excel saves your macro sheet in the add-in format.

5. Choose File ➤ Close or press ⌘-W to close the macro sheet.

NOTES

You can save an add-in macro sheet in Excel's startup folder, named Excel Startup Folder (4). As a result, the add-in macro sheet is automatically opened at the beginning of each session with

Excel, and all of the sheet's macros are available for use. (This is an alternative to using the Options ➤ Add-ins command to install an add-in macro, a procedure described later in this entry.) In System 7, the startup folder is in the Preferences Folder, which is in turn located in the System Folder. In earlier system versions, you'll find the startup folder in the System Folder.

To Open an Add-In Macro
for Use in the Current Session

Choose File ➤ Open and select the name of the add-in macro that you want to open. Then click OK. Although the add-in macro sheet is not displayed as an open document, all of its command and function macros are now available for you to use.

SHORTCUTS

Click the Open File tool on the Standard toolbar, or press ⌘-O to view the Open dialog box.

NOTES

The command macros of an open add-in sheet are not included in the list presented by the Macro ➤ Run command, but you can run an add-in macro by pressing its shortcut key. In contrast, function macros in an .UL ON open add-in macro sheet *are* listed in the Formula ➤ Paste Function dialog box when a worksheet is active. A call to an add-in function macro has the same format as a call to any of Excel's built-in functions; the name of the source macro sheet is not required before the call.

You can also call an open add-in macro from within another macro. Again, you do not need to include the name of the add-in macro sheet in the call statement. (When a macro sheet is active, the Formula ➤ Paste Function command lists the names of command and function macros on all open add-in macro sheets.)

Several of Excel's most important analysis tools—including the Solver, the Scenario Manager, and the Analysis ToolPak—are themselves stored and implemented as add-in macros. You run these macros by choosing the corresponding menu commands—for example Formula ➤ Solver and Formula ➤ Scenario Manager—or by entering a function that is stored on one of these add-in macro sheets.

Excel opens an add-in file as a hidden macro sheet that you cannot unhide. However, you can open and display an add-in file as a regular macro sheet when you want to edit the file. See the next section of this entry for details.

To Open an Add-In Macro as a Regular Macro Sheet

1. Choose File ➤ Open. Select the macro sheet that you want to open and edit.

2. Hold down the Shift key and click the Open button. (If the macro sheet is currently open as a hidden add-in macro sheet, Excel asks you if you want to revert to the saved file. Click OK.)

3. If Excel does not display the macro sheet, choose the Window ➤ Unhide command. Select the name of the macro sheet from the Unhide list and click OK. You can now edit the macro sheet and then save the file back to disk.

To Install Add-In Macros in the Add-In Startup List

1. Choose the Options ➤ Add-ins command. When the Add-In Manager dialog box appears on the screen, you'll see the Add-Ins Installed box with the current startup list—that is, the list of add-in macros that are automatically available at the beginning of each session with Excel.

2. Click the Add button. In the resulting dialog box, select the name of an add-in macro and click Open. When the

Add-In Manager dialog box reappears, you'll see the name of the selected macro file in the Add-Ins Installed list.

3. Optionally, repeat step 2 to install other add-in macro sheets.

4. Click the Close button to complete the operation. All the macros on the newly installed add-in sheets are now available for use in this and subsequent sessions with Excel.

NOTES

Another way to build a library of permanently available macros is to save new macros in Excel's global macro sheet, Global Macros. See the MACRO RECORDING entry for details.

To Remove an Add-In Macro from the Add-In Startup List

1. Choose Options ➤ Add-ins. The Add-In Manager dialog box appears on the screen.

2. From the Add-Ins Installed list, select the name of the add-in macro sheet that you want to remove.

3. Click the Remove button. Excel asks you to confirm that you want to remove this add-in from the startup list. Click OK.

4. When the Add-In Manager dialog box reappears, notice that the file is no longer in the Add-Ins Installed list. Click the Close button.

NOTES

This operation removes the add-in macro from the startup list but does not delete the add-in file from disk. You can choose File ➤ Open to reopen the add-in macro sheet for use in the current Excel session.

SEE ALSO

Analysis Tools, Crosstab ReportWizard, Customizing Excel, Engineering Functions, Folders, Hiding, Macros SnapGuide, Macro Library, Macro Recording, Opening Files, Reports, Scenarios, Solver, Statistical Functions.

Alignment

Excel offers a variety of horizontal and vertical alignments and orientations for displaying text and numeric entries in a cell or range. You can also change the alignment and orientation of the text displayed in a text box, the label on a button, or attached text in a chart.

To Change the Alignment of Entries in a Cell or Range

1. Select the cell or range of cells that you want to realign.

2. Choose the Format ➤ Alignment command. The Alignment dialog box appears on the screen.

3. In the Horizontal box, select the Left, Center, or Right option to change the alignment of text and numeric entries within the current column-width settings.

4. Optionally, choose Top, Center, or Bottom in the Vertical box to adjust the placement of entries within the current row height.

5. Click OK.

SHORTCUTS

Select a cell or range and click one of the three alignment tools in the Standard toolbar—Left Align, Center Align, or Right Align. Alternatively, pull down the shortcut menu for the current cell or range selection (point to the selection and press ⌘-Option while you click the mouse button) and choose the Alignment command.

NOTES

The General option in the Horizontal box represents the default alignment settings: left-alignment for text entries, right-alignment for numeric entries, and centering for logical and error values.

When you change column widths or row heights, Excel adjusts the placement of entries according to the current alignment settings. For example, if you increase the column width for a range of centered entries, Excel centers the entries within the new width.

To Rotate Entries within Cells

1. Select the cell or range of cells that you want to rotate.

2. Choose Format ➤ Alignment.

3. Select one of the samples displayed in the Orientation box—for vertically arranged text, text rotated to read from bottom to top, or text rotated to read from top to bottom.

4. Click OK.

NOTES

Excel automatically adjusts the row height to accommodate the length of a rotated entry. If you later restore the default horizontal orientation, you may also want to restore the appropriate row height by double-clicking the line below the corresponding row heading.

To Justify a Long Text Entry within its Cell

1. Select the cell containing the long text entry that you want to justify.

2. Choose Format ➤ Alignment and select the Justify option in the Horizontal box. Then click OK. In response, Excel wraps the text within the cell, increasing the row height as necessary. To the extent possible, the text is aligned along the left and right sides of the cell.

3. Optionally, adjust the column width and row height at the cell's location to achieve the justified text arrangement that you want.

SHORTCUTS

Select the cell containing the long text entry, and click the Justify Align Tool on the Formatting toolbar.

To Realign Long Text Entries in a Column of Cells

1. Select a range consisting of a column of long text entries and the adjacent columns (to the right) where you want to realign the text.

2. Choose Format ➤ Justify. In response, Excel redistributes the text within the cells in the first column of the range selection to make the lines roughly the same length.

EXAMPLE

In this worksheet, the cells in A5:A12 contain long text entries:

	A	B	C	D	E	F
1	Memo					
2	*To: Staff*					
3	*From: MH*					
4						
5	Tomorrow we will host five visiting					
6	executives from the central office. Please get ready					
7	to show and explain your best recent work					
8	to visitors who stop by your work area.					
9	I will try to give you advance					
10	notice---at least 15 minutes---before we stop by,					
11	but the day is unscheduled, so be prepared.					
12	We'll all be going to lunch at 12:30.					
13						

To realign these entries, select the range A5:C12 and choose For-mat ➤ Justify. Here is the result:

	A	B	C	D	E	F
1	Memo					
2	*To: Staff*					
3	*From: MH*					
4						
5	Tomorrow we will host five visiting executives					
6	from the central office. Please get ready to					
7	show and explain your best recent work to					
8	visitors who stop by your work area. I will try to					
9	give you advance notice---at least 15					
10	minutes---before we stop by, but the day is					
11	unscheduled, so be prepared. We'll all be going					
12	to lunch at 12:30.					
13						

NOTES

If the range you select is not large enough for the realignment of text entries, Excel displays the message "Text will extend below range" and then increases the range by the number of rows neces-sary to realign the lines of text.

To Change the Text Alignment of a Text Box or a Button

1. If a macro is assigned to the text box or button, select the object by holding down the Control key while you click it with the mouse. If no macro is assigned, simply click the object (or click the border of the object in the case of a text box) to select it.

2. Choose Format ➤ Text. This command is available when a text box or button is selected.

3. On the resulting Text dialog box, select options for the horizontal and vertical text alignment and orientation, and then click OK.

SHORTCUTS

Pull down the graphic object's shortcut menu (point to the object and press ⌘-Option while you click the mouse button) and choose the Text command.

To Change the Alignment of Attached Text in a Chart

In a chart window, select the attached text that you want to realign, and choose Format ➤ Text. Select options for alignment and orientation from the Text dialog box and click OK.

SHORTCUTS

Pull down the shortcut menu for the attached text and choose the Text command.

NOTES

In an Excel chart you can change the alignment and orientation of titles as well as text that appears along axes.

SEE ALSO

Attached Text, Centering across Columns, Charting SnapGuide, Column Widths, Filling Ranges, Formatting Worksheet Data, Graphic Objects, Row Height, Text Box, Toolbars, Wrapping Text.

Analysis Tools

The Analysis ToolPak is a collection of add-in macros stored in the folder Macro Library:Analysis Tools within the folder where Excel itself is installed. Given an input range of relevant worksheet data, the macros in this collection are designed to perform specific statistical and engineering analyses.

To Run a Macro from the Analysis ToolPak

1. Create or open a worksheet containing the data that you want to analyze, and select the range of data. This becomes the input range for the upcoming analysis.

2. Choose Options ➤ Analysis Tools. The Analysis Tools dialog box appears on the screen.

3. Select the analysis that you want to perform and click OK. The dialog box for the corresponding analysis tool appears on the screen, and a reference to the selected range of data appears in the Input Range text box.

4. In the Output Range text box, enter a reference to the location where you want Excel to display the results of the analysis. (You can enter a reference to a single cell to specify the upper-left corner of the output range.)

Respond to other options that appear in the dialog box. Click Help for more information about a particular analysis tool.

5. Click OK to perform the analysis. The results appear in the output range you have indicated.

Analysis Tools	
Anova: Single-Factor	OK
Anova: Two-Factor With Replication	
Anova: Two-Factor Without Replication	Cancel
Correlation	
Covariance	Help
Descriptive Statistics	
Exponential Smoothing	
F-Test: Two-Sample for Variances	

NOTES

The following tools are available in the Analysis ToolPak:

▲ Anova: Single-Factor produces an analysis of variance for an input range that contains two or more data samples.

▲ Anova: Two-Factor with Replication produces an analysis of variance for two or more groups of samples.

▲ Anova: Two-Factor without Replication produces an analysis of variance for two or more data samples.

▲ Correlation calculates the statistical relationship between two sets of data.

▲ Covariance calculates the statistical relationship between two sets of data.

▲ Descriptive Statistics supplies a table of statistical measurements, including mean, standard deviation, minimum, maximum, and so on.

▲ Exponential Smoothing implements a mathematical forecasting technique.

▲ F-Test: Two-Sample for Variances produces a comparison of variances, given an input range containing two columns or rows of data.

▲ Fourier Analysis calculates the coefficients of a periodic function.

▲ Histogram calculates frequency distributions, given an input range of numeric data and a range of bins in which to perform the distribution.

▲ Moving Average supplies a forecasting tool.

▲ Random Number Generation produces an output range of random numbers; optionally, the numbers can match a particular distribution scheme that you specify in this tool's dialog box.

▲ Rank and Percentile determines the ordinal and percentile rank of each value in an input range, in relation to the other values in the range.

▲ Regression performs a linear regression analysis, calculating the best straight-line fit through a data sample.

▲ Sampling produces a representative data sample from a larger population in the input range.

▲ t-Test calculates the correlations between paired sets of measurements in an input range. (Three variations of this test are available.)

▲ z-Test compares two sets of measurements in the input range.

EXAMPLE

The following worksheet shows an example of the Descriptive Statistics tool. The input range is B1:B13, and the output range is D1:E15.

	A	B	C	D	E
1	Patient	Age at Start of Symptoms		Age at Start of Symptoms	
2	Alcott	76			
3	Baker	15		Mean	55.5
4	Denton	62		Standard Error	6.995128
5	Eller	83		Median	58
6	Ferber	34		Mode	81
7	Hines	81		Standard Deviation	24.23183
8	Jones	54		Variance	587.1818
9	Kim	35		Kurtosis	-1.28629
10	Minton	51		Skewness	-0.42423
11	Nelson	72		Range	68
12	Quincy	81		Minimum	15
13	Smith	22		Maximum	83
14				Sum	666
15				Count	12

SEE ALSO

Add-In Macros, Crosstab ReportWizard, Data Tables, Engineering Functions, Iteration, Scenarios, Solver, Statistical Functions.

Arithmetic Operations

Along with the four most familiar arithmetic operations—addition, subtraction, multiplication, and division—Excel supports exponentiation and percentage operations in arithmetic formulas.

To Write an Arithmetic Formula

Use any combination of the following operands:

+ addition

− subtraction

* multiplication

/ division

% percentage

^ exponentiation

NOTES

Excel offers tools for inserting any of the six arithmetic operators into a formula. You can view these tools by choosing Options ➤ toolbars, clicking the Customize button, and then selecting the Formula category in the resulting dialog box. These tools are not initially part of a toolbar, but you can add them to a toolbar by dragging them from the Customize dialog box. See TOOLBARS for more information.

In a formula that contains more than one arithmetic operand, Excel performs operations in this order: percentage, exponentiation, multiplication and division (left to right), addition and subtraction (left to right). Use parentheses in a formula to override this default order of operations.

EXAMPLE

In the following formula, Income, Expenses, and Taxrate are names defined for three cells on the current worksheet:

=(Income–Expenses)*Taxrate%

To evaluate this formula, Excel performs the percentage operation first (dividing the value of Taxrate by 100), then the subtraction (enclosed in parentheses), and finally the multiplication.

SEE ALSO

Formula Bar, Formulas SnapGuide, Functions SnapGuide, Logical Functions, Text Operations, Toolbars.

*A*rray Formulas

An array formula can be an efficient and economical way to perform an operation involving multiple rows and columns of data, or to enter the same formula into multiple cells in a range. In addition, several of Excel's built-in functions take arrays as arguments or return array results.

To Enter an Array Formula

1. Select the cell or cells where you want the formula to appear.

2. Enter the elements of the formula. To include a range as an operand in the formula, point to the range with the mouse or enter the range reference directly from the keyboard.

3. Press ⌘-Enter (or Control-Shift-Enter) to complete the formula. In response, Excel encloses the array formula in braces, { and }.

EXAMPLE

In the following worksheet example, the range B5:E5 contains an array formula to calculate quarterly tax estimates:

	A	B	C	D	E
1		Q1	Q2	Q3	Q4
2	Income	$75,000	$62,000	$87,000	$125,000
3	Expenses	$9,500	$5,300	$8,200	$11,500
4	Tax Rate	28	28	28	28
5	Tax Due	$18,340	$15,876	$22,064	$31,780

To create the array formula, select the range B5:E5 and then enter the following in the formula bar:

    =(B2:E2–B3:E3)*B4:E4%

When you press ⌘-Enter, Excel enters the array formula into each cell in the range B5:E5:

    {=(B2:E2–B3:E3)*B4:E4%}

As you can see, this formula produces a different quarterly tax estimate in each cell of the array range.

In this second example, an array formula in cell B6 calculates the total tax estimate for the year:

	A	B	C	D	E
1		Q1	Q2	Q3	Q4
2	Income	$75,000	$62,000	$87,000	$125,000
3	Expenses	$9,500	$5,300	$8,200	$11,500
4					
5	Tax Rate	28			
6	Total Tax	$88,060			

The array formula in cell B6 is:

$$\{=SUM((B2:E2-B3:E3)*B5\%)\}$$

As you can see, this single array formula performs two intermediate calculations on each column of quarterly data in order to compute the total year's tax amount. First it subtracts each quarter's expense amount from the income to find the net after-expense income, and then it multiplies the result by the estimated quarterly tax. The SUM function then adds these quarterly tax amounts together to produce the year's total.

NOTES

You can include an array constant as an operand in an array formula. An array constant is a sequence of numeric or text values enclosed in braces. Within the braces, the sequence of constant values requires specific punctuation: commas to separate columns of data, and semicolons to separate rows. For example, in the following array formula, each value in the five-column by three-row range A1:E3 is multiplied by the corresponding value in a five-by-three array constant:

$$\{=A1:E3*\{1,2,3,4,5;2,2,2,2,2;9,8,7,6,5\}\}$$

The result is an array consisting of five columns and three rows, as
you can see in the range A5:E7 of the following worksheet:

	A	B	C	D	E
1	1	1	1	1	1
2	1	1	1	1	1
3	1	1	1	1	1
4					
5	1	2	3	4	5
6	2	2	2	2	2
7	9	8	7	6	5

To Select the Range of an Array Formula

1. Select any cell within the range where the array formula is
entered.

2. Choose Formula ➤ Select Special.

3. In the Select Special dialog box, click the Current Array
option, and then click OK.

SHORTCUTS

Select any cell within the array range, and press Control-/.

To Edit an Array Formula

1. Select the entire array range or any cell within the range.

2. Activate the formula bar by clicking the bar with the
mouse, or by pressing ⌘-U. (The braces around the formula disappear.)

3. Edit the formula and then press ⌘-Enter to re-enter the
array formula.

ATTACHED TEXT

SEE ALSO

Copying Formulas, Formula Bar, Formulas SnapGuide, Functions
SnapGuide, References.

Attached Text

In a chart, attached text is a title or label that has a predetermined
position in the chart area—a chart title, an axis title, or a label
attached to a data point.

To Attach Text to a Chart

1. Activate the chart window, or double-click an embedded
   chart on a worksheet to open a chart window.

2. Choose the Chart ➤ Attach Text command. The Attach Text
   dialog box appears on the screen.

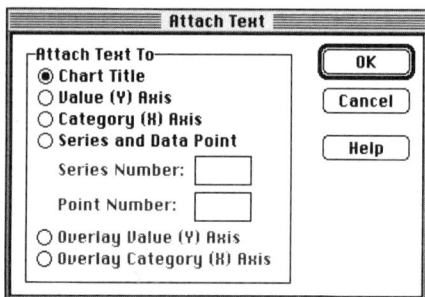

```
╔══════════════ Attach Text ══════════════╗
║ ┌Attach Text To──────────┐              ║
║ │ ● Chart Title          │   ┌────OK────┐║
║ │ ○ Value (Y) Axis       │   └──────────┘║
║ │ ○ Category (H) Axis     │  ┌──Cancel──┐ ║
║ │ ○ Series and Data Point │  └──────────┘ ║
║ │                        │   ┌───Help───┐ ║
║ │   Series Number: [   ] │   └──────────┘ ║
║ │                        │               ║
║ │   Point Number:  [   ] │               ║
║ │ ○ Overlay Value (Y) Axis│              ║
║ │ ○ Overlay Category (H) Axis│           ║
║ └────────────────────────┘              ║
╚══════════════════════════════════════════╝
```

3. In the Attach Text To box, select the chart item where you
   want to display text—the title, x-axis, y-axis, or a
   specific data point. If you select the Series and Data Point
   option, enter the series number and the data point number.

4. Click OK. In response, Excel displays a generic text value at
   the location you have selected—for example, "Title," "X,"

18

or "Y." Selection handles appear around the perimeter of the text.

5. Type the actual text that you want to appear at the selected location. Your entry initially appears in the formula bar; press Enter to complete the entry.

SHORTCUTS

Position the mouse pointer over the chart area, the plot area, an axis, or a data point. To select a data point, hold down the Control key while you click the point with the mouse. Pull down the shortcut menu for the selected chart item (point to the selected item and press ⌘-Option while you press the mouse key), and then choose the Attach Text command. The Attach Text dialog box appears, and the current item is selected in the list.

To Delete Attached Text

Select the text and choose Edit ➤ Clear.

SHORTCUTS

Press ⌘-B, or pull down the shortcut menu for the item and choose the Clear command.

To Format Attached Text

Select the text item, and then choose any combination of formatting commands: Format ➤ Patterns changes the background and foreground of the text area; Format ➤ Font changes the font, style, size, or color of the text; Format ➤ Text changes the alignment and orientation of the text.

SHORTCUTS

Select an item of attached text, and click one of the text formatting tools in the Standard toolbar: Bold, Italic, Increase or Decrease Font Size.

SEE ALSO

Charting SnapGuide, ChartWizard, Text Box.

AutoFill

By dragging the fill handle—the small black box at the lower-right corner of a selected cell or range—you can easily create series, copy data, or replicate formulas across rows or down columns in a worksheet.

To Create a Series by Dragging the Fill Handle

1. Enter the first elements of the series in consecutive cells in a column or adjacent cells in a row, and then select the range of cells containing these entries.

2. Position the mouse pointer over the fill handle for the current selection. The pointer changes to a cross-hair shape.

3. Drag the mouse down or across to the cells where you want to extend the series. Excel fills the selection with sequential elements of the series you defined in the initial cell entries.

EXAMPLE

To create a series of integers in column A, enter 1 in cell A1 and 2 in cell A2. Select the range A1:A2. Then drag the fill handle at the lower-right corner of cell A2 down column A to the last cell you want to fill. Excel fills the column with integers 3, 4, 5, 6, 7, and so on. Use the same technique to create numeric series with step values other than 1—for example 5, 10, 15, 20…

To enter a series of month names in column A, enter January in A1, and drag the cell's fill handle down to A12. From A2 to A12, Excel fills the column with the text entries February, March, April, and so on. Use the same technique to create a column of quarter labels (Quarter 1, Quarter 2, Quarter 3, Quarter 4), or other numbered labels (for example, Product 1, Product 2, Product 3; or 1st, 2nd, 3rd, 4th, 5th, and so on.)

NOTES

To fill a column or row with an identical sequence of entries—rather than a series—hold down the Option key while you drag the fill handle. For example, suppose you want to fill the range A1:A12 with repetitions of the labels Product 1, Product 2, and Product 3. To do so, enter these three labels into A1, A2, and A3. Then select A1:A3 and hold down the Option key while you drag the fill handle from A3 to A12.

You can also drag the fill handle to copy a formula from an initial cell to consecutive cells down a column or adjacent cells across a row. If the formula contains relative references, Excel adjusts the references accordingly as it copies the formula to new positions.

SEE ALSO

Copying Data, Copying Formulas, Filling Ranges, References, Series.

AutoFormat

In the AutoFormat command, Excel offers over a dozen predesigned table formats that you can choose from. These designs include specific selections from Excel's border, font, pattern, alignment, and numeric formatting options, as well as adjustments in column widths and row heights. If one of the available designs suits the data you have entered into a given worksheet, you can save time by selecting the format directly from the AutoFormat dialog box, rather than applying formats individually.

To Use the AutoFormat Feature

1. Select the table of data where you want to apply a predesigned format. (Alternatively, select a single cell within the data table, and Excel will select the contiguous table range.)

2. Choose the Format ➤ AutoFormat command. The Auto-Format dialog box appears on the screen.

3. Select the name of a predesigned table format in the Table Format list, and examine the sample of the selected format that appears in the Sample box.

AutoFormat						
Table Format:						OK
Classic 1	Sample					Cancel
Classic 2		Jan	Feb	Mar	**Total**	
Classic 3	East	$7	$7	$5	$19	Options >>
Financial 1	West	6	4	7	17	
Financial 2	South	8	7	9	24	
Financial 3	Total	$21	$18	$21	$60	Help
Colorful 1						
Colorful 2						
Colorful 3						

4. Repeat step 3 until you find a format that suits the current data table. Then click OK to apply this format to your data.

SHORTCUTS

Select the data table and click the AutoFormat tool in the Standard toolbar. By default, this tool applies the last format design that you selected from the AutoFormat dialog box. Alternatively, hold down the Shift key and click the AutoFormat tool repeatedly to step through all of the available format designs.

NOTES

If you wish to apply only certain parts of a predesigned format to your data table, click the Options button on the AutoFormat dialog box. In response, the dialog box expands to display six check boxes labeled Number, Border, Font, Patterns, Alignment, and Width/Height. By default, all of these options are checked. Click a check box to remove the X and disable a given category of formatting.

SEE ALSO

Borders, Colors, Column Widths, Copying Formats, Custom Number Formats, Fonts, Formatting Worksheet Data, Patterns, Shading, Styles.

Borders

Using the Borders command, you can draw a border around the perimeter of a selected range of cells in a worksheet, or around the individual cells within a range selection. Alternatively, you can choose to draw borders along specified sides of cells in a range. You can select from a variety of border styles and colors.

To Draw Borders

1. Select the range of cells where you want to create a border.

2. Choose the Format ➤ Border command. The resulting Border dialog box contains a list of border locations and a group of available border styles.

3. From the Border options, select the location for a border you want to draw. The Outline option draws a border around the perimeter of the current range selection. The Left, Right, Top, and Bottom options apply borders to all the cells within the current range.

4. From the Style options, select a border style for the current Border location. Eight style options are available: dotted, thin, medium, thick, double, small dashed, long dashed, and none.

5. Optionally, pull down the Color list and select a color for the current border style.

6. Repeat steps 3 to 5 for each additional location where you want to apply a border. Note that you can apply different border styles and colors to particular locations within the current range of cells.

7. Click OK to apply the borders you have selected.

 **SHORTCUTS**

Select a range of cells, pull down the shortcut menu for the selection, and choose the Border command. Alternatively, select a range of cells and click the Outline Border tool on the Standard toolbar (or press ⌘-Option-Zero) to draw a thin black border around the perimeter of the range. Click the Bottom Border tool to draw a thin black border at the bottom of each cell in the selected range.

NOTES

Excel has several additional border tools that are not initially displayed on any of the toolbars. To see these tools, choose Options ➤
Toolbars, click the Customize button, and then click the Formatting option in the Categories box. The border tools are displayed
in the first row of the Tools box. You can drag any combination
of these tools to any open toolbar. (See TOOLBARS for more
information.)

To Remove a Border

1. Select the range of cells that contain the border you want
   to remove.

2. Choose Format ➤ Border.

3. In the Style frame, select the no-border option. Then, in the
   Border frame, select the location where you want to remove
   the border.

4. Repeat step 3 for all the locations where you want to
   remove a border.

5. Click OK.

SHORTCUTS

Select the range of cells where you want to remove the borders,
and press ⌘-Option-minus sign (−) to remove all borders from
the range.

SEE ALSO

AutoFormat, Patterns, Shading.

Centering across Columns

Worksheet titles and other text or numeric entries can be centered across a horizontal range of cells.

To Center an Entry across a Range of Columns

1. Starting from the cell that contains a text or numeric entry, select a horizontal range of cells. The selected cells to the right of the entry should be blank.

2. Choose Format ➤ Alignment. In the list of Horizontal options, choose Center across selection. Then click OK. Excel centers the entry across the range you have selected.

SHORTCUTS

Select a range of cells and click the Center Across Columns tool on the Standard toolbar.

NOTES

For editing and formatting purposes, a centered entry is stored in the cell where you originally entered it.

SEE ALSO

Alignment.

SnapGuide to Charting

A chart in Excel is created from—and linked to—a table of work-sheet data. You can create a chart as an embedded graphic object in a worksheet, or you can work with a chart in a separate window of its own. Either way, Excel offers a great variety of chart types and formats for you to choose from. You can select chart types from the Chart toolbar or from the Gallery menu.

Creating a Chart

The first step in creating a chart is to select a target range of work-sheet data. Then you can choose from three techniques for creat-ing the chart: Click a chart type tool in the Chart toolbar to create an embedded chart, choose the File ➤ New command to open a chart window, or use Excel's ChartWizard tool. See the CHARTWIZARD entry to learn about this third technique.

To Create an Embedded Chart

1. If the Chart toolbar is not currently displayed, choose Options ➤ Toolbars, select Chart from the list of toolbars, and click the Show button.

2. Select the worksheet data from which you want to create the chart. If you want Excel to copy labels to the chart from your worksheet, include a row and/or column of text entries in your range selection.

3. Click one of the chart type tools in the Chart toolbar. Then move the mouse pointer back to the worksheet; the pointer appears in a cross-hair shape.

4. Drag the mouse pointer over the worksheet area where you want to display the chart. Optionally, hold down the Shift key while you drag to create a square chart box, or hold down the ⌘ key to create a chart box that is aligned with the worksheet grid. Release the mouse button when you have defined an appropriate area for the chart box. Excel draws the embedded chart on your worksheet.

5. If you are not satisfied with the chart as it initially appears, experiment with other chart types by clicking other tools in the Chart toolbar.

6. Optionally, click the Legend tool in the Chart toolbar to add a legend to your chart.

NOTES

Most typically, you create a chart from a single contiguous range, but Excel can also create a chart from nonadjacent ranges—as long as the range dimensions together form a usable data table. See SELECTING A RANGE to learn how to select nonadjacent cells.

The first seventeen tools on the chart toolbar represent the following variety of chart types and formats: area chart, bar chart, column chart, stacked column chart, line chart, pie chart, X-Y (scatter) chart, 3-D area chart, 3-D bar chart, 3-D column chart, 3-D column chart with a 3-D plot area, 3-D line chart, 3-D pie chart, 3-D surface chart, radar chart, combination chart (column chart overlayed by line chart), and combination chart for stock prices.

Select an embedded chart by clicking it with the mouse. When an embedded chart is selected, Excel displays handles—small black squares—around the perimeter of the chart box. (Excel also normally displays the Chart toolbar when an embedded chart is selected.) You can change the size of the embedded chart by dragging one of its selection handles, or you can move the chart to a new position in the worksheet by dragging the entire chart box with the mouse. Delete an embedded chart by selecting it and pressing the Delete key.

Deselect an embedded chart by clicking elsewhere in the worksheet.

Editing and Formatting a Chart

Excel has many commands and options for changing the appearance of a chart. But before you can use the chart menu commands, you must activate a chart window rather than a worksheet that contains an embedded chart.

To Edit and Format an Embedded Chart

1. Double-click the embedded chart. In response, Excel creates a chart window and copies the embedded chart to the window. (The name of this window consists of the name of the source worksheet itself followed by a generic chart name such as Chart 1, Chart 2, and so on.) Also, a new collection of chart-related menus appear in the menu bar.

2. Choose commands from the Gallery, Chart, and Format menus to make changes in the appearance of the chart.

   ▲ The Gallery menu provides a list of Excel's standard chart types and formats.

   ▲ The Chart menu allows you to add new items to your chart, such as attached text, a legend, arrows, and gridlines.

   ▲ The Format menu offers commands for changing the appearance of the chart or of selected items in the chart.

   Many of the commands in these three menus are also represented as tools in the Chart toolbar.

3. When you are finished editing the chart, choose File ➤ Close to close the chart window. Excel copies all the changes to the embedded chart in your worksheet.

NOTES

In a chart window you can select individual items or areas of the chart for editing. To do so, click the item or area with the mouse; Excel displays selection handles around or within the element that you select. For example, you can select the entire chart area, the plot area, an axis, the legend, or the chart title. After selecting an item in the chart, pull down the Format menu to see the list of the relevant formatting commands. Alternatively, point to a chart item and press ⌘–Option while you click the mouse to view a shortcut menu of commands that apply to the selection.

You can also select a series in the chart—that is, all the chart markers representing a particular range of numbers from the source worksheet table. Finally, you can select an individual data marker—that is, a single bar, point, wedge, or other chart item that represents one numeric value on the source worksheet table. To select a data marker, hold down the ⌘ key or the Control key and click the marker itself. Excel displays selection handles around the perimeter of the marker. In some chart formats—for example, column charts, bar charts and line charts—you can drag a black selection handle to change the value that the marker represents. When you do so, Excel automatically changes corresponding value in the source worksheet table.

EXAMPLE

The embedded chart in the worksheet below is a column chart created from the data in the range A1:E3. Notice that Excel displays the entries from row 1 as labels along the x-axis; these are known as the category names. The entries from column A appear as labels in the legend; these are the series names. The y-axis shows a scale of values appropriate to the range of data that the graph represents:

	A	B	C	D	E	F	G	H
1		1989	1990	1991	1992			
2	Admission Offers	900	1100	1200	1350			
3	Enrollment	750	775	1050	1295			
4								
5								

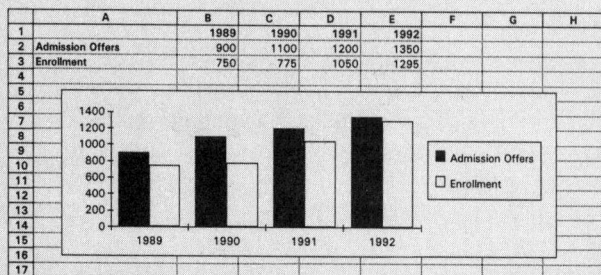

To add the title to this chart, double-click the embedded graph to create a chart window. Then choose Chart ➤ Attach Text, select the Chart Title option, and click OK. See the ATTACHED TEXT entry for more details.

Changing the chart type is as simple as clicking a tool on the Chart toolbar. These tools work either on an embedded chart or a chart window. For example, in the following worksheet the embedded chart has been changed to a combination chart:

	A	B	C	D	E	F	G	H
1		1989	1990	1991	1992			
2	Admission Offers	900	1100	1200	1350			
3	Enrollment	750	775	1050	1295			
4								

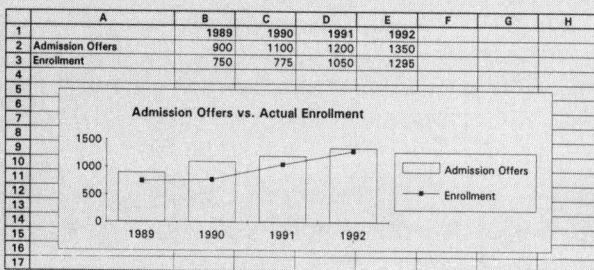

Working with a Series

When you select a series or a data point in a chart, the formula bar shows the series formula that links the series to the corresponding worksheet range. The series formula consists of a call to Excel's built-in SERIES function. The charts in the two examples above contain two data series. The first series, shown in the column chart as a set of black columns, represents the data in row 2 of the worksheet table. The second, shown as a set of white columns (or a line in the combination chart), represents the data in row 3. Each data series contains four data markers representing the four years of data. Given a source worksheet named Enroll, here are the SERIES functions for these two series:

```
=SERIES(Enroll!$A$2,Enroll!$B$1:$E$1,
    Enroll!$B$2:$E$2,1)
=SERIES(Enroll!$A$3,Enroll!$B$1:$E$1,
    Enroll!$B$3:$E$3,2)
```

As you can see, the SERIES function takes four arguments. Here the arguments are external references representing the series name, the category names, the series data, and the series number.

In these first examples, the chart series are plotted from rows of data. In general, Excel uses the number of rows and columns in the source worksheet selection to decide how to form the data series. By default, if there are more columns than rows (or an equal number of rows and columns), the rows of data are plotted as series. Conversely, if there are more rows than columns, the columns of data become the series. You can easily change this arrangement using the ChartWizard.

To Change Series from Rows to Columns or Columns to Rows

1. Click the embedded chart to select it.

2. Click the ChartWizard tool on the Standard toolbar or the Chart toolbar. (Notice that the same tool appears on both toolbars.)

3. In the first dialog box—named "ChartWizard–Step 1 of 2"—click the Next button.

4. In the second dialog box, select an option under the Data Series in label. If the current selection is Rows, click Columns; conversely, if Columns is selected, click Rows. Notice the resulting change in the Sample Chart box.

5. Click OK to copy the new series arrangement to the embedded chart on your worksheet.

EXAMPLE

In the following chart, the series are formed from four columns of worksheet data—columns B, C, D, and E. As you can see, the four series names displayed in the legend are now taken from row 1 of the worksheet. The category names, displayed along the x-axis, are from column A of the worksheet:

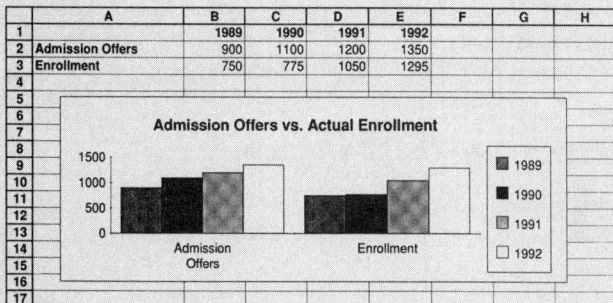

	A	B	C	D	E	F	G	H
1		1989	1990	1991	1992			
2	Admission Offers	900	1100	1200	1350			
3	Enrollment	750	775	1050	1295			
4								

Admission Offers vs. Actual Enrollment

NOTES

You can use the ChartWizard as a guide for all the steps of creating a chart; see the CHARTWIZARD entry for details.

When the current window is a chart, the Chart ➤ Edit Series command is also available for modifying the chart series. You can use this command to insert or delete series, or to change a series definition. Four text boxes in the Edit Series dialog box correspond to the four arguments of the SERIES function: the series name (Name), the category names (X Labels), the series data (Y Values), and the series number (Plot Order).

Chart Windows

You can save a chart as a separate file by first creating a chart window from an embedded chart. Alternatively, you can initially create a chart as a separate document rather than as an embedded object.

To Save an Embedded Chart as a Separate File

1. Double-click the embedded chart to create a chart window.

2. Choose File ➤ Save As and save the chart to disk.

NOTES

When a chart window is active, you can print the chart by choosing File ➤ Print or by clicking the Print tool in the Standard toolbar. See PRINTING CHARTS for more information.

To Create a New Chart Window

1. In the source worksheet, select the range of data from which you want to create a new chart.

2. Choose File ➤ New.

3. In the New dialog box, select the Chart option. Click OK. Excel opens a new chart window and creates a chart in the current preferred chart format.

SHORTCUTS

Press ⌘-N to view the New dialog box.

NOTES

The column chart is initially the preferred chart format.

To Change the Preferred Chart Format

1. Activate a chart window.

2. Optionally, change the chart's format by clicking a tool in the Chart toolbar or by choosing a command from the Gallery menu.

3. Choose the Gallery ➤ Set Preferred command. The format of the current chart becomes the preferred format.

NOTES

To change any chart to the preferred format, choose Gallery ➤ Preferred, or click the Preferred Chart tool in the Chart toolbar.

To Create an Embedded Chart from a Chart Window

1. Select the chart window and choose the Chart ➤ Select Chart command.

2. Choose Edit ➤ Copy. A moving border appears around the chart.

3. Switch to the worksheet window and select the worksheet location where you want to place the embedded chart.

4. Choose Edit ➤ Paste.

SHORTCUTS

Press ⌘–A to select the chart area, ⌘–C to copy the chart, and ⌘–V to paste the chart.

SEE ALSO

Attached Text, ChartWizard, Colors, Graphic Objects, Links between Worksheets, Printing Charts, References, Text Box, Toolbars.

ChartWizard

The ChartWizard is Excel's step-by-step guide through the process of creating an embedded chart. Using the ChartWizard you can easily make specific decisions about the type, format, and structure of your chart, and about the link between the chart and the source data. You can also add elements such as a title, axis labels, and a legend during the ChartWizard procedure. Many Excel users find the ChartWizard the most efficient and effective way to create charts.

To Use the ChartWizard

1. On the source worksheet, select the data from which you want to create a chart. In the range selection you can include a first row and a first column of labels that describe or identify the numeric data.

2. Click the ChartWizard tool in the Standard toolbar. Then drag the mouse pointer over the worksheet area where you want to display the chart you are about to create. (Optionally, hold down the Shift key while you drag to create a square chart box, or hold down the Control key to create a chart box that is aligned with the worksheet grid.) When you release the mouse button, Excel displays the first of five dialog boxes, this one named "ChartWizard–Step 1 of 5."

3. In the first ChartWizard dialog box you can change or confirm the source data range for the chart. If the reference displayed in the Range box is correct, click the Next button.

4. In the second ChartWizard dialog box, Excel displays icons representing the fourteen available chart types. Select one of these icons and click the Next button.

5. In the third dialog box, Excel displays icons representing a variety of formats for the chart type you have selected. Select a format and click Next to continue.

6. In the fourth ChartWizard dialog box, you make decisions that will affect the link between the worksheet data and the chart. First, select Rows or Columns to specify whether the data series for the chart should be read from the rows or the columns of the source data table. Then specify whether the first column and first row of the data table contain entries that should be used as labels or as data points in the chart. Study the Sample Chart box to see if the resulting chart is the one you want to create. Click Next to continue.

7. Finally, the fifth dialog box gives you options for including a legend, a chart title, and axis titles. Enter the titles in the appropriate text boxes, and study the sample chart to confirm that your entries are correct.

8. When you are finished, click OK. Excel creates an embedded chart on your worksheet, following the specifications you have supplied in the five ChartWizard dialog boxes.

NOTES

In addition to Next, the ChartWizard dialog boxes have these buttons:

Back   returns you to the previous dialog box.

| goes back to the first dialog box.

>>   skips the remaining dialog boxes.

After you have created an embedded chart, you can click the ChartWizard button again to revise the chart's structure. See the CHARTING SNAPGUIDE entry for details and an example.

SEE ALSO

Charting SnapGuide, Colors.

Clearing Data

Excel offers two efficient ways to clear data—and optionally to clear the formats you have applied to the data—from a worksheet selection: You can choose the Edit ➤ Clear command, or you can drag the fill handle back over the data you want to clear.

To Clear Data with the Edit ➤ Clear Command

1. Select the range of worksheet data that you want to delete.

2. Choose Edit ➤ Clear, and select one of the four options from the Clear list:

▲ All deletes all entries, formats, and notes;

▲ Formats deletes formatting only;

▲ Formulas deletes text, numbers, and formula entries;

▲ Notes deletes any notes you have saved in the worksheet range.

3. Click OK to complete the clear operation.

SHORTCUTS

Select the worksheet range and press ⌘-B to delete data values and formulas (not formats or notes) from the selection. Alternatively, point to the selection, press ⌘-Option while you click the mouse button, and choose the Clear command from the shortcut menu. In addition, Excel provides Clear Formulas and Clear Formats tools, neither of which is initially part of a toolbar. (See TOOLBARS for instructions about adding these tools to a toolbar.)

NOTES

To undo an inadvertent Clear operation, choose Edit ➤ Undo Clear or press Control-Z immediately after the clear.

To Use the Dragging Technique for Clearing Data

1. Select the range of data that you want to clear.

2. Position the mouse pointer over the fill handle, the small black square located at the lower-right corner of the selection. The mouse pointer is displayed as a cross-hair shape.

3. Drag the fill handle up or to the left, over the data that you want to delete. (Optionally, hold down the Option key while you drag if you want to delete data, formats, and notes.) The range that you drag over is displayed in gray.

4. Release the mouse button. Excel clears the data from the range.

SEE ALSO

AutoFill, Formatting Worksheet Data, Notes.

Clipboard

The Clipboard is a storage area that Macintosh applications use during cut-and-paste and copy-and-paste operations.

To Copy a Range of Worksheet Data to the Clipboard

Select the data and choose the Edit ➤ Copy command.

SHORTCUTS

Press Control-C or ⌘-C to copy the current selection to the clipboard.

To Copy a Picture of Data to the Clipboard

1. Select a worksheet range.

2. Hold down the Shift key, and choose the Edit ➤ Copy Picture command. (This command appears in the Edit menu only when you hold down the Shift key.)

3. In the Copy Picture dialog box, select an option to specify the type of picture you want to copy. Then click OK.

NOTES

The Copy Picture command creates a worksheet picture that you can insert into a document as a graphic object.

To View the Clipboard

Choose Window ➤ Show Clipboard.

NOTES

The Clipboard window does not need to be open during cut-and-paste and copy-and-paste operations.

SEE ALSO

Copying Data, Moving Data.

Colors

Several menu commands in Excel provide a color palette—with a set of 16 colors—from which you can select display colors for worksheets and charts. For worksheets, the color palette appears on the dialog boxes for the Font, Patterns, and Border commands, all from the Format menu. For charts, the palette is available for the Patterns and Font commands, also from the Format menu. You can use the Options ➤ Color Palette command (or the Chart ➤ Color Palette command, if a chart window is active) to customize the color entries in the palette for a given document.

To Display Worksheet Entries in Color

1. Select the range of worksheet data and choose the Format ➤ Font command. The Font dialog box appears on the screen.

2. Click the arrow at the right side of the Color box to view the color palette.

3. Select a color from the palette and click OK.

NOTES

When you select a range on the worksheet, the colors change due to the selection highlight. To view the true colors, deselect the range.

Excel provides a Text Color tool for changing the color of worksheet entries and other text. To use this tool, you must first add it to a toolbar. (See TOOLBARS for instructions.) Each time you click the Text Color tool, the entries in the current worksheet selection are changed to the next color in the palette. This button also works on text boxes and text items in a chart.

To Change the Cell Color (Foreground) of a Worksheet Range

1. Select the worksheet range and choose the Format ➤ Patterns command.

2. Click the arrow at the right of the Pattern box to view the available patterns. Select the solid pattern.

3. Click the arrow at the right of the Foreground box to view the color palette.

4. Select a color and click OK.

SHORTCUTS

Select a range and click the Color tool on the Drawing toolbar. Each time you click this tool, the selected cells change to the next color in the palette.

NOTES

A shading pattern consists of a combination of foreground and background colors. When you select the solid pattern, only the foreground color applies. See PATTERNS for more information.

To Change the Border Color
in a Worksheet Selection

I. Select the worksheet range and choose Format ➤ Border.

2. In the Border dialog box, select a border location and style. See the BORDERS entry for details.

3. Click the arrow at the right of the Color box and select a color for the border. Click OK.

SHORTCUTS

Point to the selected range, press ⌘-Option while you click the mouse button, and choose the Border command from the shortcut menu.

To Change the Color of the
Worksheet Headings and Grid

I. Activate a worksheet window.

2. Choose the Options ➤ Display command. The Display Options dialog box appears on the screen.

3. Click the arrow at the right side of the box labeled Gridline & Heading Color.

4. Select a color and click OK.

To Change the Color of a Text Item in a Chart

I. In a chart window, select a text item (a title, axis, legend, attached text, or unattached text box).

2. Choose the Format ➤ Font command and select a color from the Color palette. Then click OK.

SHORTCUTS

If you have added the Text Color tool to a toolbar, select a text item and then click this tool one or more times to cycle through the available colors.

To Change the Color of a Chart Area or Chart Item

1. In a chart window, select the area or item that you want to change, and choose the Format ➤ Patterns command.

2. On the Patterns dialog box, choose a color from the Foreground palette and click OK.

To Customize a Color in a Document's Color Palette

1. Switch to the document in which you want to customize the color.

2. Choose Options ➤ Color Palette (or Chart ➤ Color Palette if the active document is a separate chart window, created through the File ➤ New command).

3. In the Color Palette dialog box, select the color that you want to customize. Then click the Edit button. A color editing dialog box appears.

4. Adjust the selected color by clicking inside the color wheel or by adjusting the digital settings labeled Hue, Saturation, Brightness, Red, Green, and Blue. When the color appears as you want it, click OK in the dialog box.

5. Repeat steps 3 and 4 to change any other colors in the palette for the active document.

6. Click OK in the Color Palette dialog box to apply the new color palette to the document.

NOTES

Changes in the color palette apply only to the active document and to any embedded objects (including embedded charts) in the document. To copy a customized color palette from an open document to the active document, select a document name from the Copy Colors From list in the Color Palette dialog box. To revert to the default color palette, click the Default button in the Color Palette dialog box.

SEE ALSO

Borders, Charting SnapGuide, Copying Formats, Customizing Excel, Fonts, Graphic Objects, Patterns, Shading, Styles.

Column Widths

Adjusting the widths of worksheet columns allows you to display large amounts of data as effectively as possible.

To Change the Width of a Single Column

1. Select a cell in the column, or click the column heading to select the entire column.

2. Choose Format ➤ Column Width.

3. Enter a new value in the Column Width text box. (This value is the width of the column in characters, given the current font and point size.) Then click OK.

SHORTCUTS

Position the mouse pointer over the line located just to the right of the column's heading, and drag the line to the right for a wider column or the left for a narrower one. Double-click the line to adjust the columns width to the best fit for the current contents. Alternatively, point to the column heading, press ⌘-Option while you press the mouse button, and choose Column Width from the shortcut menu.

NOTES

To change the widths of a group of columns, select the columns and choose the Format ➤ Column Width command.

The standard column width for a worksheet is the width of all columns that you have not adjusted individually. To change the standard width setting, choose Format ➤ Column Width and enter a new value in the Standard Width text box.

SEE ALSO

Alignment, Hiding, Row Height.

Consolidating Data

The Data ➤ Consolidate command provides flexible techniques for combining data from multiple worksheet sources in a single destination worksheet. By default, the Consolidate command uses the SUM function to combine the corresponding values from source worksheets; but you can choose from eleven different functions—including AVERAGE, MAX, MIN, and others—to perform the consolidation. Optionally, you can create links between the source worksheets and the destintation worksheet, so that the destination is updated whenever the data changes in any one of the sources.

To Consolidate Data from Multiple Source Worksheets

1. Activate the destination worksheet and select the location where you want to consolidate data. You can specify the destination area by selecting the upper-left corner cell, the top-row range, the left-column range, or the entire range. (During the consolidation process, Excel expands the desination area accordingly.)

2. Choose Data ➤ Consolidate. The Consolidate dialog box contains boxes labeled Function, Reference, and All References, along with several buttons and check boxes. The Reference text box is active initially.

3. Optionally, click the Browse button if your source worksheets are not currently open. In the resulting dialog box, find and select the name of a source worksheet, and click OK. Back in the Consolidate dialog box, Excel enters a reference to the source worksheet in the form NAME!. (Alternatively, you can type this worksheet reference directly into the Reference text box without using the Browse facility.)

4. Immediately after the worksheet name, type a range name or range reference identifying the data that you want to consolidate from the source worksheet. (If the source worksheet is open, you can select the source area with the mouse or the keyboard. Excel enters a reference to your selection in the Reference text box.) The source area may contain numeric entries alone, from a worksheet range that matches the size, shape, and location of other source areas you are including in the consolidation; in this case, Excel consolidates by position. Alternatively, the source area may include an identifying row and/or column of labels, and the range may be in a different location than other source areas; in this case, Excel consolidates by category. See the "Notes" section below for more information about this distinction.

5. Click the Add button. Excel adds the current source area reference to the All References list, and reactivates the Reference text box.

6. Repeat steps 3, 4, and 5 for all the source areas that you want to include in the consolidation.

7. If you are performing a consolidation by category, click one or both of the Use Labels In options: Top Row if the category labels are at the top of each source area; Left Column if the category labels are at the left side of each source area. (In response, Excel will copy the selected category labels to the destination area.)

8. Optionally, pull down the Functions list and select an entry other than the default SUM function.

9. Optionally, select the Create Links to Source Data check box, if you want Excel to generate external references to the source worksheet area in the destination area.

10. Click OK. Excel consolidates the data and displays it in the destination area you have selected.

NOTES

You can consolidate as many as 255 source worksheets in a destination worksheet.

If you have created the source worksheets in a consistent format—placing the source data in the same location in each worksheet—you can consolidate the data by position. (Note that the Options ➤ Group Edit command offers a convenient technique for creating any number of source worksheets in a consistent format. See Group Editing for details.) When you consolidate by position, Excel does not copy labels from the source worksheets to the destination area. You should therefore begin your work by entering any necessary labels at the top row or left column of the destination area, and formatting the area appropriately.

On the other hand, if you are consolidating data from diverse ranges in the source worksheets, the source areas should include consistent category labels that identify particular rows or columns of data. When you consolidate by category, Excel copies the category labels from the source to the destination.

The Function list in the Consolidation dialog box offers the following eleven functions:

Function	Description
AVERAGE	calculates the average of corresponding values in the source areas.
COUNT	produces a count of the corresponding numeric entries in the source areas.
COUNTA	produces a count of corresponding nonblank cells in the source areas.
MAX	selects the largest among corresponding values in the source areas.
MIN	selects the smallest among corresponding values in the source areas.
PRODUCT	multiplies corresponding values together.
STDEV and STDEVP	calculate standard deviations of corresponding values.
SUM	finds the sum of corresponding values in the source areas.
VAR and VARP	calculate the variances of corresponding values.

If you select the Create Links to Source Data option, Excel reorganizes the destination area as an outline, and inserts rows into the area for external references to the source data. You can then expand the outline to view the source data along with the consolidated data, or collapse the outline to view the consolidated data alone.

The consolidation references reappear in the Consolidate dialog box for the destination worksheet, whether or not you choose to link the source worksheets. You can revise the consolidation at any time—adding new source areas, deleting source areas, or changing the references to source areas—by activating the destination worksheet and choosing Data ➤ Consolidate again.

If you save the source worksheets with similar names, you can use the wildcard characters * and ? to identify sources in the Consolidate dialog box. For example, suppose you have four weekly data worksheets named Week1, Week2, Week3, and Week4, and you have assigned the range name Weektable to the source area on each worksheet. To consolidate all four of these sources in one efficient operation, you can enter the following name into the Reference text box of the Consolidate dialog box:

   Week?!Weektable

SEE ALSO

Group Editing, Links between Worksheets, Names, Outlines, References, Statistical Functions.

Copying Data

Along with the familiar Copy and Paste commands, Excel has a simple drag-and-drop operation that you can use to copy a range of data from one worksheet area to another.

To Copy Data Using the Copy and Paste Commands

1. Select the range of data that you want to copy, and choose Edit ➤ Copy. Excel displays a moving border around the range, and copies the data to the Clipboard.

2. Select a cell or range for the destination, and choose Edit ➤ Paste. Excel copies the data to the paste range.

SHORTCUTS

To copy the selected data to the Clipboard, press Control-C or
⌘-C, or click the Copy tool on the Standard toolbar. To paste the
data, press Control-V or ⌘-V, or click the Paste tool. The Paste tool
is not initially part of any toolbar; see the TOOLBARS entry for instructions on adding it to a toolbar. The Copy and Paste commands
are also available on the shortcut menu for worksheet cells. See
SHORTCUT MENUS. Finally, on a keyboard that includes function
keys, F3 represents the Copy operation and F4 represents Paste.

NOTES

If you select a paste area that already contains data, the Paste command overwrites the previous data entries with the copied data.
Choose Edit ➤ Undo Paste or press ⌘-Z if you want to restore the
original data.

To Insert Data During a Copy-And-Paste Operation

1. Select the range of data that you want to copy, and choose
   Edit ➤ Copy.

2. Select a cell or range for the destination, and choose the
   Edit ➤ Insert Paste command.

3. On the Insert Paste dialog box, select the Shift Cells
   Right or Shift Cells Down option and click OK. Excel
   pastes the data and moves existing entries into the cells
   to the right or the cells below the paste area.

SHORTCUTS

Press ⌘-I to view the Insert Paste dialog box.

To Copy a Selection to Multiple Locations

1. Select the copy range and choose Edit ➤ Copy.

2. Select the first paste range, and then hold down the ⌘ key or the Control key as you select each additional range.

3. Choose Edit ➤ Paste. Excel copies the data to all of the paste ranges at once.

NOTES

If the copy range contains hidden cells, or collapsed outline rows, the Copy and Paste commands normally produce a copy of the entire copy range, including the hidden or collapsed ranges.

To Copy Only the Cells that Are Visible

1. Select a range of cells that includes hidden or collapsed ranges.

2. Choose the Formula ➤ Select Special command.

3. In the Select Special dialog box, select the Visible Cells Only option, and click OK. This step results in a multiple range selection consisting of the visible cells.

4. Choose Edit ➤ Copy. A moving border appears around the copy range.

5. Select a cell or range for the paste area, and choose Edit ➤ Paste.

To Copy Data Using the Drag-and-Drop Technique

1. Select the range of data that you want to copy.

2. Position the mouse pointer along the border of the selection. The pointer shape changes to a black arrow.

3. Hold down the Option key or the Control key and drag the mouse pointer to the location where you want to paste the data. A small plus sign appears next to the arrow pointer when you hold down the Option or Control key. A gray frame representing the copy area follows the mouse pointer as you drag.

4. Release the mouse button, and then release the Option or Control key. Excel copies the data from the copy range to the paste range.

To Insert a Copy Range Using the Drag-and-Drop Technique

1. Select the range of data that you want to copy and insert.

2. Position the mouse pointer along the border of the selection. The pointer shape changes to a black arrow.

3. Hold down the Option (or Control) key and the Shift key together. Then drag the mouse pointer to the location where you want to insert the copy range. A horizontal or vertical insertion bar follows the mouse pointer as you drag. (To switch between a horizontal and vertical insertion, drag the pointer toward a row or column gridline.)

4. Release the mouse button, and then release the keys. Excel copies the data from the copy range to the paste range and shifts existing entries down or to the right.

SEE ALSO

AutoFill, Copying Formats, Copying Formulas, Deleting, Filling Ranges, Hiding, Inserting, Links between Worksheets, Moving Data, Outlines, Selecting a Range.

Copying Formats

You can use the Edit ➤ Paste Special command—or the Paste Formats tool—to copy formatting from one worksheet range to another without copying data values to the paste range. This operation copies all the formats that you assign to a range by choosing commands from the Format menu—formats such as alignments, fonts, borders, patterns, and number formats.

To Copy Formats from One Range to Another

1. Select the range from which you want to copy the formats, and choose Edit ➤ Copy. A moving border appears around the copy range.

2. Select a cell or range to which you want to copy the formatting from the copy range.

3. Choose Edit ➤ Paste Special. In the Paste Special dialog box, select the Formats option and click OK. In response, Excel applies all the formats from the copy range to the paste range.

SHORTCUTS

Instead of choosing the Edit ➤ Paste Special command, click the Paste Formats button in the Standard toolbar. The effect is the same: Excel copies the formats from the copy range to the paste range.

NOTES

If you press the Shift key while clicking the Paste Formats tool, the tool changes to Paste Values. Clicking this tool pastes all the data values from the copy area without copying the formatting.

To Clear Formats from a Range

1. Select the range from which you want to clear the formats.

2. Choose Edit ➤ Clear. The Clear dialog box appears on the screen.

3. Select the Formats option and click OK. Excel clears all formats in the selected range.

SEE ALSO

Alignment, AutoFormat, Borders, Clearing Data, Colors, Custom Number Formats, Fonts, Formatting Worksheet Data, Number Formats, Patterns, Point Size, Shading.

Copying Formulas

When you copy a formula from one location to another in a worksheet, the result depends significantly upon the types of references included in the original formula:

▲ An absolute reference is copied verbatim from the original formula to the copy; each copy refers to a fixed location on the worksheet.

▲ A relative reference is adjusted according to the location of the copy, so that the row and/or column portions of the reference may be different for each copy of the formula.

▲ A mixed reference contains a mixture of absolute and relative elements.

You can use copy-and-paste, AutoFill, or drag-and-drop operations to copy formulas from one location to another. In addition, you can use the Copy and Paste Special commands to copy a range of formulas to itself, converting all the formulas to fixed values.

To Create and Copy a Formula

1. While you enter the first copy of a formula, decide whether each reference should be absolute, relative, or mixed—depending on how you want the reference to be copied across rows and/or down columns. Enter a reference into the formula bar by pointing with the mouse or by typing the reference directly from the keyboard, and then press ⌘-T repeatedly or choose the Formula ➤ Reference command to step through the possible reference types: relative, absolute, or mixed. In each reference type, Excel inserts a dollar sign ($) before the absolute portions of the reference.

2. After you complete the original formula, use any of the techniques available in Excel for copying an entry from one location to another. See AUTOFILL and COPYING DATA for the steps of these various techniques.

EXAMPLE

The following formula contains two mixed references and one absolute reference:

=(C$4+$B5)*$B$1

Suppose you enter this formula into cell C5 of a worksheet. If you then copy the formula down column C to cells C6 and C7, the first mixed reference (C$4) is copied unchanged, but the row portion of the second mixed reference ($B5) is adjusted in each copy:

C6   =(C$4+$B6)*$B$1
C7   =(C$4+$B7)*$B$1

Conversely, if you copy the formula across row 5 to cells D5 and E5, the first reference is adjusted but the second reference remains unchanged in each copy:

D5   E5
=(D$4+$B5)*$B$1   =(E$4+$B5)*$B$1

Notice that the absolute reference, $B$1, remains unchanged in all copies of the formula.

To Convert Formulas to Fixed Values in a Worksheet Range

1. Select the range of cells containing the formulas you want to convert, and choose Edit ➤ Copy.

2. Without changing the range selection, choose Edit ➤ Paste Special.

3. In the Paste Special dialog box, select the Values option and click OK. Excel converts each formula entry in the range to its current value. In other words, the range now contains only constant entries and the background formulas are lost.

NOTES

To restore the background formulas, choose Edit ➤ Undo Paste Special or press Control-Z immediately after this operation.

To convert a formula in the formula bar to its current value, press ⌘-= or the F9 function key while the formula bar is active.

SEE ALSO

AutoFill, Copying Data, Formula Bar, Formulas SnapGuide, References.

Crosstab ReportWizard

Crosstab ReportWizard is an add-in macro that guides you through the process of creating a summary "cross-tabulation" report from a database. The ReportWizard displays a sequence of dialog boxes on the screen, prompting you to select the row and column fields that will define the report's structure, and the value fields that will become the content of the report.

To Create a Crosstab Report from an Excel Database

1. Activate the worksheet that contains the database. Make sure you have defined the database range by choosing the Data ➤ Set Database command. Optionally, you can also define a criteria range for the database; if you do, the crosstab report will include only those records that match your selection criteria.

2. Choose Data ➤ Crosstab. The first dialog box that appears on the screen is named "Crosstab ReportWizard–Introduction." Read the information in this dialog box, and click the Explain button for additional information. (Each subsequent ReportWizard dialog box also has an Explain button, which you can click for specific illustrations during each step of the process.)

3. Click the button labeled Create a New Crosstab. The next dialog box, named "Crosstab ReportWizard–Row Categories," contains a list of the fields defined in the current database.

4. Select a database field that contains data entries you want to include as row categories along the left side of the crosstab table. (The field itself should contain repeated values, typically text entries that can conveniently serve as categories in the crosstab table.) Then click Add. The selected field name appears in the box labeled Include as Row Categories.

5. Repeat step 4 for each field that you want to add to the Row Categories list. (If you change your mind about a particular field, click the Remove button.) The order in which you select the fields determines the vertical structure of the table itself: Each new selection becomes an additional sequence of rows at a level beneath the previous category.

6. After you add the final row category, click the Next button at the bottom of the dialog box. A new dialog box appears on the screen, named "Crosstab ReportWizard– Column Categories."

7. Select a field that contains database entries you want to include as column categories at the top of the crosstab table. Then click Add. The selected field name appears in the box labeled Include as Column Categories.

8. Repeat step 7 for each field that you want to add to the Column Categories list. (If you change your mind about a particular field, click the Remove button.) The order in which you select the fields determines the horizontal organization of the table itself: Each new selection becomes another level of column headings beneath the previous selection.

9. Click the Next button to view the next dialog box, named "Crosstab ReportWizard–Value Fields."

10. Click a field containing entries—typically numeric data— that you want to consolidate in the table. Click the Options button, and then select a calculation method in the Options dialog box. For example, select Sum to find the total of the value entries, or Average to calculate the average value. Click OK to confirm the option selection.

11. Repeat step 10 for each value field you want to add to the table's contents.

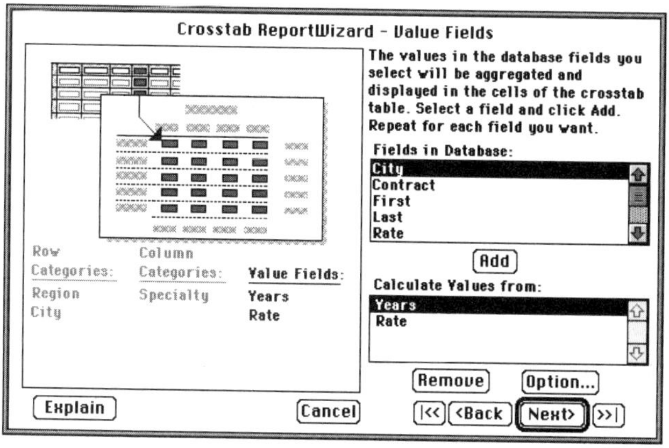

12. Click the Next button. If you have selected two or more value fields, the next dialog box to appear on the screen is named "Crosstab ReportWizard–Multiple Value Field Layout." In this dialog box you can select one of four layout options for the value fields in your report. When you make a selection, the left side of the dialog box displays an illustration of your report's structure. Click Next when you have selected the layout you want.

13. The Crosstab ReportWizard–Final dialog box appears next. You have supplied all the information that Excel needs to create a table. Click the Create It button to complete the procedure.

EXAMPLE

The crosstab report below was created from a database of computer consultants who work in major cities of four regions. The database contains fields for each consultant's name, region, city, specialty area, hourly rate, and number of years in business. In this report, the row category fields are Region and City, and the column category field is Specialty. The Value fields are Years and Rate, and the operation selected for these fields is Average.

	A	B	C	D	E	F	G
1				Specialty			
2	Region	City		Database	Spreadsheet	WP	Grand total
3	E	Boston	Average Years	5.8	5.5	6.2	5.8
4			Average Rate	$100.00	$150.00	$125.00	$125.00
5		New York	Average Years	5.7	6.1	5.2	5.7
6			Average Rate	$125.00	$100.00	$150.00	$125.00
7	E Average		Years	5.8	5.8	5.7	5.8
8			Rate	$112.50	$125.00	$137.50	$125.00
9	N	Chicago	Average Years	4.8	0.9	1.4	2.4
10			Average Rate	$150.00	$100.00	$100.00	$116.67
11	N Average		Years	4.8	0.9	1.4	2.4
12			Rate	$150.00	$100.00	$100.00	$116.67
13	S	Atlanta	Average Years	1.8	4.5	5.7	4.0
14			Average Rate	$125.00	$125.00	$75.00	$108.33
15		Dallas	Average Years	5.1	1.5	5.8	4.1
16			Average Rate	$150.00	$150.00	$100.00	$133.33
17	S Average		Years	3.4	3.0	5.8	4.1
18			Rate	$137.50	$137.50	$87.50	$120.83
19	W	Los Angeles	Average Years	2.1	5.1	1.1	2.8
20			Average Rate	$75.00	$100.00	$150.00	$108.33
21		San Francisco	Average Years	6.5	#N/A	5.1	5.8
22			Average Rate	$75.00	#N/A	$150.00	$112.50
23	W Average		Years	4.3	5.1	3.1	4.0
24			Rate	$75.00	$100.00	$150.00	$110.00
25	Grand total		Average Years	4.5	3.9	4.4	4.3
26			Average Rate	$114.29	$120.83	$121.43	$118.75

As you can see, the report contains rows for the average years in business and the average hourly rate for the consultants in each city. Columns D, E, and F provide the averages for the three specialty areas, and column G gives the city-wide and region-wide averages.

NOTES

In addition to Next, the ReportWizard dialog boxes have the following buttons:

Back — returns to the previous dialog box.

|<< — moves back to the beginning of the process.

>>| — skips to the end of the process.

By default, Excel opens a new worksheet for the crosstab table, and creates an outline structure for the report. You can override these defaults by clicking the Set Table Creation Options button on the Final dialog box, and selecting options on the resulting dialog box.

The Row Categories and Column Categories dialog boxes also have Option buttons. Click these buttons to view additional options for the structure of the crosstab report.

If you want to revise the structure of an existing crosstab report, select the report and choose Data ➤ Crosstabs again. Make revisions in any or all of the dialog boxes.

To create the crosstab report, Excel enters CROSSTAB functions into specified cells of the crosstab worksheet. You can revise any CROSSTAB function directly in the formula bar.

SEE ALSO

Add-in Macros, Databases SnapGuide, Database Criteria, Outlines.

Custom Number Formats

The Format ➤ Number command provides over two dozen built-in numeric display formats in these categories: Number, Currency, Date, Time, Percentage, Fraction, and Scientific. You can add your own custom formats to these built-in formats by editing an existing format or by devising an entirely new format.

To Create a Custom Number Format

1. Select the cell or range of cells to which you want to apply the custom format, and then choose Format ➤ Number. The resulting Number Format dialog box contains a Value Type list and a Format Codes list.

2. Optionally, select a starting format from the Format Codes list. This format appears in the Code text box, where you can edit it to create your custom format.

3. Activate the Code text box. Edit or enter the code for the custom format you want to create. Use new combinations of the same formatting symbols that are used in the built-in format codes.

4. Click OK. Excel applies the new format to the current selection of worksheet cells, and adds the custom format to the Format Codes list in the Number Format dialog box. You can reuse this custom format anywhere in the active worksheet.

SHORTCUTS

Point to the selection where you want to apply a custom format, press ⌘–Option while you click the mouse button, and choose the Number command from the resulting shortcut menu.

EXAMPLE

The following custom code is designed to format cells for phone-number entries:

(000) 000-0000" ext. "0000

For example, if you apply this custom format to a cell and then enter the number 41555598761234, the entry will be displayed as follows in the cell:

(415) 555-9876 ext. 1234

This custom code produces a complete date-and-time format:

dddd, mmmm d, yyyy "at" h:mm AM/PM

If you apply this format to a cell and then enter 33750.75, the number appears as

Monday, May 27, 1996 at 6:00 PM

This is the result under the 1904 serial date system, the default for Excel on the Macintosh. See DATE ENTRIES for details.

 **NOTES**

You can divide a custom format into four different sections of formatting code, each section separated from the next by a semicolon (;). The resulting format depends upon the kind of data entered in the cell:

▲ The first section of formatting code applies to positive numeric entries.

▲ The second section applies to negative numeric entries.

▲ The third section applies to entries of zero.

▲ The fourth section applies to text entries.

To Delete a Custom Number Format

1. Choose Format ➤ Number.

2. In the Format Codes list, select the custom format that you want to delete. (You cannot delete Excel's built-in formats.)

3. Click the Delete button.

4. Click OK.

 **NOTES**

When you delete a custom format, any cells to which the format was applied revert to the general format.

 **SEE ALSO**

Copying Formats, Date Entries, Formatting Worksheet Data, Number Formats, Time Entries.

Customizing Excel

Several important techniques are available for adding features to Excel or for changing its operation. You can use these techniques to make Excel conform to your own work requirements.

To Customize Excel

▲ Create and install an add-in macro sheet. See ADD-IN MACROS.

▲ Create a custom color palette. See COLORS.

▲ Enter the code for a custom number format. See CUSTOM NUMBER FORMATS.

▲ Create dialog boxes and custom data forms. See DIALOG EDITOR.

▲ Write or record your own macro commands and macro functions. See MACROS SNAPGUIDE and MACRO RECORDING.

▲ Assign a macro to a button. See MACROS SNAPGUIDE.

▲ Change the tools on a toolbar, or create a new toolbar. See TOOLBARS.

Data Form

A data form is a dialog box designed to simplify your work with an Excel database. You can use a data form to examine and edit the fields of individual records, to scroll through the database one record at a time, to add new records to the database, to delete records from the database, and to search for records that match specific criteria. Excel's standard data form layout is available for any database. Alternatively, you can create a custom data form in the Dialog Editor for use in a particular database application.

To Open a Data Form for Viewing Records

1. Open or activate a worksheet that contains a database. Make sure you have used the Data ➤ Set Database command to define the database range.

2. Choose Data ➤ Form. The data form for the current database appears on the screen. At the left side of the form are labels identifying the fields of the database, and text boxes showing the field entries for the first record. At the right side is a column of command buttons you can use to perform specific operations on your database.

Consultants		
		1 of 20
Last:	Abrams	New
First:	P.	Delete
City:	Atlanta	Restore
Region:	S	Find Prev
Specialty:	Database	Find Next
Rate:	125	Criteria
Contract:	10/20/1990	Close
Years:	1.8	Help

3. Use the vertical scroll bar in the middle of the data form to scroll one record at a time through the database, or to move quickly from one position to another in the database. At the upper-right corner of the data form, Excel displays the current record number and the total number of records; for example, "5 of 40."

4. Click the Close button to close the data form when you are finished viewing records of the database.

NOTES

A defined criteria range on the database worksheet has no effect on the selection of records shown in the data form. In general, a data form is independent of worksheet-based operations you perform on your database.

If a database has too many fields for the standard data form layout, Excel displays only as many fields as will fit. There is no way to scroll to the undisplayed fields.

To Edit a Record in the Data Form

1. Choose Data ➤ Form to open the data form for the current database.

2. Scroll to the record that you want to edit, and make changes in any of the text boxes displaying the fields of the record.

3. Scroll to a different record. Excel copies the changes in the edited record to the database itself.

NOTES

Before scrolling to a different record, you can click the Restore button to bring back the original unedited version of the current record. Once you scroll to a different record, however, any changes you have made are copied to the database.

Computed fields cannot be edited in the data form. The data form displays the current value of each calculated field, but not in a text box.

To Add New Records to the Database in the Data Form

1. Choose Data ➤ Form to open the data form for the current database.

2. Click the New button. The data form displays blank text boxes for all of the fields that can be edited. The words

"New Record" appear at the upper-right corner of the data form.

3. Enter a data item for each of the fields of the new record

4. Press Enter to add the new record to the database. The data form displays blank fields for the next new record.

5. Repeat steps 3 and 4 for each new record you want to add to the database.

6. Click the Close button to close the data form.

NOTES

The data form always appends new records to the end of the database, regardless of the current order of other records. Choose Data ➤ Sort to rearrange the database after you have added one or more records. (See SORTING for details.)

If your database contains one or more computed fields, Excel automatically copies the field formulas into each new record that you add into the data form.

To Delete a Record in the Data Form

1. Choose Data ➤ Form to open the data form for the current database.

2. Scroll to the record that you want to delete.

3. Click the Delete button. A message box appears on the screen asking you to confirm the deletion.

4. Click OK to delete the record from the database, or click Cancel to back out of the deletion.

NOTES

You cannot undo a record deletion that you complete in the data form. In contrast, if you delete a database record by deleting its row directly from the worksheet (select the row and choose Edit ➤ Delete), you can use the Edit ➤ Undo Delete command to bring back the record.

To Search for Records in the Data Form

1. Choose Data ➤ Form to open the data form for the current database.

2. Click the Criteria button. The data form displays a blank text box for each of the fields in the database, including the computed fields. The word "Criteria" appears in the upper-right corner of the data form, and the scroll bar is temporarily removed.

3. Enter a comparison criterion into any one of the field boxes. The criterion can be any text or numeric entry that you want to search for. Alternatively, you can begin the criterion expression with any of Excel's six comparison operators (=, <, >, <=, >=, <>), or you can include wildcard characters (* or ?) to search for variations of matching text. See DATABASE CRITERIA for more information about criteria expressions.

4. Repeat step 3 for each field in which you want to include a criterion. If you enter multiple criteria into the data form, Excel reads them as "and" conditions—that is, a record must meet all of the criteria to be selected as a match.

5. Click the Find Next button to find the first record that matches your criteria, and then click the same button repeatedly to find subsequent matching records. Optionally, click the Find Prev button to scroll backwards through the matching records. Excel beeps in response to either button when there are no more matching records in the specified direction.

6. Click Close to close the data form when you are finished examining the matching records.

NOTES

Excel does not retain the criteria when you close the data form. The next time you open the data form and click the Criteria button, all of the field boxes will be blank.

You can revise the search criteria at any time while the data form is open. Click the Criteria button to view the current criteria, and edit the entry in any of the field boxes. Click Clear to erase all the current criteria, or click Restore to bring back the previous criteria.

To Create a Custom Data Form

1. Open the folder in which the Excel files are stored.

2. Double-click the Dialog Editor icon to start the application. An empty dialog box appears in the center of the Macintosh desktop .

3. Choose Item ➤ Text from the Dialog Editor's menu. A text item is added to the dialog box. Type a label that will serve to identify a field in the data form. Optionally, include an ampersand (&) in the label, just before the character that you want to designate as the ⌘ key for selecting the field. The current text item displays the label as you type it. (Do not press Enter.)

4. Choose Item ➤ Edit Box. In the resulting dialog box, click OK without changing the Text option selection. An edit box item appears in the dialog box you are building.

5. Choose Edit ➤ Info. This command allows you to define the characteristics of the current edit box item. In the dialog box resulting from the command, select the text box labeled Init/Result and enter the name of the database field that the current edit box item will represent. Then click OK.

6. Repeat steps 3, 4, and 5 for each field that you want to include in the custom data form. As you add new items to the form, drag the borders of the dialog box to change its size and shape. When you have added all the field items, arrange them inside the form in any way you want. To move an item to a new position in the form, drag it with the mouse.

7. Choose Edit ➤ Select Dialog, and then choose Edit ➤ Copy to copy the dialog box to the Clipboard. Choose File ➤ Quit to close the Dialog Editor application.

8. Return to the Excel application, and activate the worksheet that contains your database. Select a location to the right of the database itself, and out of the way of any criteria range you may have already entered into the worksheet. Then choose Edit ➤ Paste. A seven-column table of information—known as the dialog box definition table—appears in your worksheet. The first row in this table represents the characteristics of the dialog box itself, and each subsequent row represents the characteristics of one item you added to the dialog box.

9. Select the entire table and choose Formula ➤ Define Name. Enter the name Data_Form in the name text box and click OK. This completes the definition of your custom data form.

10. Scroll back to the database range, and choose Data ➤ Form. Instead of Excel's standard data form layout, your custom data form now appears on the screen. (The column of command buttons at the right side of the data form is the same as in the standard layout.)

EXAMPLE

The table below defines a custom data form for a database of software consultants. (See DATABASES SNAPGUIDE to view the database example itself.) The Data_Form range is N1:T17.

	N	O	P	Q	R	S	T
1							
2	5	40	50			&First	
3	6	40	25	40			First
4	5	104	50			&Last Name	
5	6	104	25	120			Last
6	5	40	100			&City	
7	6	40	75	160			City
8	5	216	100			&Region	
9	6	216	75	40			Region
10	5	40	149			&Specialty	
11	6	40	125	160			Specialty
12	5	216	150			Ra&te	
13	6	216	125	64			Rate
14	5	40	200			Contract &Date	
15	6	40	175	160			Contract
16	5	112	230			Years of Experience	
17	6	40	225	64			Years

In this example, the first row of the table, which normally
describes the position and dimensions of the dialog box itself,
is blank. Whether this first row is blank or not, it must be included in the Data_Form range. From left to right, the seven
columns of the table represent the following characteristics of a
given item in the custom form: the item type (5 for a text label,
and 6 for a text edit box); the item's horizontal position (x coordinate); the item's vertical position (y coordinate); the item's
width; the item's height (left blank for automatic adjustment); the
text entry for a label (blank for an edit box); and the Init/Result
entry for an edit box (blank for a label). Here is the resulting
custom data form:

NOTES

To restore Excel's default data form layout for the current database, choose Formula ➤ Define Name, select the Data_Form name, and click the Delete button. This deletes the Data_Form name without deleting the dialog box definition table itself. If you later want to restore the custom data form, you can simply redefine the Data_Form name.

A database worksheet can contain any number of dialog box definition tables for custom data forms. The active data form is the one that is currently named Data_Form.

You can fine-tune a custom data form definition by editing the entries in the definition table. For major changes, however, you'll probably want to return to the Dialog Editor. You can copy the table to the Clipboard and then paste it into the Dialog Editor; when you do so, the Dialog Editor displays the data form graphically rather than as a definition table.

SEE ALSO

Databases SnapGuide, Database Criteria, Database Operations, Dialog Editor, Sorting.

Data Tables

In a data table, Excel calculates multiple results from a formula that contains one or two variables. A one-input data table includes a column or a row of values to be substituted into a single variable. A two-input table has both a column and a row of values to be substituted into two variables. In either case, you choose the Data ➤ Table command to fill in the table after you set up a worksheet for this operation.

To Create a One-Input Data Table with One Formula

1. Enter a single column of values and then enter a target formula in the cell one row above and one column to the right of the values. Or, enter a single row of values and a target formula just below and to the left. The formula includes a reference to an input cell elsewhere on the worksheet; this is the formula's "variable."

2. Select the two-column or two-row range that includes the values and the formula.

3. Choose Data ➤ Table. In the resulting dialog box, enter a reference to the input cell into the Column Input Cell box for a column-oriented table, or the Row Input Cell box for a row-oriented table. Click OK, and Excel immediately fills in the table.

EXAMPLE

In the following column-oriented data table, cell B8 contains a formula for calculating the break-even point in the unit sales of a manufactured product:

    =B4/(B5–B3)

Cell B4 shows the fixed costs associated with the product. B5 is the wholesale price per unit, and B3 is one estimate of the anticipated per-unit manufacturing cost. The columns of cells in A9:A17 contains a range of other estimates for the per-unit manufacturing cost. The goal is to find the break-even point corresponding to each of these per-unit cost estimates. To create the table of break-even points, you select the range A8:B17 and choose the Data ➤ Table command. In the Table dialog box, enter a reference to the input cell, B3, in the Column Input Cell box, and click OK. Excel substitutes each of the entries in A9:A17 into the input

cell B3, and produces the resulting break-even calculations in
B9:B17, as follows:

	A	B	C	D
1	Product X			
2				
3	Manufacturing cost per unit	$1.25	<- column input cell	
4	Fixed costs	$28,000		
5	Wholesale price per unit	$8.25		
6				
7	*Break-even point analysis*			
8		4000		
9	$0.95	3836		
10	$1.05	3889		
11	$1.15	3944		
12	$1.25	4000		
13	$1.35	4058		
14	$1.45	4118		
15	$1.55	4179		
16	$1.65	4242		
17	$1.75	4308		

NOTES

A one-input data table can contain more than one formula. For example, in the break-even point worksheet, you could enter the
following formula into cell C8 to calculate the dollar sales at the
break-even point:

$$=B5*B4/(B5-B3)$$

To fill in the two-formula data table, select the range A8:C17 and
then choose the Data ➤ Table command.

To Create a Two-Input Data Table

1. Enter the target formula into the upper-left corner cell of
   the range where you want to create the data table. The formula includes references to two input cells elsewhere on
   the worksheet; these are the formula's two "variables."

2. Enter a column of input values beneath the formula, and a row of input values to the right of the formula.

3. Select the two-dimensional range of cells that includes the formula and the row and column of input values.

4. Choose Data ➤ Table. Enter references to the two input cells into the Row Input Cell and Column Input Cell text boxes. Click OK, and Excel fills in the data table.

EXAMPLE

In the following break-even point worksheet, A9:A17 contains a range of per-unit manufacturing cost estimates, and B8:F8 contains a range of fixed cost estimates. The break-even point formula in cell A8 is the same as in the previous example:

=B4/(B5–B3)

To fill in the data table, select the range A8:F17, and choose Data ➤ Table. Enter a reference to B4 as the Row Input Cell, and B3 as the Column Input Cell. Here is the resulting table:

	A	B	C	D	E	F
1	Product X					
2						
3	Manufacturing cost per unit	$1.25	<- column input cell			
4	Fixed costs	$28,000	<- row input cell			
5	Wholesale price per unit	$8.25				
6						
7	Break-even point analysis					
8	4000	$24,000	$26,000	$28,000	$30,000	$32,000
9	$0.95	3288	3562	3836	4110	4384
10	$1.05	3333	3611	3889	4167	4444
11	$1.15	3380	3662	3944	4225	4507
12	$1.25	3429	3714	4000	4286	4571
13	$1.35	3478	3768	4058	4348	4638
14	$1.45	3529	3824	4118	4412	4706
15	$1.55	3582	3881	4179	4478	4776
16	$1.65	3636	3939	4242	4545	4848
17	$1.75	3692	4000	4308	4615	4923

 NOTES

Excel enters an array formula into the worksheet to calculate a one-input or two-input data table. Consequently, you can change any one of the input values in the column at the left side of the table or the row at the top of the table, and the corresponding table results are automatically recalculated.

 SEE ALSO

Array Formulas.

SnapGuide to Databases

An Excel database is a rectangular arrangement of information stored in a worksheet. The columns in the database range are known as fields, and the rows are records. The top row of the database contains the field names. After you create and define a database you can use the commands in Excel's Data menu to perform a variety of operations—such as searching for records that match specified criteria, extracting records, deleting records, and sorting the database. Excel also provides a special data form dialog box that simplifies several basic database operations.

Planning, Creating, and Defining a Database

The first task in creating a database is deciding how you want to structure the information it will contain. How many fields should there be, and what type of data will each field represent? What are the most appropriate field names to use? Will your database include computed fields with values calculated from information in other fields? In what order should you enter the records of the database? The answers to these questions will help you plan your database before you begin the actual process of data entry.

To Create an Excel Database

1. In a worksheet, enter a row of field names at the top of the range where you plan to create the database. Enter a unique field name in each cell.

2. Enter one record of information in each row after the field names. A field entry may be text, a number, a date, a time value, or even a formula, but the entries in a given field column should all contain the same type of data. Do not leave any rows blank between records.

3. Select the entire database range, including the row of field names and all the records you have entered beneath it. Optionally, include a blank row after the last record in the database range. (This blank row makes it easier to append new records to the database.)

4. Choose Data ➤ Set Database. As a result of this command, Excel assigns the name Database to the selected range.

EXAMPLE

The database below contains records of information about software consultants working in major cities. The database has eight fields—providing the last name, first initial, city, region, specialty area, hourly rate, first contract date, and years of experience for each consultant. There are twenty records in the database:

	A	B	C	D	E	F	G	H
1								
2	Abrams	P.	Atlanta	S	Database	$125	20-Oct-90	1.8
3	Alexander	E.	Los Angeles	W	WP	$150	14-Jun-91	1.1
4	Ballinger	I.	Boston	E	Spreadsheet	$150	12-Feb-87	5.5
5	Cody	L.	Los Angeles	W	Database	$75	20-Jun-90	2.1
6	Davis	G.	San Francisco	W	WP	$150	09-Jul-87	5.1
7	Fitzpatrick	P.	New York	E	Database	$125	07-Nov-86	5.7
8	Garrison	V.	Boston	E	WP	$125	06-May-86	6.2
9	Gill	P.	Los Angeles	W	Spreadsheet	$100	22-Jun-87	5.1
10	Harris	P.	Dallas	S	Spreadsheet	$150	12-Feb-91	1.5
11	Hayes	S.	San Francisco	W	Database	$75	07-Feb-86	6.5
12	Jones	L.	Atlanta	S	Spreadsheet	$125	10-Feb-88	4.5
13	Jordan	E.	Dallas	S	WP	$100	06-Oct-86	5.8
14	Kwan	O.	New York	E	Spreadsheet	$100	21-Jun-86	6.1
15	Lambert	S.	Dallas	S	Database	$150	26-Jun-87	5.1
16	Leung	M.	Chicago	N	WP	$100	26-Mar-91	1.4
17	Manning	P.	Atlanta	S	WP	$75	09-Nov-86	5.7
18	Meyer	J.	New York	E	WP	$150	05-May-87	5.2
19	Roberts	P.	Chicago	N	Spreadsheet	$100	21-Aug-91	0.9
20	Taylor	F.	Boston	E	Database	$100	24-Oct-86	5.8
21	Williams	C.	Chicago	N	Database	$150	02-Oct-87	4.8

NOTES

A field name is any text entry. In writing field names you do not necessarily have to follow the same rules that Excel imposes on range names. See NAMES for information about range names. Some database operations are simplified, however, if field names are written as legal range names.

A computed field is a database column that contains formula entries. To create a computed field, enter a formula for the first record, and then copy the formula down the column to each subsequent record. The Years field in the consultant database is a computed field, calculated as the difference in years between the first contract date (the Contract field) and the current date.

Working with a Database

In addition to the database range itself, you can define two other special worksheet ranges for performing particular operations with your database:

▲ A criteria range contains special expressions that Excel uses for selecting records from the database. In the first row of a criteria range you copy field names from your database. Below the field names you enter one or more rows of criteria expressions. Once you have created the range, you choose the Data ➤ Set Criteria command to define the range. In response, Excel assigns the name Criteria to the range. See the DATABASE CRITERIA entry for more information.

▲ An extract range is a location where Excel can copy a selection of fields and records from your database. In an extract operation, Excel finds records that match the expressions in a defined criteria range and copies those records to the extract range. You create an extract range by entering a row of field names and then using the Data ➤ Set Extract command to define the range. Excel assigns the name Extract to the range.

With these three defined ranges—Database, Criteria, and Extract—you can perform any database operation available in Excel.

Specifically, you can choose the following commands from the Data menu:

Command	Use
Find	locates records that match the expressions in the current criteria range.
Extract	copies selected records to an extract range, as described above.
Delete	removes selected records permanently from the database.

You can learn more about all of these commands in the DATABASE OPERATIONS entry.

You can also use Excel's data form to work with a database. In a data form you can view, edit, append, find, and delete database records. Excel's data form is a simple and convenient alternative to the process of setting up a criteria range on your database worksheet. See DATA FORM for more information.

Finally, you can use Excel's library of database functions to calculate statistical values from selections of records in the database. Each database function uses defined database and criteria ranges to select records for a particular operation. DATABASE FUNCTIONS explains how to use this collection of tools.

SEE ALSO

Crosstab ReportWizard, Data Form, Database Criteria, Database Functions, Database Operations, Queries on External Databases, Sorting.

Database Criteria

To perform operations on a selection of records in a database, you create a criteria range. Excel uses the expressions in this range to determine whether a given record matches your selection criteria. In the criteria range you can write comparison criteria to find records that contain a certain value or a range of values; or computed criteria to find records based on a formula. Once you have created a criteria range, you can use Excel's database commands to find matching records, to extract matching records to a separate table, or to delete matching records from the database.

To Create a Criteria Range

1. Go to a location in your database worksheet that will not interfer with the database. (Use columns located to the right or left of the database range, or rows above the database. Do not enter the criteria range in the rows beneath the database range, because this might limit the growth of the database itself.)

2. Enter a row of field names for the criteria range. The row may contain all of the field names from the database, or only a selection of names. (For a computed criterion, enter a name that is not the same as any field name in the database.)

3. In the row or rows beneath the field names, enter the criteria expressions. Multiple criteria in the same row denote an "and" condition—that is, a record must match all of the criteria in the row to be selected. Multiple criteria in different rows denote an "or" condition; a record is selected if it matches all the criteria in any one row.

4. Select the field names and the row or rows of criteria, and then choose the Data ➤ Set Criteria command.

EXAMPLE

The following criteria range contains two rows of criteria. To be selected, a record must match the criteria in either row:

	J	K
1	City	Rate
2	Los Angeles	< = 100
3	New York	< = 100

The criteria range is J1:K3. Each row in the range contains two comparison criteria. The first row searches for records in which the City field contains the entry "Los Angeles" *and* the Rate field contains a value that is less than or equal to 100. The second row searches for records in which the City field is "New York" *and* the Rate is less than or equal to 100.

NOTES

The Set Criteria command defines the name Criteria for the criteria range. For convenience, you typically create the criteria range on the same worksheet as the database itself. However, Excel allows you to define an external reference to a criteria range located on another worksheet. To do so, choose Formula ➤ Define Name and create an external reference to the name Criteria on the worksheet that contains the criteria range. See LINKS BETWEEN WORKSHEETS for information about external references.

A comparison criterion consists of a simple text or numeric entry, or an expression that begins with one of Excel's six comparison operators: =, <, >, <=, >=, or <>. In addition, comparison criteria can use the wildcard characters * and ? to search for patterns of text entries.

A computed criterion is a formula that includes a relative reference to at least one of the fields in the database. The reference may appear as a field name, whether or not you have actually defined field names as range names in your worksheet. See NAMES for information about defining range names.

For example, in a database of salespeople you might use the computed criterion

=Sales*CommRate>5000

to find all records in which the product of the Sales field and the commission rate is greater than 5000. (The name CommRate could be a field name, or it could be a range name defined elsewhere on the worksheet.) Keep in mind that the name for a computed criterion—that is, the name you enter above the criterion in the criteria range—should not be the same as any of the field names.

SEE ALSO

Crosstab ReportWizard, Data Form, Database SnapGuide, Database Functions, Database Operations, Links between Worksheets, Names.

Database Functions

Excel provides a set of statistical and arithmetic functions that operate on selected records in a database. Each of these functions takes three arguments: a database range, a target field name enclosed in quotes, and a criteria range. Given a selection of records that match the criteria, each function performs a particular calculation on the data in the target field.

To Perform Calculations on Matching Records in a Database

Create a database and criteria range, and then enter any of the following functions at another location in the worksheet:

▲ DAVERAGE(Database,"Field",Criteria) finds the average of the target numeric field entries in the records that match the criteria.

▲ DCOUNT(Database,"Field",Criteria) counts the numeric entries in the target field of the selected records. (Omit the "Field" argument to count all the records that match the criteria.)

▲ DCOUNTA(Database,"Field",Criteria) counts the nonblank entries in the target field of the selected records.

▲ DGET(Database,"Field",Criteria) reads a field value from a single record that matches the criteria. (DGET returns the error value #NUM! if there are multiple records that match the criteria, or #VALUE! if no record matches the criteria.)

▲ DMAX(Database,"Field",Criteria) returns the largest of the target numeric field values in the selected records.

▲ DMIN(Database,"Field",Criteria) returns the smallest of the target numeric field values in the selected records.

▲ DPRODUCT(Database,"Field",Criteria) finds the product of the target numeric field values in the selected records.

▲ DSTDEV(Database,"Field",Criteria) calculates the standard deviation of the target numeric field values in the selected records. (The DSTDEVP function performs the same statistical calculation based on an entire "population.")

▲ DSUM(Database,"Field",Criteria) returns the sum of the target numeric field values in the selected records.

▲ DVAR(Database,"Field",Criteria) calculates the variance of the target numeric field values in the selected records. (The DVARP function performs the same statistical calculation based on an entire "population.")

EXAMPLE

The following function returns the average of the Rate field entries in the records that match the current critieria:

=DAVERAGE(Database,"Rate",Criteria)

NOTES

If you have chosen the Data ➤ Set Database and Data ➤ Set Criteria commands to define the database and criteria ranges on your worksheet, you can use the range names Database and Criteria as the first and third arguments in the database functions. Otherwise, if you have not formally defined the database and criteria ranges, enter range references for these arguments.

The second argument can appear as a field name in quotation marks, or a field number. For example, the following function returns the average of the numeric entries in the sixth field:

=DAVERAGE(Database,6,Criteria)

The database fields, left to right, are numbered consecutively from 1 up to the number of fields.

SEE ALSO

Crosstab ReportWizard, Databases SnapGuide, Database Criteria, Database Operations.

Database Operations

Given a database and a criteria range, you can choose three commands in the Data menu to perform database operations: Data ➤ Find searches for and highlights records that match the selection criteria; Data ➤ Delete permanently deletes database records that match the criteria; and Data ➤ Extract copies matching records to a separate table, in a location that you define as the extract range.

To Find Records that Match the Selection Criteria

I. Activate the database worksheet, and make sure you have defined both the database range and a criteria range. See DATABASE SNAPGUIDE and DATABASE CRITERIA for details.

2. Choose Data ➤ Find. Excel highlights the first record that matches your criteria, and displays special scroll bars for use during the find operation.

	A	B	C	D	E	F	G	H	I	J	K	
						Consultants						
1	Last	First	City	Region	Specialty	Rate	Contract	Years				
2	Abrams	P.	Atlanta	S	Database	$125	20-Oct-90	1.8		*Criteria range:*	
3	Alexander	F.	Los Angeles	W	WP	$150	14-Jun-91	1.1			Region	
4	Ballinger	I.	Boston	E	Spreadsheet	$150	12-Feb-87	5.5			W	
5	Cody	L.	Los Angeles	W	Database	$75	20-Jun-90	2.1				
6	Davis	G.	San Francisco	W	WP	$150	09-Jul-87	5.1				
7	Fitzpatrick	P.	New York	E	Database	$125	07-Nov-86	5.7				
8	Garrison	V.	Boston	E	WP	$125	06-May-86	6.2				
9	Gill	P.	Los Angeles	W	Spreadsheet	$100	22-Jun-87	5.1				
10	Harris	P.	Dallas	S	Spreadsheet	$150	12-Feb-91	1.5				
11	Hayes	S.	San Francisco	W	Database	$75	07-Feb-86	6.5				
12	Jones	L.	Atlanta	S	Spreadsheet	$125	10-Feb-88	4.5				
13	Jordan	E.	Dallas	S	WP	$100	06-Oct-86	5.8				
14	Kwan	O.	New York	E	Spreadsheet	$100	21-Jun-86	6.1				
15	Lambert	S.	Dallas	S	Database	$150	26-Jun-87	5.1				
16	Leung	M.	Chicago	N	WP	$100	26-Mar-91	1.4				
17	Manning	P.	Atlanta	S	WP	$75	09-Nov-86	5.7				
18	Meyer	J.	New York	E	WP	$150	05-May-87	5.2				
19	Roberts	P.	Chicago	N	Spreadsheet	$100	21-Aug-91	0.9				
20	Taylor	F.	Boston	E	Database	$100	24-Oct-86	5.8				
21	Williams	C.	Chicago	N	Database	$150	02-Oct-87	4.8				
22												

3. Press ↓ or click the down-arrow on the vertical scroll bar to find the next matching record. Excel beeps if no more matching records are beneath the record that is currently highlighted.

4. Press ↑ or click the up-arrow on the vertical scroll bar to find the previous matching record.

5. To exit from the find operation take any one of these actions: Choose Data ➤ Exit Find, press Esc, or select a cell that is outside of the database range.

SHORTCUTS

Press ⌘-F to begin a find operation or to exit from an ongoing find operation.

To Extract Records that Match the Selection Criteria

1. Activate the worksheet on which you have defined a database and a criteria range.

2. Go to the location where you want to copy the extracted records, and enter a row of field names as the top row of the extract range. Each name should be identical to a field name in the database, but not necessarily in the same order. The extract range does not need to include all of the field names from the database.

3. Select the row of field names in the extract range and choose Data ➤ Set Extract. Excel defines the name "Extract" for the selected range.

4. Choose Data ➤ Extract. On the Extract dialog box, select the Unique Records Only option if you want the extract range to contain only one copy of any duplicate extract records.

5. Click OK to perform the extract operation. Excel copies information from matching database records to the fields of the extract range.

Extract range:		
Last	**City**	**Years**
Alexander	Los Angeles	1.1
Cody	Los Angeles	2.1
Davis	San Francisco	5.1
Gill	Los Angeles	5.1
Hayes	San Francisco	6.5

SHORTCUTS

Press ⌘-E to perform the Extract operation.

NOTES

Before extracting records from the database, Excel clears any data from all the cells beneath the field names in the extract range. For this reason, you should be careful to place the extract range in columns where there is no other important data. If you choose Data ➤ Extract more than once for the same extract range, Excel first clears the result of the previous extract operation before performing the current operation.

If you have not yet chosen Data ➤ Set Extract to define the extract range on your worksheet, you can perform an extract operation simply by selecting a range of field names and choosing Data ➤ Extract. Note that this shortcut does not assign the name Extract to the range.

Use the Extract command cautiously. The Edit ➤ Undo command is not available after an extract operation.

To Delete Records that Match the Selection Criteria

1. Activate the worksheet on which you have defined a database and a criteria range.

2. Choose Data ➤ Delete. Excel displays a dialog box with the warning message "Matching records will be deleted permanently."

3. If you are sure you want to carry out the deletion, click OK. If you have any doubts about the operation, click Cancel.

NOTES

After deleting a record, Excel moves other records up to fill in the blank rows. Record deletions take place within the column range of the database, so that entries in columns to the left or the right of the database are left intact.

The effects of the Data ➤ Delete command are permanent, and cannot be undone by choosing Edit ➤ Undo. Write the selection criteria for a delete operation carefully.

SEE ALSO

Crosstab ReportWizard, Data Form, Database SnapGuide, Database Criteria, Database Functions, Names, Sorting.

Date and Time Functions

Excel provides a useful collection of date and time functions that you can use for the following general purposes: entering the current date and time into a cell; converting values between various date and time formats; performing date arithmetic for special business applications; and reading specific calendar or chronological information from a serial number.

To Enter the Current Date and Time into a Cell

Use one of these two functions:

▲ NOW() returns a complete serial number representing the current date and time. The integer portion of the number is the date, and the fractional portion represents the time. For more information about serial numbers, see DATE ENTRIES and TIME ENTRIES.

▲ TODAY() returns a serial integer representing the current date.

NOTES

Neither NOW nor TODAY takes an argument, but both must be followed by an empty pair of parentheses.

To Convert between Formats

Use these functions:

▲ DATE(yy,mm,dd) returns a serial number for the specified date.

▲ DATEVALUE("DateString") returns the serial equivalent of a date string.

▲ TIME(hh,mm,ss) returns a serial number for the specified time value.

▲ TIMEVALUE("TimeString") returns the serial equivalent of a time string.

To Perform Date Arithmetic for Business Applications

Use one of these functions:

▲ DAYS360(date1,date2) returns the number of days between the two dates, based on a 360-day business year.

▲ NETWORKDAYS(date1,date2,{holidays}) returns the number of business days between the two dates, not including weekends or the specified holidays. (The holidays argument is an array of dates.)

▲ YEARFRAC(date1,date2,basis) returns the fraction of the year represented by the difference between the two dates.

▲ EDATE(date,months) returns the date that is a specified number of months from the given date.

▲ EOMONTH(date,months) returns the date at the end of the month, a specified number of months from the given date.

▲ WORKDAY(date,workdays,{holidays}) returns the date that is a specified number of work days from the given date, not counting the holidays listed in the array.

NOTES

All but the first of these date arithmetic functions are supplied by the Analysis Toolpak add-in. See ADD-IN MACROS.

To Get Date or Time Information from a Serial Number

Use these functions:

▲ YEAR(date) returns the year from a serial date.

▲ MONTH(date) returns the month, from 1 to 12.

▲ DAY(date) returns the day of the month, from 1 to 31.

▲ WEEKDAY(date) returns the day of the week, from 1 to 7, where 1 is Sunday.

▲ HOUR(date) returns the hour, from 0 to 23, from a serial time value.

▲ MINUTE(date) returns the minute, from 0 to 59.

▲ SECOND(date) returns the second, from 0 to 59.

SEE ALSO

Add-in Macros, Date Entries, Functions SnapGuide, Time Entries.

Date Entries

You can enter a date value into a worksheet cell in any of several date formats that Excel recognizes. In response, Excel applies a date format to the cell, but stores the date itself as a special type of numeric value known as a serial number. The serial number format allows you to perform date arithmetic operations in a worksheet.

To Enter a Date into a Worksheet Cell

Select the cell and type the date in a recognizable format.

EXAMPLE

Here are some examples of date entry formats that Excel recognizes:

3/14/93

3-14-93

March 14, 1993

14 Mar 1993

In response to these entries, Excel applies one of its built-in date formats to the cell and displays the date either as 3/14/93 or 14-Mar-93. Excel stores the date internally as 32580, which is the serial number for March 14, 1993.

NOTES

The starting date of Excel's default serial number system on the Macintosh is January 1, 1904; this date has a serial number of 0. The last date in the system is December 31, 2078, which has a serial number of 63918.

A full serial number contain digits both before and after the decimal point. In this case, the integer portion before the decimal point represents the date, and the fractional value after the decimal point represents the time. (Specifically, the fraction is the portion of the day that has elapsed at a given time.) For example, 32580.25 represents the date/time value March 14, 1993 6:00 AM.

To provide compatibility with other software environments, an alternate serial date system is also available in Excel. In this alternate system, day 1 is January 1, 1900. To switch to the 1900 system, choose Options ➤ Calculation and click the 1904 Date System option to remove the X from the corresponding check box. Make this switch cautiously, however; any existing date entries on a worksheet will be reinterpreted according to the new system.

To Find the Difference between Two Dates in a Worksheet

Enter a formula that subtracts one date from the other.

EXAMPLE

Suppose you have entered date values in cells B1 and C1. The following formula gives the difference between the two dates:

    =C1–B1

Internally, Excel subtracts one date's serial number from the other, resulting in the difference in days between the dates.

NOTES

To include a date in a formula, enclose the date in double quotation marks and use a date format that Excel recognizes. For example, the formula

    ="3/14/93"+90

adds 90 days to the date 3/14/93. The result is the serial number equivalent of the date 6/12/93.

To View the Serial Number for a Date Entry

1. Select the cell that contains the entry displayed in a date format.

2. Choose Format ➤ Number. The Number Format dialog box appears.

3. Select All in the Category box, and then select General in the Format Codes box. Click OK.

SHORTCUTS

Select the cell that contains a date entry and press Control-Shift-+ to apply the General Format.

SEE ALSO

Copying Formats, Custom Number Formats, Date and Time Functions, Formatting Worksheet Data, Time Entries.

Deleting

You can use either the Delete command or a special dragging technique to delete rows, columns, or a selection of cells from a worksheet. When you do so, Excel shifts other cells up or to the left to fill in the deleted area.

To Delete Entire Rows or Columns

1. Select the rows or columns by dragging the mouse along the appropriate row or column headings. (To select a single row or column, click the row or column heading.)

2. Choose Edit ➤ Delete. Or, hold down the Shift key and drag the fill handle up (for rows) or to the left (for columns).

SHORTCUTS

▲ Select the rows or columns and press ⌘-K or Control-minus sign.

▲ Point to the selected rows or columns, press ⌘-Option while you click the right mouse button, and then choose the Delete command from the shortcut menu.

▲ Select any range of cells within the target rows or columns, and click the Delete Row or Delete Column tool. These tools are not initially part of any toolbar; see TOOLBARS for information about installing them.

NOTES

When you select entire rows, the fill handle is located at the lower-left corner of the selection. When you select entire columns, the fill handle is at the upper-right corner of the selection.

The Delete dialog box does not appear when you choose Edit ➤ Delete for a selection of entire rows or columns. If you select a range of cells within the target rows or columns and then choose Edit ➤ Delete, you can select the Entire Row or Entire Column command on the Delete dialog box.

To undo a deletion, take one of these actions immediately after the deletion: choose Edit ➤ Undo Delete, press ⌘-Z or Control-Z, or click the Undo tool on the Utility toolbar.

To Delete a Range of Cells

1. Select the range you want to delete.

2. Choose Edit ➤ Delete.

3. On the Delete dialog box, select the Shift Cells Left or Shift Cells Up option, depending how you want Excel to fill in the empty area.

4. Click OK.

SHORTCUTS

▲ Select the range, hold down the Shift key, and drag the fill handle left to shift cells left, or up to shift cells up. Release the mouse button before releasing the Shift key. No dialog box appears.

▲ Select the range and click the Delete tool. Excel shifts cells to fill in the space. This tool is not initially part of any toolbar. See TOOLBARS.

SEE ALSO

Clearing Data, Inserting, Selecting a Range.

Deleting Files

By using the File ➤ Delete command, you can delete files permanently from disk.

To Delete a File from Disk

1. Choose File ➤ Delete. The resulting Delete Document dialog box has a list of folders and a group of command buttons.

2. If necessary, use the folder list to locate the target file, and then select the name of the file you want to delete. (Click the Desktop button to view all the disks and folders on the desktop level.)

3. Click Delete. Excel asks you to confirm the file deletion. Click Yes if you are sure you want to delete the file, or click No to cancel.

4. Optionally, repeat steps 2 and 3 to delete additional files. Then click Close to close the Delete Document dialog box.

NOTES

In the Delete Document dialog box you can delete only one file at a time. (In other words, you cannot select multiple files in the file list box.)

SEE ALSO

Folders, Opening Files, Saving Files.

Dialog Editor

The Dialog Editor is a separate Macintosh application that comes with Excel. Using this application you can design custom dialog boxes for your own macro programs, or you can create custom data forms for database applications. You design a dialog box graphically in the Dialog Editor window, and then you use the Clipboard to transfer the design to Excel in the form of a dialog box definition table. This table can be stored either on a worksheet or macro sheet.

To Create a Custom Dialog Box

1. Open the folder in which the Excel files are stored. Double-click the Dialog Editor icon to start the application. An empty dialog box appears in the center of the Macintosh desktop .

2. Pull down the Item menu and choose the type of item you want to add to the dialog box. You can add buttons (including command buttons, option buttons, check boxes, and picture buttons), text items to serve as labels in a dialog box, edit boxes to receive user input, group boxes to enclose sets of other items, list boxes, and icons. To add an item to a group box, select the group box first and then choose the item type from the Item menu. (A custom data form uses only text items and edit boxes.)

3. Repeat step 2 for as many items as you want to add to your custom dialog box. Drag the borders of the dialog box to change its size, and drag the items inside the box to rearrange their positions.

4. When the dialog box is complete, choose Edit ➤ Select Dialog to select the dialog box, and then choose Edit ➤ Copy to copy the dialog box definition table to the Clipboard. Choose File ➤ Quit to close the Dialog Editor application.

5. Return to Excel and activate the macro sheet or worksheet on which you want to store the dialog box definition table. Go to a location where the table will not interfere with other data. Select the upper-left corner of the range where you want to paste the table, and choose Edit ➤ Paste.

6. Choose Formula ➤ Define Name, and define a name for the entire range of the dialog definition table. If you are using the table in a macro sheet, assign it a name of your choice. But if the table is designed as a custom data form in a database worksheet, assign the table the name Data_Form. See DATA FORM for more information.

NOTES

The top row of the dialog box definition table defines the characteristics of the dialog box itself. Each row thereafter defines one of the items inside the dialog box.

The table is seven columns wide. The columns are for the following information:

Column	Contains
1	an integer code from 1 to 24, specifying the item type.
2 and 3	the horizontal and vertical positions of the item inside the dialog box.
4 and 5	the width and height of the item.

Column	Contains
6	the text displayed on a label or button.
7	the default initial value or the value that the user enters into the item.

To Use a Custom Dialog Box in a Macro Program

Include a DIALOG.BOX function in your macro. This macro function takes as its one argument the range name of the dialog box definition table:

=DIALOG.BOX(DialogTableName)

The function displays the dialog box on the screen and waits for the user's response. Upon return from the dialog box, any items of information that the user entered into the box (for example, entries in edit boxes, or selections from groups of option buttons) are stored in the dialog box definition table. By reading this table, your macro can find out how the user responded to the items on the dialog box.

SEE ALSO

Customizing Excel, Data Form, Macro SnapGuide, Names.

Dynamic Links between Applications

Under System 7, there are two ways to exchange data dynamically between documents in different Macintosh applications: Dynamic Data Exchange (DDE) and publisher-subscriber links.

Using either of these techniques, you can update the data in the destination document whenever there is a change in the source data.

In Dynamic Data Exchange, the origin of the data is known as the *source document* and the destination is known as the *dependent document*. DDE creates a link between the two documents. An Excel worksheet can be either a source or a dependent document. For a dependent worksheet, Excel creates a *remote formula* that includes three items of information: the name of the linked application, the name of the source document, and a reference to the data that is being shared.

DDE may sometimes prove impractical, due to memory limitations. In this case, an alternative approach is to establish the source document as a *publisher*. This results in a special file, known as an *edition*, which serves as the medium for the data exchange between applications. In this scheme, the destination document is called the *subscriber*.

To Create a DDE Link from a Source Worksheet

1. Activate the Excel worksheet and select the range of cells containing the data that you want to share between documents. (A chart window can also be the source document. In this case, activate the chart window and choose the Chart ➤ Select Chart command.)

2. Choose Edit ➤ Copy.

3. Switch to the other application and activate the document that will be the destination of the data.

4. In the other application, choose Edit ➤ Paste Link, or Edit ➤ Paste Special. (The exact command sequence for establishing the link depends upon the DDE features of the other application.)

EXAMPLE

You can use this technique to create a link between an Excel worksheet and a Word document. Select the worksheet range, choose Edit ➤ Copy, and then switch to the Word document. In the Word menu, choose Edit ➤ Paste Special. In the Paste Special dialog box, select a format for the data exchange, and click the Paste Link button. A table containing the worksheet data appears in the Word document. Whenever you change a value in the source Excel worksheet, the table in the linked Word document is automatically updated.

	Q1	Q2	Q3	Q4
Product 1	$12,345	$11,738	$5,601	$14,167
Product 2	$13,088	$10,426	$8,542	$10,063
Product 3	$12,159	$5,013	$7,244	$12,621
Product 4	$14,462	$14,102	$13,949	$14,264
Product 5	$9,715	$9,932	$7,767	$5,450
Product 6	$8,014	$9,917	$6,790	$5,674
Product 7	$13,562	$13,423	$9,191	$13,406
Product 8	$9,426	$9,095	$7,051	$6,096
Product 9	$7,636	$11,032	$10,552	$5,968
Product 10	$9,796	$10,977	$14,947	$5,894

Worksheet3

	A	B	C	D	E
1		Q1	Q2	Q3	Q4
2	Product 1	$12,345	$11,738	$5,601	$14,167
3	Product 2	$13,088	$10,426	$8,542	$10,063
4	Product 3	$12,159	$5,013	$7,244	$12,621
5	Product 4	$14,462	$14,102	$13,949	$14,264
6	Product 5	$9,715	$9,932	$7,767	$5,450
7	Product 6	$8,014	$9,917	$6,790	$5,674
8	Product 7	$13,562	$13,423	$9,191	$13,406
9	Product 8	$9,426	$9,095	$7,051	$6,096
10	Product 9	$7,636	$11,032	$10,552	$5,968
11	Product 10	$9,796	$10,977	$14,947	$5,894
12					

To Create a DDE Link to a Dependent Worksheet

1. Start the other application and select the data that you want to send to Excel.

2. From the other application's menu, choose Edit ➤ Copy.

3. Switch to Excel and select the upper-left corner cell of the location where you want to create the link.

4. From the Excel menu, choose Edit ➤ Paste Link.

EXAMPLE

You can use this technique to create a link between a Word table and an Excel worksheet. Select the table in the Word document and choose Edit ➤ Copy from the Word menu. Then switch to Excel, select the location where you want to paste the data, and choose Edit ➤ Paste Link from the Excel menu. In response, Excel enters the remote reference as an array formula into the range of the linked data:

$$\{=WordDocument\,|\,Doc!LINK1\}$$

Notice the three parts of the remote reference: the application reference, WordDocument; the document name, Doc in this example; and the data reference, LINK1. (Also note the punctuation used in this remote reference: a solid vertical bar ($|$) separates the application name from the document name, and an exclamation point separates the document name from the data reference.)

NOTES

To view the source document for a dependent worksheet, double-click the mouse in any cell that contains the remote reference. In response, the Finder switches you to the other application and activates the source document.

By default, a dependent worksheet document is automatically updated whenever a change occurs in the data of the source document. This may not be the most convenient way to operate a link if you are planning many changes in the source document. Accordingly, you can use Excel's File ➤ Links command to switch to manual updating.

To Switch to Manual Updating in a Dependent Worksheet

I. Activate the worksheet that is the dependent document in a DDE link.

2. Choose File ➤ Links. The Links dialog box appears on the screen.

3. If necessary, choose the DDE/OLE Links option in the Link Type list. (If this option is already displayed, the links for the active worksheet are displayed in the Links box.)

4. In the Links box, select and highlight the remote formula for the link that you want to modify.

5. Click the Options button. In the resulting Dynamic Data Exchange Options dialog box, click the Automatic option to remove the X from the corresponding check box.

6. Click OK in the Dynamic Data Exchange Options dialog box, and then click Close in the Links dialog box. The DDE link is now in manual mode, and will be updated only on command.

To Update a Manual Link

1. Activate the dependent worksheet and choose File ➤ Links from the Excel menu.

2. If necessary, choose the DDE/OLE Links option in the Link Type list. In the Links box, select and highlight the remote formula for the link that you want to modify.

3. Click the Update button, then click Close. Any changes that have taken place in the data of the source document are now transferred to the dependent worksheet.

NOTES

You can also use the File ➤ Links command to change the remote reference for a link in a dependent worksheet. In the Links dialog box, click the Change button, and then edit the reference in the resulting Change Links dialog box.

To Create a Publisher-Subscriber Link from a Source Worksheet

I. Select the range of worksheet data that you want to share with another document, and choose Edit ➤ Create Publisher. The dialog box that appears on the desktop gives you a variety of options for defining and creating the edition.

2. In the folder box, select the folder in which you want to save the edition file. Then enter a name for the edition file in the text box labeled Name of new edition.

3. Click the Publish button. Excel creates an edition file for the current selection of data.

4. Switch to the other application, and activate the document that is to become the subscriber.

5. Choose Edit ➤ Subscribe To from the other application's menu bar. The subscribe dialog box appears on the desktop.

6. Select the name of the edition file you created in Excel, and then click the Subscribe button. The data from the edition is copied to the subscriber document.

NOTES

After you choose Edit ➤ Create Publisher, you can click the Options button on the resulting dialog box if you want to change the format of the data in the edition. The Publisher Options dialog box contains option buttons and check boxes for controlling the appearance and contents of the edition.

To Update an Edition from a Worksheet Publisher

I. Activate the Excel worksheet that serves as the publisher in the link. Make any necessary changes in the data itself.

2. Choose File ➤ Links. In the Links dialog box, select and highlight the name of the edition from the Links box.

3. Click the Update button, and then click the Close button. The changes in the data are updated in the edition.

SHORTCUTS

Double-click the shared data in the publisher document; in the resulting dialog box, click the button labeled Send Edition Now. This updates the edition and the subscriber document.

To Create a Subscriber Worksheet

I. Switch to the application that will be the source of the data, and activate the document that you want to designate as the publisher. Select the data that you want to share.

2. From the application's menu bar, choose Edit ➤ Create Publisher, and enter a name for the edition. Then click the Publish button.

3. Switch to Excel and activate the worksheet that is to become the subscriber. Select the cell or range where you want to create the link.

4. Choose Edit ➤ Subscribe To. In the dialog box, highlight the name of the edition and click the Subscribe button. Data is copied from the edition to the worksheet.

NOTES

When you designate a worksheet as the subscriber in a link, Excel enters a SUBSCRIBER function as an array formula into the range of the link. The SUBSCRIBER function takes a text argument, identifying the location and the name of the edition.

 **EXAMPLE**

Suppose you select a data table in a Word document, and then use the table to create an edition named Word Edition. You save the edition in a folder named Word Files on the Macintosh hard disk, and then you create an Excel worksheet as the subscriber. Here is the array formula that Excel enters into the link range:

=SUBSCRIBER("MacintoshHD:Word Files:Word Edition")

To Update a Subscriber Worksheet

1. Double-click any cell in the link range.

2. In the resulting dialog box, click the Get Edition Now button. The data in the subscriber worksheet is updated from the latest changes in the edition.

 **NOTES**

If the data in the subscriber is not updated as expected, make sure edition file has been updated from the publisher.

 **SEE ALSO**

Links between Worksheets, Object Linking and Embedding (OLE).

Engineering Functions

The Analysis ToolPak add-in supplies a library of over forty mathematical and technical functions suitable for engineering applications. If you have installed the add-in, you can enter these functions directly into worksheets, or you can select them from the Formula ➤ Paste Function command.

To Select an Engineering Function

1. Select the cell or cells where you want to enter the function and choose Formula ➤ Paste Function.

2. In the Function Category list, select the Engineering category. In response, Excel lists the engineering functions in the Paste Function box. (If this category is not available, the Analysis TookPak has not been installed.)

3. Select a function name and click OK.

4. In the formula bar, enter actual arguments for the function, and then press Enter.

NOTES

The engineering function category includes the following groups of tools:

▲ Base conversion functions for converting between binary, octal, decimal, and hexidecimal numbers (BIN2DEC, BIN2HEX, BIN2OCT, DEC2BIN, DEC2HEX, DEC2OCT, HEX2BIN, HEX2DEC, HEX2OCT, OCT2BIN, OCT2DEC, OCT2HEX).

▲ Bessel functions (BESSELI, BESSELJ, BESSELK, BESSELY).

▲ Complex number functions (COMPLEX, IMABS, IMAGINARY, IMARGUMENT, IMCONJUGATE, IMCOS, IMDIV, IMEXP, IMLN, IMLOG2, IMLOG10, IMPOWER, IMPRODUCT, IMREAL, IMSIN, IMSQRT, IMSUB, IMSUM).

▲ Degree and radian conversion functions (DEGREES, RADIANS).

▲ Error functions (ERF, ERFC).

▲ A measurement conversion function (CONVERT).

▲ Miscellaneous (DELTA, GESTEP).

SEE ALSO

Add-in Macros, Functions SnapGuide, Mathematical Functions.

Excel Window

You can choose the Options ➤ Workspace command to select the elements you want displayed in the Excel application window.

To Display or Hide Elements of the Excel Window

Choose Options ➤ Workspace, and click any combination of check box options in the Display box. You can choose to display or hide the status bar, the information window, the scroll bars, the formula bar, and the note indicators. (You can also switch to the R1C1 reference format.)

SEE ALSO

Formula Bar, Info Window, Notes, References, Toolbars.

Exiting Excel

When you close Excel, the program gives you the opportunity to save any documents that have been edited but not updated to disk.

To Exit Excel

Choose File ➤ Quit. For each unsaved document, Excel displays a prompt asking you for instructions: Click Yes to save the document to disk, or click No to abandon the changes in the document. Click Cancel to return to the Excel application window.

 **SHORTCUTS**

Press ⌘-Q.

 **SEE ALSO**

Window Operations.

File Formats

You can use the File ➤ Save As command to save files in the formats used by software other than Excel. Likewise, the File ➤ Open command allows you to open files created in other programs and convert those files to the Excel worksheet format.

To Save a File in a Selected Format

1. Activate the Excel worksheet that you want to save in a new format, and choose File ➤ Save As. In the resulting dialog box, enter a file name into the Save Worksheet as text box and select a folder from the list of folders.

2. Click the Options button. In the Save Options dialog box, pull down the File Format list, and select the format in which you want to save the file.

3. Click OK to confirm the file type selection, and then click Save to save the file.

 **NOTES**

The File Format list includes the following file formats:

▲ Normal is the Excel worksheet format.

▲ Template is the format for Excel template files. See TEMPLATES for details.

111

▲ Excel 3.0 and Excel 2.2 are formats for previous versions of Excel.

▲ SYLK (Symbolic Link) is a data transfer format that many applications can read and write. (It is most commonly associated with Multiplan.)

▲ Text is a column-oriented text file, where data items are separated by tabs. (The File Format list also has versions of this format for Windows, OS/2, and DOS systems.)

▲ CSV (Comma Separated Values) is a text file in which data items are separated by commas. (The File Format list also has versions of this format for Windows, OS/2, and DOS systems.)

▲ WKS, WK1, and WK3 are formats for versions of Lotus 1-2-3. (When appropriate, Excel creates an associated format file with an extension name of FMT or FM3.)

▲ DIF (Data Interchange Format) is a data-transfer format that many applications can read and write. (It was introduced with VisiCalc, the first popular spreadsheet program for personal computers.)

▲ DBF 2, DBF 3, and DBF 4 are formats for versions of the dBASE II, III, and IV database-management programs.

To save a worksheet in one of the dBASE formats, you must first choose Data ➤ Set Database to define the database range.

You can use the Apple File Exchange application to read and translate files from disks formatted under DOS. After translating an Excel for Windows file, you can then open the file directly into Excel for the Macintosh.

To Open a File in a Selected Format

1. Choose File ➤ Open. In the resulting dialog box, select the folder that contains the file you want to open, and then highlight the file name.

2. If the file is in a text format, click the Text button. In the Text File Options dialog box, click one of the options in the Column Delimiter box. These options identify the

character that separates each data item in a line of the target text file.

3. If the file is from Windows, DOS, or OS/2, select one of the options in the File Origin box.

4. Click OK and then Open to open the file.

NOTES

If you correctly identify the separator character in a text file, Excel places individual data items from the file into separate columns of your worksheet. Otherwise, each line of text is placed in a single cell in column A; you can then use the Data ➤ Parse command to separate the lines of data into columns.

The File ➤ Open command recognizes and translates files in any of the formats in the File Formats list of the Save Options dialog box.

SEE ALSO

Lotus 1-2-3 Help, Opening Files, Parsing, Saving Files.

Filling Ranges

The Edit ➤ Fill commands are designed to fill a range of cells by copying the contents of a single cell located at the beginning or end of the range. Alternatively, you can fill all the cells of a range by selecting the range before you begin an entry.

To Use the Fill Commands to Copy Entries

I. Enter a number, text entry, or formula into the beginning cell of the range you want to fill. Optionally, apply any combination of formats to the entry.

2. Starting from the cell containing the entry, select the row or column range that you want to fill.

3. Choose Edit ➤ Fill Right to fill a row, or Edit ➤ Fill Down to fill a column. Excel copies the entry and formats in the first cell to all the cells in the range.

SHORTCUTS

Press ⌘-R or Control-R to fill a row to the right. Press ⌘-D or Control-D to fill down a column. Or, select the range and click the Fill Right or Fill Down tool. (These tools are not initially part of any toolbar. See TOOLBARS for instructions on adding them to a toolbar.)

NOTES

Excel also provides the Fill Left and Fill Up commands for copying entries from the *last* cell of a row or the bottom cell of a column selection. To choose either of these commands, hold down the Shift key and pull down the Edit menu. To reverse the direction of the Fill tools, hold down the Shift key while you click Fill Right or Fill Down.

You can use the Fill commands to fill multiple rows or columns at once. To fill rows, select a range in which the first or last column contains the data you want to copy, and choose Edit ➤ Fill Right or Edit ➤ Fill Left. To fill columns, select a range in which the first or last row contains the data, and choose Edit ➤ Fill Down or Edit ➤ Fill Up.

To Enter Data or Formulas into an Entire Range at Once

1. Select the range into which you want to enter the data or formulas.

2. Type the entry into the formula bar.

3. Press Option-Enter or Control-Enter to complete the entry. Excel copies the entry into each cell of the range.

SEE ALSO

Array Formulas, AutoFill, Copying Data, Copying Formats, Copying Formulas, Selecting a Range.

Financial Functions

Excel provides a library of fifty financial functions in a variety of categories. Many of these functions are part of the Analysis Toolpak add-in macro.

To Use a Financial Function

1. Select the cell or range where you want to enter the function, and choose Formula ➤ Paste Function.

2. In the Function Category list, select the Financial category. Excel displays a list of the financial functions in the Paste Function box.

3. Select a function name and click OK.

4. In the formula bar, enter arguments for the function and press Enter.

NOTES

The financial function category includes the following groups of tools:

▲ Conversion functions (DOLLARDE, DOLLARFR).

▲ Coupon functions (COUPDAYBS, COUPDAYS, COUP-DAYSNC, COUPNCD, COUPNUM, COUPPCD).

▲ Depreciation functions (DB, DDB, SLN, SYD, VDB).

▲ Internal rate of return functions (IRR, MIRR, XIRR).

▲ Loan payment calculation functions (CUMIPMT, CUMPRINC, EFFECT, IPMT, NOMINAL, NPER, PMT, PPMT, RATE).

▲ Net present value, present value, and future value functions (FV, FVSCHEDULE, NPV, PV, XNPV).

▲ Security functions, to calculate interest, discount rate, duration, price, yield, and amount received at maturity (ACCRINT, ACCRINTM, DISC, DURATION, INTRATE, MDURATION, ODDFPRICE, ODDFYIELD, ODDLPRICE, ODDLYIELD, PRICE, PRICEDISC, PRICEMAT, RECEIVED, YIELD, YIELDDISC, YIELDMAT).

▲ Treasury bill functions (TBILLEQ, TBILLPRICE, TBILLYIELD).

EXAMPLE

One of the most frequently used of all these functions is PMT. You can use PMT to calculate the monthly payment on a fixed-rate loan or mortgage. For example, suppose you want to know the monthly mortgage payment on a 30-year home loan of $120,000 at 9.5 percent interest. Enter the PMT formula as follows:

=PMT(9.5%/12,30*12,120000)

Notice that the first and second arguments—giving the interest rate and the term of the loan—are both expressed as monthly amounts. This function calculates the monthly payment as $1,009.03. The return value is a negative amount in this example.

SEE ALSO

Formulas SnapGuide, Functions SnapGuide, Mathematical Functions, Statistical Functions.

Finding Worksheet Data

The Formula ➤ Find command searches for a sequence of text in the formulas, values, or notes of a worksheet or macro sheet.

To Search for Data in a Worksheet or Macro Sheet

1. Activate the document in which you want to perform the search, and choose Formula ➤ Find. The Find dialog box appears on the screen.

2. In the Find What box, enter the text that you want to search for.

3. In the Look in group, select the kind of cell contents that you want to search through: Formulas, Values, or Notes.

4. In the Look at group, select the Whole option if the text you have entered in the Find What box represents an entire cell entry; or select Part if you want to search for the text as a portion of a cell entry.

5. In the Look by group, select Rows to search from the top to the bottom of your worksheet, or Columns to search from left to right.

6. Click the Match Case option, placing an X in its check box, if you want Excel to search for the text in the exact upper-case and lowercase combinations you have entered into the Find What box. Leave this option unchecked if you want to perform the search without regard for alphabetic case.

7. Click the OK button to begin the search.

SHORTCUTS

Press ⌘-J to open the Find dialog box. To search for the next occurrence of the text you last entered into the Find dialog box, press ⌘-H. To search for the previous occurrence, press ⌘-Shift-H.

NOTES

If Excel does not find the target text in your worksheet, a dialog box appears on the screen with the message "Could not find matching data." If the search is unsuccessful, but you believe the text does exist in your worksheet, reopen the Find dialog box and make sure you have selected appropriate options in the Look in and Look at boxes.

You can use wildcard characters in the search text: ? stands for a single unspecified character, and * stands for a string of unspecified characters.

To restrict the search to a specific range of cells on your worksheet, select the range before choosing the Find command or before pressing ⌘-H to repeat the search. Otherwise, Excel searches through the entire worksheet for the target text.

SEE ALSO

Database Operations, Formulas SnapGuide, Notes, Replacing Worksheet Data.

Folders

The File ➤ Open command contains a folder list and a file list box that you can use to change the current folder for opening Excel documents.

To Change the Folder for Opening a File

1. Choose File ➤ Open. The name of the current disk or folder is displayed in a pop-up menu at the top of the Open Document dialog box. The names of all the files and folders within the current disk or folder appear in a scrollable list box.

2. To move up to the level of a containing folder, click the down-arrow next to the name of the current folder and select Desktop, a disk name, or a folder name. (Alternatively, click the Desktop button to move to the desktop level.)

3. To open a folder within the current folder, double-click the folder name in the list box.

SEE ALSO

Deleting Files, Opening Files, Saving Files.

Fonts

You can display and print worksheet data in any of the fonts available on your Macintosh system. You can also select a point size and any combination of styles—including bold, italics, underlining, and others.

To Change the Font of a Selection

1. Select the target data, and choose Format ➤ Font. The resulting Font dialog box has Font, Size, Style, and Color selections.

2. Select a font name from the Font box, and a numeric setting from the Size box.

3. Click any combination of the Style options: Bold, Italic, Underline, Strikeout, Outline, and Shadow.

4. Click OK to apply the font to the current selection.

SHORTCUTS

Press Control-F to view the Font dialog box; however, if an open toolbar contains a Font list box, pressing Control-F instead activates the Font list. Press Control-B, Control-I, or Control-U to apply bold, italics, or underlining to the current selection. Alternatively, click the Bold or Italics tool on the Standard toolbar, or the Underline tool on the Formatting toolbar.

NOTES

As you select options in the Font dialog box, the Sample box shows what the resulting text will look like. To undo all selections and return to the *normal* font, place an X in the Normal Font check box. The normal font is the default for a given worksheet, as defined by the style named Normal in the Style list.

The Format ➤ Font command is also available for a text selection on an active chart window.

To Change the Default Font for a Worksheet

1. Activate the worksheet, and choose Format ➤ Style. The Style dialog box appears on the screen.

2. In the Style Name list, choose Normal if this style name is not already displayed.

3. Click the Define button to expand the Style dialog box. Then click the Font button in the Change box.

4. Choose a new font in the resulting Font dialog box, and then click OK.

5. Click OK on the Style dialog box. The font selection is now the default for the active worksheet.

SEE ALSO

Copying Formats, Formatting Worksheet Data, Point Size, Styles.

Formatting Worksheet Cells

The formatting characteristics of a cell or range in a worksheet include numeric display format, alignment, font, borders, patterns, and cell protection.

To Change the Format of a Range of Cells

Select the range, and choose any of the following commands from the Format menu:

Number	changes the display format of numeric values in the range. See NUMBER FORMATS and CUSTOM NUMBER FORMATS for details.
Alignment	determines the horizontal and vertical alignment, and the orientation of individual data entries in their cells. See ALIGNMENT.
Font	provides a variety of fonts, sizes, styles, and display colors for the data in a range. See FONTS.
Border	displays borders in several styles along selected sides of cells in a range. See BORDERS.
Patterns	changes the background pattern and color of a range of cells. See PATTERNS and COLORS.
Cell Protection	creates a protection scheme of locked cells and/or hidden formulas. See PROTECTING CELLS.

To Change the Default Formats for a Worksheet

Choose Format ➤ Style and modify the definition of the worksheet's Normal style. See STYLES for details.)

Formula Bar

The formula bar is the line beneath the menu bar (and beneath the default location for the Standard toolbar), where you enter or edit data.

To Enter Text or a Numeric Value into a Worksheet Cell

1. Select the cell and begin typing the entry. Your entry appears on the formula bar. The active formula bar also displays an enter box (a check-mark icon) and a cancel box (an X icon).

2. When you finish typing the entry, press Enter or click the enter box to complete the entry.

NOTES

When you first begin a new entry, the word "Enter" appears on the status bar. In the Enter mode, you can complete your text or numeric entry and control the subsequent cell selection by pressing any of the following keys or key conbinations:

Return	completes the entry and moves the selection to the next cell down the current column.
Shift-Return	completes the entry and moves the selection to the previous cell up the current column.
↑, ↓, ←, or →	completes the entry and moves the cell selection in the indicated direction.
Enter	completes the entry without changing the cell selection.

Press ⌘–Option-Return to enter a carriage-return into a text entry in the formula bar. This results in a multiple-line entry in the current cell. (After you complete the entry, choose Format ➤ Alignment and check the Wrap Text option to display multiple lines within the cell. See ALIGNMENT for more information.) Press ⌘–Option-Tab to enter a tab character into a cell.

Press ⌘–U to toggle into the Edit mode while the formula bar is active. In the Edit mode, pressing an arrow key moves the insertion point within the formula bar itself.

To cancel an entry without changing the contents of the current cell, click the Cancel box, or press ⌘–period.

To Edit the Current Entry in a Cell

Select the cell and press ⌘–U to activate the formula bar or click the mouse inside the formula bar.

NOTES

In the Edit mode, press Home or ↑ to move the insertion point to the beginning of the formula bar. Press End or ↓ to move to the end of the current entry. Press ← or → to move the insertion point left or right by one character.

You can use cut-and-paste or copy-and-paste operations to move or copy information within the active formula bar. Drag the mouse to select text in the formula bar, and then press ⌘–X to cut the text or ⌘–C to copy it to the Clipboard. Move the insertion point and press ⌘–V to paste the text to a new position in the formula bar.

SEE ALSO

Alignment, Clipboard, Date Entries, Filling Ranges, Formulas SnapGuide, Time Entries.

SnapGuide to Formulas

A formula in Excel is an entry that performs a calculation or other operation on one or more operands. In a worksheet, the formula's result is displayed in the cell where you enter the formula. The formula itself appears in the formula bar when you select the cell.

Creating Formulas on a Worksheet

A formula begins with an equal sign (=) and may include values, references, names, functions, and operations. When you type the equal sign, Excel activates the formula bar, where you can develop your formula using a combination of keyboard techniques, mouse actions, and menu commands.

To Enter a Formula into a Cell

1. Type = to begin the formula.

2. Enter an operand. To enter a reference as the operand, type the reference directly from the keyboard, or point to the cell or range with the mouse or the keyboard. Alternatively, enter a name you have defined to represent a cell or range, or choose Formula ➤ Paste Name and select the name from the Paste Name list.

3. Optionally, enter an arithmetic operator (+, −, *, /, ^, or %), a comparison operator (<, >, <=, >=, <>, or =), or a text operator (&).

4. Optionally, enter a function by typing the function name and arguments directly from the keyboard, or by choosing Formula ➤ Paste Function.

5. Repeat any combination of steps 2, 3, and 4 to complete the formula, and then press Enter.

Working in the Formula Bar

To insert a cell reference into the active formula bar, you can click the cell with the mouse or select the cell by using the arrow keys. To insert a range reference, drag the mouse over the range or select the range by holding down the Shift key and pressing any combination of arrow keys. The word "Point" appears on the status bar and Excel displays a moving border around the range you have pointed to. If you use the mouse to point to multiple cells or ranges in succession without entering operators, Excel automatically inserts a plus sign (+) between each reference in the formula bar.

To step through the possible reference types—relative, absolute, and mixed—press % – T repeatedly while the insertion point is positioned next to a reference in the formula bar. See COPYING FORMULAS AND REFERENCES for more information.

To replace a formula with its current value while the formula bar is active, press % – = or F9.

You can enter formulas into a each cell of a selected range in a single entry operation. See ARRAY FORMULAS and FILLING RANGES for details.

Precedents and Dependents

A precedent is a cell that is referred to by a formula located elsewhere on the worksheet. Conversely, a dependent is a cell containing a formula that refers to other cells. When you need to explore or review the precedents and dependents on a worksheet, you can use the Formula ➤ Select Special command.

To Find Formulas that Refer to a Selected Worksheet Cell

1. Select a precedent cell.
2. Choose Formula ➤ Select Special. In the Select Special dialog box, click the Dependents option.

3. If you want to find only those formulas that contain an explicit reference to the selected cell, select the Direct Only option. If you want to find all formulas that are dependent on the cell, directly or indirectly, select the All Levels option.

4. Click OK. In response, Excel selects cells containing formulas that are dependent on the original cell.

SHORTCUTS

Select the precedent cell and press ⌘-] or Control-] to find direct dependents. Press ⌘-Shift-} or Control-Shift-} to find all dependents.

To Find Cells that a Formula Refers To

1. Select a cell that contains a formula with one or more references; this is the dependent cell.

2. Choose Formula ➤ Select Special. In the Select Special dialog box, click the Precedents option.

3. If you want to find only those cells that appear as explicit references in the current formula, select the Direct Only option. If you want to find all cells on which the formula is dependent, directly or indirectly, select the All Levels option.

4. Click OK. In response, Excel selects cells to which the current formula refers.

SHORTCUTS

Select the cell containing a formula and press ⌘-[or Control-[to find direct precedents. Press ⌘-Shift-{ or Control-Shift-{ to find all precedents.

NOTES

Excel displays the message "No cells found" if no precedents or dependents exist for the active cell.

SEE ALSO

Arithmetic Operations, Array Formulas, Copying Formulas, Filling Ranges, Formula Bar, Functions SnapGuide, Info Window, Names, References, Selecting a Range, Text Operations.

SnapGuide to Functions

A function is a tool that performs a predefined calculation or operation in Excel. Each function has a name and may require one or more arguments as the operands of the calculation. The result of a function is known as the return value. In other words, a function performs its calculation on the arguments that you send, and then "returns" the resulting value to the cell where you make the entry. Excel has many built-in functions for specific categories of applications (for example, statistics, engineering, date and time operations, and so on). You can add to this large collection of built-in functions by writing your own custom functions on macro sheets.

Using Functions in a Worksheet

You can enter a function directly into a cell from the keyboard, or you can select a function from the categories listed in the Formula ➤ Paste Function dialog box. A complete function entry begins with an equal sign, followed by the name of the function. If a function takes arguments, they are enclosed in parentheses after the function name and separated by commas. A function that does not take arguments still requires a pair of empty parentheses after the name.

To Enter a Function into a Worksheet Cell

1. Select the cell where you want to enter the function, and choose Formula ➤ Paste Function. The resulting Paste Function dialog box has a list of function categories and a box that lists all the functions in a selected category.

2. Select a function category. Then, from the Paste Function box, select the function that you want to enter into the active cell. (Use the vertical scroll bar to move up or down the Paste Function box, or activate the box and type the first letter of the function you are looking for.)

3. Optionally, click the Paste Arguments option to display or remove the X from the corresponding check box. (When this option is checked, Excel inserts argument names in the function entry to guide you through the process of entering arguments.)

4. Click OK. Excel pastes the selected function into the formula bar, preceded by an equal sign.

5. Enter the appropriate arguments between parentheses after the function name and press Enter. The result of the function appears in the active cell.

SHORTCUTS

To display the Paste Function dialog box, press Shift-F3 or click the Paste Function tool on the Macro toolbar.

Alternatively, select a cell and type = to begin the formula; then type the name of the function you want to use. Press Control-A, and Excel inserts the names of the arguments that the function requires.

Entering the Arguments of a Function

You can express the arguments of a function in a variety of formats, depending on the requirements of your worksheet. An argument can appear as a value, a reference, a name, an expression, another function, or any combination of these. Some of these formats are illustrated in the following example, where window 1 displays a worksheet comparing three car loans and window 2 displays the formulas behind the worksheet:

	A	B	C	D
		Car #1	Car #2	Car #3
2	Purchase Price	$19,000	$23,500	$13,750
3	Percent Financed	80%	90%	50%
4	Term of Loan	5	4	2
5	Interest Rate	10.25%	8.75%	9.50%
6				
7	Monthly Payment	$324.83	$523.81	$315.66
8				
9				
10		Average Price	Total Monthly Payment	
11		$18,750	$1,164	
12				

Car Loans:1

	B	C	D
1	Car #1	Car #2	Car #3
2	19000	23500	13750
3	0.8	0.9	0.5
4	5	4	2
5	0.1025	0.0875	0.095
6			
7	=-PMT(0.1025/12,60,19000*0.8)	=-PMT(C5/12,C4*12,C2*C3)	=-PMT(Rate3/12,Term3*12,Price3*Loan3)
8			
9			
10	Average Price	Total Monthly Payment	
11	=AVERAGE(Price1,Price2,Price3)	=SUM(B7:D7)	

Car Loans:2

One function can appear as an argument for another function, in an arrangement known as a nested function call. Consider the following example:

$$=IF(AVERAGE(B7:D7)>375,"Increase the down payments.", "Loans are OK.")$$

The IF function takes three arguments. The first argument is a condition that results in true or false value. The second argument is the value that the function will return if the condition is true, and the third is the return value if the condition is false. See LOGICAL FUNCTIONS for further information and examples. In this case, the first argument contains a call to the Average function. If the average of the monthly payments in the range B7:D7 is greater than $375, this IF function returns the text message "Increase the down payments." Otherwise, if the average is less than or equal to $375, the function returns the message "Loans are OK."

Using Custom Functions

If a macro sheet containing custom functions is open—or if you have created and installed an add-in macro sheet for your own library of custom functions—the names of the functions appear in the Paste Function list. Unless you have designated a specific category for a function macro you have written, all custom functions are listed when you select the User Defined category.

When a macro sheet is active, the Paste Function dialog box lists all the worksheet functions along with Excel's large library of command functions that you can use in a macro program.

SEE ALSO

Add-in macros, Array Formulas, Charting SnapGuide, Copying Formulas, Database Functions, Date and Time Functions, Engineering Functions SnapGuide, Financial Functions, Formulas SnapGuide, Information Functions, Logical Functions, Lookup Functions, Macros SnapGuide, Macro Library, Mathematical Functions, Statis-tical Functions, Text Functions.

Goal Seek

The Goal Seek command achieves a target result from a formula by adjusting a numeric entry that the formula depends on.

To Change the Result of a Formula with Goal Seek

1. Select the cell containing a formula whose result you want to change, and choose Formula ➤ Goal Seek. The Goal Seek dialog box has three text boxes, labeled Set cell, To value, and By changing cell. The Set cell box shows a reference to the cell containing the formula.

2. In the To value text box, enter the result that you want from the selected formula.

3. In the By changing cell box, enter a reference to a cell that the formula depends on. The cell must contain a numeric entry.

4. Click OK. The Goal Seek Status dialog box appears on the screen, and Excel finds the target solution.

5. Click OK to accept the solution. Excel records the new data value in the worksheet.

EXAMPLE

In the following worksheet, the calculated profit from the sales of a manufactured product depends upon development and production costs, the number of sales, and the price per unit:

	A	B
1	Product Profit Analysis	
2		
3	Development costs	$57,500
4	Production cost per unit	$5.25
5		
6	Number of units pre-sold	15,000
7	Estimated price per unit	$17.95
8	Profit	$133,000

The profit formula in cell B8 is:

$$=(B7-B4)*B6-B3$$

Suppose you want to know what the price per unit should be changed to in order to arrive at a target profit amount of $150,000. Select cell B8 (the estimated profit), and choose Formula ➤ Goal Seek. Enter 150000 in the To value box, and a reference to cell B7 in the By changing cell box. Click OK. To arrive at the target profit, Excel calculates a new per-unit price of $19.08:

	A	B
1	Product Profit Analysis	
2		
3	Development costs	$57,500
4	Production cost per unit	$5.25
5		
6	Number of units pre-sold	15,000
7	Estimated price per unit	$19.08
8	Profit	$150,000

Notes

To revert to the worksheet's original data, click the Cancel button on the Goal Seek Status dialog box. Or, if you complete the Goal Seek operation, you can either choose the Edit ➤ Undo Goal Seek command or press ⌘-Z.

SEE ALSO

Iteration, Scenario Manager, Solver.

Graphic Objects

Using tools on the Drawing and Utility toolbars, you can add a variety of graphic objects to a worksheet. The drawing objects include lines, arrows, freehand drawings, and four geometric shapes: rectangles, ovals, arcs, and polygons. (The four geometric shapes can be drawn as opaque or filled objects.) The Utility tool-bar has tools for adding buttons and pictures. You can move and resize a graphic object, and you can make changes in its other visual pro-perties. In addition, you can attach a macro to an ob-ject so that the macro runs whenever the the object is clicked.

To Add a Graphic Object to a Worksheet

1. Choose Options ➤ Toolbars, then select the Drawing or Utility option from the Show Toolbars box, and click the Show button. (Your choice between the Drawing and Utility toolbars depends upon which graphic object you want to add to your worksheet. Open both toolbars at once if you want to add a combination of graphic objects.)

2. Activate the worksheet in which you want to display graphic objects.

3. Click the tool representing the object you want to add, and then drag the mouse over the worksheet area where you want the object to be displayed. When you release the mouse button, Excel displays selection handles around the object.

4. Click elsewhere on the worksheet to deselect the object.

SHORTCUTS

To draw more than one object of the same type, double-click the appropriate drawing tool, and then drag the mouse over each area where you want to draw the object. To quit drawing objects, select a cell or click another tool.

EXAMPLE

The following worksheet uses an oval, an arrow, and a text box to draw attention to a particular part of the data:

	Q1	Q2	Q3	Q4	Total
Product 1	$5,447	$8,369	$5,300	$9,584	$28,700
Product 2	$8,635	$7,488	$9,327	$6,618	$32,068
Product 3	$6,122	$8,897	$5,040	$6,093	$26,152
Product 4	$6,252	$6,542	$5,088	$5,332	$23,214
Product 5	$8,933	$5,884	$8,194	$9,988	$32,999
Product 6	$8,704	$6,790	$5,599	$8,403	$29,496
Product 7	$6,150	$8,233	$7,539	$5,311	$27,233
Product 8	$8,235	$8,675	$6,741	$6,765	$30,416
Product 9	$8,361	$8,311	$5,711	$8,096	$30,479
Product 10	$5,908	$5,863	$7,251	$6,465	$25,487
Total	$72,747	$75,052	$65,790	$72,655	$286,244

Best performance!

See TEXT BOX for more information.

NOTES

To select an object, click its border; the selection handles reappear around the object. Move a selected object by dragging it with the mouse. Change its size and shape by dragging individual selection handles.

To delete an object, select it and choose Edit ➤ Clear, or press ⌘-B. To copy a selected object, choose Edit ➤ Copy (or press ⌘-C), and then select a location for the copy and choose Edit ➤ Paste (or press ⌘-V).

The process of drawing a polygon is different from drawing other objects. Click the Polygon tool on the Drawing toolbar, and then click the mouse at each position in turn where you want to place the corners of the polygon. Excel draws a line between one corner and the next. Complete the drawing by clicking a final time at the object's starting point (creating an enclosed polygon), or double-clicking the mouse at any position (creating an open shape).

In a chart window you can add arrows and text boxes (unattached text), but not other graphic objects.

To Select Multiple Graphic Objects

Click the border of one object to select it, and then hold down the
Shift key while you click the borders of other objects.

NOTES

By selecting multiple objects, you can change the patterns or
properties of all the objects at once.

You can create a single object out of multiple drawings by selecting the objects and choosing Format ➤ Group. Restore the drawings as individual objects by choosing Format ➤ Ungroup.
(Alternatively, click the Group or Ungroup tool on the Drawing
toolbar.)

To Change the Patterns and Colors of an Object

1. Select the object, and choose Format ➤ Patterns. The Patterns dialog box contains options for changing the appearance of the object's border and fill pattern.

2. Select a style, color, and weight for the object's border, and
   optionally click the Shadow check box to display a shadow
   behind the object.

3. Select a pattern style and foreground and background
   colors for filling the interior of the object. The Sample box
   shows what your object will look like after these changes.

4. Click OK to confirm the pattern selections.

SHORTCUTS

Double-click an object's border to view the Patterns dialog box.
Or, point to the object's border and press ⌘–Option while you

click the mouse button; then choose the Patterns command from the object's shortcut menu. To change only the foreground color inside an object, click the Color tool in the Drawing toolbar.

NOTES

To apply patterns to several objects at once, select all the objects before choosing the Patterns command.

To Change the Properties of an Object

1. Select the object and choose Format ➤ Object Properties. The Object Properties dialog box includes options for the placement of the object in relation to worksheet cells, and for inclusion of the object in printed output.

2. Select one of the three Object Placement options. See "Notes" below for an explanation of these options.

3. Optionally, change the Print Object setting. When this option is checked the object is printed with the worksheet; when it is unchecked, the object is displayed on the screen but not printed.

4. Click OK.

SHORTCUTS

Select the Object Properties command from the object's shortcut menu.

NOTES

By default, a graphic object is *attached* to its underlying cells—that is, the object changes its size and shape when you change the height and width of rows and columns where the object is located. To detach an object completely from its underlying cells, select the

Don't Move or Size with Cells option in the Object Properties dialog box. Alternatively, if you want the object to be moved but not resized, select Move but Don't Size with Cells.

To Assign a Macro to a Graphic Object

1. Open the macro sheet that contains the macro you want to assign to the object. (This is not necessary if the macro is stored in the Global Macros sheet.)

2. Select the object and choose Macro ➤ Assign to Object. The Assign To Object dialog box contains a list of all available macros.

3. Select a macro from the list and click OK.

4. Click elsewhere on the worksheet to deselect the object.

NOTES

When you point to an object that has an assigned macro, the mouse pointer changes to a pointing hand. Click the object to run the macro. To select the object without running the macro, hold down the ⌘ key and click the object.

A button object is designed to represent a macro. To create a button object, click the Button tool on the Utility toolbar, and drag the mouse over the worksheet area where you want to display the button. When you release the mouse button, Excel automatically displays the Assign To Object dialog box. Select a macro and click OK. Then click elsewhere on the worksheet to deselect the button. To change the label displayed on a button, hold down the ⌘ key and select the button, and then type the new label from the keyboard.

SEE ALSO

Charting SnapGuide, Colors, Macros SnapGuide, Printing
Worksheets, Text Box.

Group Editing

Group editing allows you to perform identical tasks on multiple
worksheets at once. The categories of operations you can perform
on worksheets in a group include data entry, formatting, filing,
and printing.

To Edit Documents in a Group

1. Open the worksheets that you want to include in the
   group editing session. Activate the worksheet from which
   you want to control the group operations.

2. Choose Options ➤ Group Edit. The Group Edit dialog box
   shows a list of open worksheets and macro sheets. Highlighted documents in the list will become part of the

group. To select or deselect a document for the group edition session, hold down the ⌘ key and click the document's name in the list.

3. Click OK to begin the group session. Excel adds the notation [Group] to the title bar of each document in the group.

4. On the active worksheet, perform the operations that you want to complete on all the documents of the group: Enter new data, edit existing data, format the worksheet, print the worksheet, save the worksheet to disk, and so on. During the group session, Excel treats each document in the group identically.

5. To end the group session, activate a different document—either by clicking the document with the mouse or by pulling down the Window menu and selecting the name of a new document.

NOTES

If you print the active document during a group session, Excel prints each document in the group, one after another. Before printing, you can choose File ➤ Page Setup to establish layouts for the documents in the group, and File ➤ Print Preview to preview each document before printing it.

When you save the active document in a group, Excel saves all the other documents to disk as well.

Choose File ➤ Close or press ⌘-W to close each document in the group. Alternatively, click a document's close box to close an individual document in the group without closing other documents. Either way, this action ends the group session.

To Copy Data to Worksheets in a Group

1. Activate the worksheet that contains the data you want to copy to other worksheets.

2. Choose Options ➤ Group Edit, select the worksheets you
   want to include in the group, and click OK.

3. On the active worksheet, select the range of data that you
   want to copy to the other worksheets in the group.

4. Choose Edit ➤ Fill Group. In the Fill Group dialog box,
   select one of the three option buttons—All to copy data
   and formats, Formulas to copy data alone, or Formats to
   copy formats alone.

5. Click OK. Excel copies the selection to the other
   worksheets in the group.

NOTES

The copied data overwrites any data in the same range on the
other worksheets in the group.

SEE ALSO

Links between Worksheets, Printing Worksheets, Saving Files,
Workbooks.

Headers and Footers

A header consists of one or more lines of text that appear at the top
of each page of a printed document. A footer appears at the bottom of
each page. Headers and footers are typically used for information
such as the date, the title of the document, and the page number.

To Create a Header and/or a Footer

I. Activate the document for which you want to create the
   header or footer, and choose FIle ➤ Page Setup.

2. On the Page Setup dialog box, click the Header button or the Footer button. The resulting dialog box divides the header or footer into three side-by-side sections represented by text boxes labeled Left, Center, and Right.

3. Enter text into any or all of the three text boxes. To change the font or style, select the text and click the Font tool (labeled A) on the Header or Footer dialog box. Make selections on the resulting Font dialog box, and click OK.

4. To include special information in a text box, type one of the following codes, or click the corresponding tool on the dialog box:

▲ &P for the page number,

▲ &N for the number of pages,

▲ &D for the date,

▲ &T for the time,

▲ &F for the file name.

5. Click OK to record your entries for the header or footer, and then click OK on the Page Setup dialog box.

EXAMPLE

The header in the following printed worksheet contains the date, the time, a title, the page number, and the number of pages:

7/21/92, 2:51 PM	*Product Sales*, 1991			Page 1 of 1
	Q1	Q2	Q3	Q4
Product 1	$10,258	$12,187	$8,176	$5,405
Product 2	$8,262	$8,079	$14,425	$5,351
Product 3	$7,783	$6,913	$13,203	$9,614
Product 4	$14,392	$8,200	$5,537	$9,245
Product 5	$14,424	$7,938	$8,268	$13,623
Product 6	$8,580	$11,652	$5,088	$7,587
Product 7	$9,015	$14,263	$14,564	$12,976
Product 8	$6,630	$12,113	$6,571	$9,414
Product 9	$9,429	$6,919	$8,056	$9,127
Product 10	$5,141	$8,465	$13,020	$8,336

To produce this header, enter the following text in the three sections of the Header dialog box:

Left	&D, &T
Center	*Product Sales*, 1991
Right	Page &P of &N

NOTES

You can enter multiple lines into any of the sections in the Header or the Footer dialog box. To start a new line, hold down the Option key and press Enter.

When you save a worksheet, the header and footer text is saved in the file, along with other settings in the Page Setup dialog box.

SEE ALSO

Page Setup, Previewing, Printer Setup, Printing Worksheets, Views.

Help

The Excel Help window provides complete information about all aspects of the Excel application. There are several ways to open the Help window and locate the topic you need: Select a topic from the Help Contents list, click the Help tool on the Standard toolbar, click the Help button that appears on Excel dialog boxes, or simply press F1 at any point in your work.

To Get Help

Try any of the following techniques:

▲ Pull down the Macintosh Help menu (click the **?** icon), and select Microsoft Excel Help to open the Help window.

Select one of the major topics in the Contents list. (To go to an underlined topic in the Help window, click the topic with the mouse.) Alternatively, press ⌘-? to open the Help window.

▲ Click the Search button at the top of the Help window, and type a topic name into the search text box. Click the Show Topics button, and Excel displays a list of topics related to your entry. Select a topic and click the Go To button to view the topic.

▲ Click the Help tool on the Standard toolbar. The mouse pointer turns into an arrow with a bold question mark. Click a tool, a menu command, or any other element in the Excel window to go directly to a relevant help topic.

▲ Click the Help button on any dialog box to view instructions for carrying out the current command.

NOTES

When the Help window is active, the menu bar at the top of the desktop provides several useful tools for using and customizing the Help facility:

▲ Choose File ➤ Print Topic to print the current help topic.

▲ Choose Edit ➤ Annotate to attach your own notes to a help topic.

▲ Choose Bookmark ➤ Define to define a marker for quick access of a particular help topic.

SEE ALSO

Lotus 1-2-3 Help.

Hiding

Use the Hide command when you want to keep a document open but out of view. Within a worksheet, you can hide individual rows or columns when you want to keep specific ranges of data out of view.

To Hide an Open Document

Activate the document that you want to hide, and choose Window ➤ Hide.

NOTES

The Global Macros sheet is hidden by default.

To Unhide a Document

Choose Window ➤ Unhide, select the name of the document you want to unhide, and click OK.

To Hide Columns or Rows on a Worksheet

1. Select the columns or rows that you want to hide, and choose Format ➤ Column Width or Format ➤ Row Height.

2. In the resulting dialog box, click the Hide button.

SHORTCUTS

To hide a single column, drag the right border to the left border in the column heading. To hide a single row, drag the bottom border up to the top border in the row heading.

To Unhide Columns or Rows

1. Select the columns on both sides of the hidden columns or select the rows above and below the hidden rows.

2. Choose Format ➤ Column Width or Format ➤ Row Height.

3. On the resulting dialog box, click the Unhide button.

SHORTCUTS

To unhide a column, drag the thick border (representing the hidden column heading) to the right. While you drag, the mouse pointer appears as two parallel vertical lines with attached arrows. To unhide a row, drag the thick border (representing the hidden row heading) down. While you drag, the mouse pointer appears as two parallel horizontal lines with attached arrows.

SEE ALSO

Add-in Macros, Macros SnapGuide, Protecting Cells, Protecting Documents.

Info Window

The Info window gives you complete information about a selected cell on the active worksheet—including the cell's formula, value, format, protection status, name, precedents and dependents, and any note that is recorded in the cell. You can open the Info window temporarily to examine the properties of a particular cell, or you can keep the window open while you develop a worksheet.

To Open the Info Window and Select Information Categories

I. Select the worksheet cell about which you want to view information.

2. Choose the Options ➤ Workspace command and click the Info Window option. An X appears in the corresponding check box.

3. Click OK. The Info window appears on the screen, and supplies information about the selected cell. While the window is active, the Excel menu bar displays menus and commands that relate to the Info window.

4. Pull down the Info menu and select an information category that you want Excel to include in the Info window. Repeat this step for all the categories you want to include in the Info window.

5. To view the Info window alongside the worksheet window, choose Window ➤ Arrange, click the Tiled option, and click OK. In this arrangement, you can select any cell on the worksheet and view the cell's properties in the Info window.

NOTES

To print the Info window, make sure the window is active and choose File ➤ Print, or simply click the Print tool on the Standard toolbar. To close the Info window, choose File ➤ Close while the window is active.

EXAMPLE

Here is an example of a printed Info window. It displays all the
categories of information available about a particular cell:

```
        Cell: F12
     Formula: =SUM(B12:E12)
       Value: 301469
      Format: Normal Style
              + $#,##0_);($#,##0)
              + General, Bottom Aligned
              + MS Sans Serif 10, Black
              + Thin Top Border
                Medium Bottom Border
              + Solid Pattern
                Light Gray Foreground
                Cyan Background
     Protect: Locked
       Names: annualTotal
   Precedents: B12:E12
  Dependents:
        Note: Four-quarter total sales of ten products.
```

SEE ALSO

Formatting Worksheet Cells, Formulas SnapGuide, Names, Notes,
Protecting Cells, Window Operations.

Information Functions

The information functions are designed to identify cell properties
and data types in a worksheet. In addition, one function, INFO,
provides information about the current operating system and
memory environment. These functions are used most commonly
in macro programs, but can also prove valuable for checking
data in worksheets.

To Use an Information Function

1. Select the worksheet cell where you want to enter the function, and choose Formula ➤ Paste Function.

2. Select the Information category, and then select a function name from the Paste Function box.

3. Click OK, and Excel enters the function in the formula bar. Enter the function's arguments and press Enter.

NOTES

The information functions include the following:

▲ Cell information function (CELL).

▲ Data-type functions, or functions that identify the type of entry in a cell (ISBLANK, ISEVEN, ISLOGICAL, ISNONTEXT, ISNUMBER, ISODD, ISREF, ISTEXT, TYPE).

▲ Error functions (ERROR.TYPE, ISERR, ISERROR, ISNA, NA).

▲ Numeric conversion function (N).

▲ Operating system function (INFO).

The functions whose names begin with IS all return logical values of TRUE or FALSE.

EXAMPLE

The following formula uses the ISNUMBER function to test the contents of a cell before performing a numeric calculation:

=IF(ISNUMBER(B1),B1*5,"")

The expression ISNUMBER(B1) is TRUE if cell B1 contains a numeric entry; in this case, the IF function returns the value of the expression B1*5. But if B1 is blank or contains a text entry, the IS-NUMBER function returns a value of FALSE, and the IF function

returns a blank text value. The cell containing this formula therefore remains blank until B1 contains a number.

SEE ALSO

Functions SnapGuide, Logical Functions, Macros SnapGuide.

Inserting

You can use either the Insert command or a special dragging
technique to insert rows, columns, or a selection of cells into a
worksheet. When you do so, Excel shifts other cells down or
to the right to make room for the insertion.

To Insert Entire Rows or Columns
with the Insert Command

I. Select the rows or columns at the position where you want
to perform the insert operation. (To select more than one
row or column, drag the mouse along the appropriate row
or column headings. To select a single row or column, click
the row or column heading.)

2. Choose Edit ➤ Insert.

SHORTCUTS

▲ Select the rows or columns and press ⌘-I or Ctrl-Shift-plus
sign (+).

▲ Point to the selected rows or columns, and press ⌘-Op-
tion while you click the mouse button; then choose the Insert command from the shortcut menu.

▲ Select any range of cells within the target rows or columns, and click the Insert Row or Insert Column tool. These tools are not initially part of any toolbar; see TOOLBARS for information on installing them.

NOTES

The Insert dialog box does not appear when you choose Edit ➤ Insert for a selection of entire rows or columns. However, if you select a range of cells within the target rows or columns and then choose Edit ➤ Insert, you can select the Entire Row or Entire Column option on the Insert dialog box.

To undo an insertion, take one of these actions immediately after the insertion: choose Edit ➤ Undo Insert, press ⌘-Z or Ctrl-Z, or click the Undo tool on the Utility toolbar.

To Insert a Range of Cells Using the Insert Command

1. Select the range at the position where you want to insert cells.

2. Choose Edit ➤ Insert.

3. On the Insert dialog box, select Shift Cells Right or Shift Cells Down, depending on how you want Excel to make room for the new blank cells.

4. Click OK.

SHORTCUTS

Select the range and click the Insert tool. Excel shifts cells to make room for the new blank cells. This tool is not initially part of any toolbar. See TOOLBARS.

To Insert Cells by Dragging the Fill Handle

I. Select the cell, range, row, or column located before the position where you want to perform the insert operation.

2. Hold down the Shift key and drag the fill handle down (to insert rows) or to the right (to insert columns). The number of rows or columns you insert depends on how far you drag the fill handle.

NOTES

When you select an entire row, the fill handle is located at the lower-left corner of the selection. When you select an entire column, the fill handle is at the upper-right corner of the selection. You cannot use this dragging technique to insert a column before column A, or a row before row 1; use Edit ➤ Insert instead.

SEE ALSO

Deleting, Selecting a Range.

Iteration

Iteration is the process of resolving a circular reference by recalculating a worksheet multiple times. A formula that depends directly or indirectly on its own result contains a circular reference. In its default calculation mode, Excel cannot resolve circular references. To find a result from a circular reference, you must activate the Iteration option.

To Resolve a Circular Reference by Iteration

I. Develop a worksheet that contains a circular reference.

2. Choose Options ➤ Calculation.

3. In the Calculation Options dialog box, click the Iteration option. An X appears in the corresponding check box.

4. Optionally, enter new values for the maximum number of iterations and for the maximum change.

5. Click OK. Excel begins the iterative calculation in an attempt to find a solution to the circular reference on your worksheet.

NOTES

The iterations continue until one of the following conditions is met:

▲ The number of iterations reaches the value entered in the Maximum Iterations box.

▲ The difference in the result of the circular formula from one iteration to the next is less than the Maximum Change value.

EXAMPLE

Suppose you want to calculate the amount you must earn in annual gross income to achieve a specific after-tax income. The formulas in the following worksheet are set up to solve this problem:

	A	B
1	Gross Income	= B2 + B5 + B6
2	Expenses	22500
3	Net Income	= B1-B2
4	Tax Rate	0.28
5	Tax	= B4*B3
6	After-Tax Income	125000

Cell B2 contains the annual expenses, B4 contains the estimated tax rate, and B6 shows the desired after-tax income. Cell B3 calculates the net income as gross income minus expenses. Cell C5 calculates the tax amount as the net income multiplied by the tax rate.

But B1—the calculated gross income—is the sum of the expenses, the tax amount, and the after-tax income. This formula is circular because the tax calculation (B5) depends indirectly on the gross income itself. When you first enter this sequence of formulas into a worksheet, Excel displays the message "Cannot resolve circular references." But as soon as you activate the Iteration option, Excel resolves the circular references as follows:

	A	B
1	Gross Income	$196,111
2	Expenses	$22,500
3	Net Income	$173,611
4	Tax Rate	28%
5	Tax	$48,611
6	After-Tax Income	$125,000

SEE ALSO

Goal Seek.

Links between Worksheets

A link between two worksheets is a means of sharing data and updating it when changes occur. In every link, one worksheet is the *source* document and another is the dependent, or destination, document. You create a link by entering an external reference into the dependent worksheet; this reference identifies the source worksheet and also the source cell or range on that worksheet. You can enter an external reference directly from the keyboard, or, more simply, you can use Excel's Copy and Paste Link commands to establish the link.

To Create a Link Using the Paste Link Command

I. Open both the worksheets that are to become the source and the destination in the link. So that you can view both worksheets at the same time, choose Window ➤ Arrange, select the Tiled option, and click OK.

2. On the source worksheet, select the data that will become the object of the link, and choose Edit ➤ Copy.

3. Activate the destination worksheet and select the cell where you want to establish the link.

4. Choose Edit ➤ Paste Link. Excel enters an external formula into the destination worksheet.

NOTES

If both the source worksheet and the destination worksheet are open, the external reference appears in the following form:

=worksheet!source

where *worksheet* is the name of the source worksheet, and *source* is the range of data in the worksheet. Notice the punctuation: The worksheet name and the source range are separated by an exclamation point. If you save the source worksheet to disk and then close it, Excel expands the external reference to include the disk and folder location of the source worksheet. In this case, the worksheet name and its location are enclosed in single quotation marks:

='disk:folder:worksheet'!source

(Excel also places quotation marks around the worksheet name alone if the name includes spaces or other special characters.)

You can establish a link by entering an external formula directly into the dependent worksheet. The end result is the same as that of the Paste Link command. You can also create a link by entering a more complex external reference formula—that is, a formula that contains an external reference as one of its operands.

If the source data is in a range consisting of more than one cell, the Paste Link command enters the external formula as an array:

{=worksheet!source}

To achieve the same effect, you can press ⌘-Enter or Control-Shift-Enter to enter an external array formula into the dependent worksheet. (See Array Formulas for further information.)

The Paste Link command creates an external formula consisting of an absolute reference to the source range of data. Excel also permits external formulas consisting of relative or mixed references. Copying such a formula within the dependent worksheet results in an additional external formula, where the relative reference is adjusted in the usual way, according to the position of the copy in relation to the original formula. See COPYING FORMULAS.

If you open a dependent worksheet at a time when the source worksheet or worksheets are not open, Excel displays a dialog box asking you if you want to update references to unopened documents. Click Yes, and Excel checks the sources for any changes in data, and updates the destination accordingly. To open a source document and view the linked data you can simply double-click a cell that contains an external reference.

When you create a chart from a range of worksheet data, Excel creates SERIES formulas in the chart document. The arguments of the SERIES function are external references to the source worksheet data. The chart is therefore a dependent document. See CHARTING SNAPGUIDE for more information.

EXAMPLE

One common use for external references is to create a master worksheet that consolidates data from other worksheets and summarizes their results. For example, suppose you have developed detailed annual worksheets for three years of sales data, and you want to combine the total sales from the three years in a single worksheet. To do so, you could use the Copy and Paste Link commands to create external references to the three source worksheets in a single dependent worksheet. If the three sales worksheets are named Sales 1989, Sales 1990, and Sales 1991, and the total on each annual worksheet is in a cell named annualTotal, the external references will look like this:

```
='Sales 1989'!annualTotal
='Sales 1990'!annualTotal
='Sales 1991'!annualTotal
```

If you save the source worksheets in a folder named Excel Files on the Macintosh hard disk, and close the files, Excel expands the external references on the dependent worksheet as follows:

```
='MacintoshHD:Excel Files:Sales 1989'!annualTotal
='MacintoshHD:Excel Files:Sales 1990'!annualTotal
='MacintoshHD:Excel Files:Sales 1991'!annualTotal
```

SEE ALSO

Array Formulas, Charting SnapGuide, Consolidating Data, Copying Formulas, Dynamic Links between Applications, Folders, Formulas SnapGuide, Names, References, Window Operations.

Logical Functions

Using Excel's six logical functions, you can introduce varieties of decision-making formulas into a worksheet. Several of these functions take logical arguments—that is, expressions that result in values of TRUE or FALSE. All but one of the logical functions return logical results.

To Enter a Logical Function into a Worksheet Cell

I. Select the cell, and choose Formula ➤ Paste Function.

2. Select Logical in the Function Category list. As a result, Excel displays the names of the six logical functions in the Paste Function list.

3. Select a logical function and click OK. Back in the formula bar, type arguments for the function and press Enter.

NOTES

The logical functions include the decision function, IF; functions representing logical operations, AND, OR, and NOT; and functions that simply return logical values, TRUE and FALSE. The logical arguments of IF, AND, OR, and NOT often appear as comparison expressions, using Excel's comparison operators <, >, <=, >=, <>, and =. Here are brief descriptions of the six functions:

IF	returns one of two values, depending upon the value of an initial logical argument. The function takes three arguments:

=IF(logicalTest,trueReturn,falseReturn)

If the value of logicalTest is TRUE, the function returns the value of its second argument, trueReturn. If logicalTest is FALSE, the IF function returns its third argument, falseReturn. The arguments trueReturn and falseReturn can be any type of data, including numeric, text, or logical values.

AND *and* OR	take as many as 30 logical arguments. AND returns a value of TRUE if all its arguments are true, or FALSE if one or more arguments are false. The OR function returns TRUE if any one or more arguments are TRUE, or FALSE if all its arguments are false.

NOT	takes a single logical argument, and returns the reverse of the argument's value. If the argument is true, NOT returns a value of FALSE; if the argument is false, NOT returns TRUE.
TRUE( ) *and* FALSE( )	return logical values of TRUE and FALSE. These two functions take no argument. Excel also recognizes the logical constants TRUE and FALSE as legal cell entries. TRUE has a numeric value of 1, and FALSE has a value of 0.

EXAMPLE

For worksheets, the IF function is the central tool in the category of logical functions. You can use this tool to decide between two values or computations for the entry in a given cell. For example, the following IF function examines the value in a cell named income. If the value is less than 75000, the function enters the result of one calculation; if not, the function performs another calculation:

$$=IF(income<75000,income*tax1,income*tax2)$$

In writing the first argument of an IF function, you may sometimes want to use the AND, OR, and NOT functions to express complex logical conditions. In the next example, the IF function examines the values in two cells, named status and income:

$$=IF(AND(status=1,income<35000),income*tax1,$$
$$income*tax2)$$

Finally, by nesting one IF function within another, you can write formulas that perform multiple levels of decision making. Consider this example:

> =IF(income<35000,income*tax1,IF(income<60000,
> income*tax2,income* tax3))

This formula chooses among three different formulas:

▲ income*tax1 if income is less than 35000;

▲ income*tax2 if income is greater than or equal to 35000,
but less than 60000; or

▲ income*tax3 if income is greater than or equal to 60000.

SEE ALSO

Database Operations, Functions SnapGuide, Information Functions.

Lookup and Reference Functions

Excel's lookup functions provide a variety of techniques for
reading individual data values from lookup tables. The reference
functions are designed to return range references from specific
arguments, or, conversely, to provide information about ranges.

To Enter a Lookup or Reference Function into a Worksheet

I. For a lookup function, begin by creating a lookup table
on a worksheet. Then select the cell or range where you
want to enter the function and choose Formula ➤ Paste
Function.

2. Select Lookup & Reference in the Function Category box, and then select a function name from the Paste Function box.

3. Click OK. In the formula bar, enter the arguments for the function, and press Enter.

SHORTCUTS

Enter the function directly from the keyboard. While the formula bar is active, press Control-A to display the function's argument names.

NOTES

The lookup and reference functions can be grouped into the following three categories:

▲ Lookup functions that read a value from a worksheet table, a list, or an array (CHOOSE, FASTMATCH, HLOOKUP, INDEX, LOOKUP, MATCH, VLOOKUP).

▲ Functions that return information about a reference or an array (AREAS, COLUMN, COLUMNS, ROW, ROWS).

▲ Functions that return a reference or an array (ADDRESS, INDIRECT, OFFSET, TRANSPOSE).

EXAMPLE

The classic example of a lookup table is a tax table, where the columns represent taxpayer status, and the rows represent income levels. The following worksheet shows a sample from an imaginary tax table; the range B2:E9 is named *taxTable*:

	A	B	C	D	E
1			Taxpayer Status		
2			1	2	3
3	Income	$28,750	5,051	4,140	4,140
4	Levels	$28,850	5,077	4,154	4,166
5		$28,950	5,104	4,169	4,193
6		$29,050	5,131	4,183	4,220
7		$29,150	5,158	4,198	4,247
8		$29,250	5,185	4,212	4,274
9		$29,350	5,212	4,226	4,301
10					
11					
12					
13		Income	$29,083		
14		Status	2		
15		Tax	$4,183		
16					

The VLOOKUP function is ideal for reading individual tax amounts from this table. The function takes three arguments:

=VLOOKUP(amount,table,column)

VLOOKUP searches down the first column of table for the largest value that is less than or equal to amount, and returns the amount from column in the same row.

Beneath the lookup table, cell C13 has the name Income and cell C14 has the name Status. Here is the formula in cell C15:

=VLOOKUP(Income,taxTable,Status+1)

As you can see, this formula reads the value $4,183 from the tax table. (Notice that the formula adds 1 to the Status value; this is because the columns of the table—B, C, D, and E—are numbered from 1 to 4 for the purposes of the VLOOKUP function.)

SEE ALSO

Arrays, Data Tables, Functions SnapGuide, References.

Lotus 1-2-3 Help

Excel has a feature called Help for Lotus 1-2-3 Users that is designed to ease the transition between 1-2-3 and Excel. This feature provides help for accomplishing 1-2-3 tasks in Excel.

To Use the Help for Lotus 1-2-3 Users Feature

1. Choose Help for Lotus 1-2-3 Users from the Macintosh Help (**?**) menu. (If you are running system software other than System 7, the Help commands are located in the Window menu.) The Lotus 1-2-3 Help dialog box appears on the screen.

2. Enter a 1-2-3 command sequence into the Command text box.

3. Click OK. In response, Excel opens up the Help window and displays the help topic that is most relevant to the 1-2-3 command you entered.

SEE ALSO

File Formats, Help.

Macro Debugging

To examine the actions of a macro in detail—and to focus on macro formulas that may be producing unexpected results—you can *step* through the performance of a macro one formula at a time.

To Step through a Macro Performance

1. Open the macro sheet that contains the macro you want to examine. (This step is not necessary if the macro is stored on the Global Macros sheet.)

2. Choose Macro ➤ Run. The Run Macro dialog box displays a list of all the macros that are currently available, including those on the Global Macros sheet.

3. Select the macro you want to step through, and click the Step button. The Single Step dialog box appears on the screen.

4. Click the Step Into button or Step Over button to step through one formula of the macro at a time. In response, Excel displays the formula in the Single Step dialog box and performs the action that the formula represents. (See the "Notes" section below for the distinction between Step Into and Step Over.)

```
╔══════════════ Single Step ══════════════╗
║                                          ║
║  Cell:   Global Macros!A18               ║
║                                          ║
║  Formula:                                ║
║  =FORMAT.NUMBER("$#,##0_);($#,##0)")      ║
║                                          ║
║                                          ║
║  ┌──────────┐ ┌──────────┐ ┌────────┐ ┌────────┐ ║
║  │Step Into │ │ Evaluate │ │  Halt  │ │  Goto  │ ║
║  └──────────┘ └──────────┘ └────────┘ └────────┘ ║
║  ┌──────────┐ ┌──────────┐ ┌──────────┐ ┌──────┐ ║
║  │Step Over │ │  Pause   │ │ Continue │ │ Help │ ║
║  └──────────┘ └──────────┘ └──────────┘ └──────┘ ║
╚══════════════════════════════════════════╝
```

5. Optionally, to see the result of a given formula, click Evaluate repeatedly until the Single Step dialog box displays the function's final result.

6. Optionally, click Pause to interrupt the program performance. Excel displays the Resume Macro tool in the Macro Paused toolbar. While the macro is paused, you can perform other actions. Click Resume Macro to continue.

7. Repeat any combination of steps 4, 5, and 6 until you have stepped through the entire macro.

SHORTCUTS

Activate the macro sheet and select the first cell of the macro (or any other cell where you want to begin the evaluation), and then click the Step Macro tool in the Macro toolbar.

NOTES

The Step Into button steps through every formula of your macro. If the current formula is a subroutine call, Step Into goes step-by-step through the subroutine. In contrast, the Step Over button treats a subroutine call as a single formula and evaluates it in a single step. If the current formula is not a subroutine call, Step Into and Step Over produce identical results.

For more elaborate debugging requirements, Excel provides a special add-in macro named Macro Debugger. This add-in is located in the Macro Library folder within the folder where Excel is installed. To use the facilities of this program, open the Macro Debugger add-in, activate the macro sheet you want to examine, and choose Macro ➤ Debug. Excel starts a debugging session, and displays a new set of menus with relevant commands. Choose Debug ➤ Exit Debug to end the debugging session and return to the standard Excel menu.

SEE ALSO

Add-in Macros, Macros SnapGuide.

Macro Library

Excel provides a library of add-in macros that are designed to expand the scope of operations you can perform on worksheets, macro sheets, databases, and charts. Some of these add-ins are available automatically when you start Excel, and are represented by commands in Excel's menus. Others need to be opened through the File ➤ Open command.

To Open an Add-in Macro

1. Choose File ➤ Open.

2. Open the Macro Library folder inside the folder where Excel is installed.

3. Select the add-in macro that you want to open and click the Open button.

NOTES

Within the Macro Library folder are several other folders that contain additional add-ins. These folders are named Analysis Tools, Crosstab, Custom Color Palettes, Slide Show, and Solver.

SEE ALSO

Add-in Macros, Analysis Tools, Crosstab ReportWizard, Reports, Scenarios, Solver, Views.

Macro Recording

The macro recorder creates a macro from the actions you perform in Excel while the recorder is on. You can record a macro in an existing macro sheet, in a new macro sheet, or in Excel's special Global Macros sheet.

To Record a Macro on an Existing Macro Sheet

1. Activate a macro sheet, and select a range or a starting cell where you want to record the macro.

2. Choose Macro ➤ Set Recorder. Excel assigns the name Recorder to the selected range or to the entire column starting from the current cell.

3. Activate the document on which you plan to work while you are recording the macro, and choose Macro ➤ Record. In the Record Macro dialog box, enter a name for the macro you are about to create.

4. Enter a letter in the Option+⌘ Key box; this letter will serve as the shortcut key for running the macro.

5. In the Store Macro In box, keep the default Macro Sheet selection. Click OK to begin recording. The word "Recording" appears on the status line.

6. Perform the actions that you want to record: Select cells or ranges, choose menu commands, click tools. Excel records your actions in the specified range of the macro sheet.

Macro1					Worksheet1			
	A				**A**	**B**	**C**	**D**
1	CompanyName (C)			**1**	Appleby Plumbing and Supplies			
2	=FORMULA("Appleby Plumbing and Supplies")			**2**	54321 Fifth Avenue			
3	=SELECT("R2C1")			**3**	San Francisco, CA 94000			
4	=FORMULA("54321 Fifth Avenue")			**4**				
5	=SELECT("R3C1")			**5**				
6	=FORMULA("San Francisco, CA 94000")			**6**				
7	=SELECT("R1C1:R3C1")			**7**				
8	=FORMAT.FONT(,,TRUE)			**8**				
9	=SELECT("R5C1")			**9**				
10				**10**				
11				**11**				
12				**12**				

7. When you are finished recording, choose Macro ➤ Stop Recorder.

NOTES

At any time before or during the recording session, you can choose Macro ➤ Relative Record or Macro ➤ Absolute Record to change the way Excel creates references during the recording. Specifically, this option determines how Excel records a new selection on the current worksheet: as a relative reference in relation to the previous selection, or as an absolute address. (Either way, references are recorded in the R1C1 style. See REFERENCES for further information.) If the Relative Record command appears in the Macro menu, you are currently recording absolute references; conversely, if Absolute Record appears, you are currently recording relative references.

To Record in a New Macro Sheet or in the Global Macro Sheet

1. Select the document that you want to work on while you are recording the macro, and choose Macro ➤ Record.

2. In the Record Macro dialog box, enter a name and a shortcut key for the macro.

3. In the Store Macro In box, select one of the two options: Macro Sheet to open a new sheet for the recording; or Global Macro Sheet to record on Excel's hidden global sheet.

4. Perform the actions you want to record, and then choose Macro ➤ Stop Recorder.

NOTES

If no document is open (or all are hidden), choose the Record Macro command from the File menu to begin recording a macro.

SEE ALSO

Hiding, Macros SnapGuide, Macro Debugging, Window Operations.

SnapGuide to Macros

A macro is a program that automates the steps of a procedure in Excel. You can create two kinds of macros: command macros and function macros. A command macro performs a task, much like a command you choose from one of Excel's menus. A function macro—also known as a "custom function"—calculates a value and returns the value to a cell, just as Excel's built-in worksheet functions do.

Developing Macros

You develop macros on a special-purpose type of document called a macro sheet. A macro consists of a sequence of formulas in a column of a macro sheet. One sheet can contain any number of macros, and all the macros are available for use whenever the sheet is open. Excel supplies a large collection of functions in several categories for use in building macro programs.

To Create a Macro

1. Choose File ➤ New. In the New dialog box, select Macro Sheet and click OK. Excel opens a new macro sheet with a default name such as Macro1.

2. In a column of the macro sheet, enter the formulas of your macro. Use the Formula ➤ Paste Function command, if you like, to insert macro-related functions into cells of the macro sheet.

3. Enter a =RETURN() function as the final formula of your macro.

4. Select the first cell of the macro and choose Formula ➤ Define Name. When a macro sheet is the active document, the Define Name dialog box allows you both to create a name for a macro and to define the macro type and category. Initially the Refers to box contains an absolute reference to the selected cell on the macro sheet.

Define Name

Names in Sheet:
ConvertToText
SerialDate

Name:
DATETEXT

Refers to:
=$B$1

Category:
User Defined

[OK]
[Close]
[Add]
[Delete]
[Help]

Macro
● Function ○ Command Option+⌘ Key: [ ] ○ None

Macro1

	A	B	C
1		DATETEXT	
2		=ARGUMENT("days",1)	*Numeric argument.*
3	SerialDate	=IF(ISNA(days),TODAY(),TODAY()+days)	*If received, add to today.*
4	ConvertToText	=TEXT(SerialDate,"dddd, mmmm d, yyyy")	*Date-to-text conversion.*
5		=RETURN(ConvertToText)	*Return text value.*

5. In the Name box, enter a name for the macro.

6. In the Macro box, click the Function option if this macro is a
custom function, or the Command option if this is a command macro. For a command macro, enter a single letter in
the Option+⌘ Key box. (This letter becomes the shortcut
key for running the macro. If you enter a lowercase
letter, the macro's shortcut is ⌘-Option-letter; for an
uppercase letter, the shortcut is ⌘-Option-Shift-letter.)

7. Optionally, pull down the Category list and select the
category under which you want to list this macro in the
Paste Function dialog box. (The default category is User
Defined.)

8. Click OK to complete the name definition of your macro.
Then choose File ➤ Save As, and save the macro sheet.

SHORTCUTS

Click the New Macro Sheet tool on the Macro toolbar to open a
new macro sheet.

NOTES

Each formula in a macro begins with an equal sign (=). When running a macro, Excel evaluates and performs each formula in turn down the column of the macro. The =RETURN() function ends the macro—and, in the case of a custom function, identifies the function's return value. Excel ignores any text entries within the macro column. Traditionally, macro programmers enter the macro's name in the first cell of the macro column range. (See the "Examples" section below for further discussion of macro sheet formats.)

By default, a macro sheet displays formulas rather than values. When you run a macro, the value resulting from a given formula is stored in the cell that contains the formula itself. To see the values stored "behind" the formulas on an active macro sheet, choose Options ➤ Display and click Formulas to remove the X from the corresponding check box. Then click OK.

When a macro sheet is active, the Paste Function dialog box includes several categories of functions that are available only for macros. In particular, the Commands category contains over 200 functions that are equivalent to individual Excel menu commands. Using these functions, you can perform the action of virtually any menu command from within the control of a macro. You can use Excel's macro recorder to create a macro that is made up of command functions; see MACRO RECORDING for details. Other categories—Customizing, Macro Control, and DDE/External—provide additional programming features for use in macros.

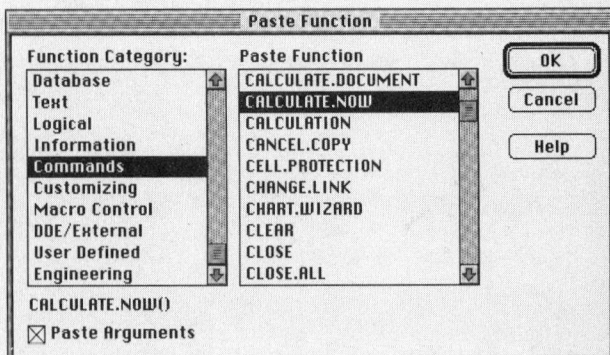

Paste Function		
Function Category:	**Paste Function**	
Database	CALCULATE.DOCUMENT	OK
Text	CALCULATE.NOW	Cancel
Logical	CALCULATION	
Information	CANCEL.COPY	Help
Commands	CELL.PROTECTION	
Customizing	CHANGE.LINK	
Macro Control	CHART.WIZARD	
DDE/External	CLEAR	
User Defined	CLOSE	
Engineering	CLOSE.ALL	

CALCULATE.NOW()
☒ Paste Arguments

In addition to assigning a name to the first cell of a macro, you might also want to name other cells within the macro column. You can then use these names in your macro to refer to values stored behind individual macro formulas.

EXAMPLE

One common use for a command macro is to automate the selection of options in a complex Excel dialog box. For example, the following short macro uses the PAGE.SETUP function to select specific settings on the File ➤ Page Setup dialog box:

A
1 PageSetup
2 =PAGE.SETUP("&CFile name: &F","",0.5,0.5,1,0.5,TRUE,TRUE,TRUE,,,,125,,)
3 =RETURN()

The PAGE.SETUP function has many arguments, corresponding to the text boxes, option buttons, and check boxes of the Page Setup dialog box. See PAGE SETUP for details. When you enter a function like this one into a macro, you include arguments for the settings you want to change and you omit arguments for settings you want to remain unchanged. An omitted argument is represented by a comma in the function's argument list.

You can use custom functions to expand Excel's already large library of built-in functions. For example, you might want to write functions to modify or simplify the use of existing functions, to add new general-purpose functions that are not already available, or to create functions that return specific information that is relevant to your own work in Excel. The following illustration is a date function named DATETEXT. As its name suggests, it returns a text value representing either today's date or a date in the past or future:

	A	B	C
1		DATETEXT	
2		=ARGUMENT("days",1)	Numeric argument.
3	SerialDate	=IF(ISNA(days),TODAY(),TODAY()+days)	If received, add to today.
4	ConvertToText	=TEXT(SerialDate,"dddd, mmmm d, yyyy")	Date-to-text conversion.
5		=RETURN(ConvertToText)	Return text value.

This function is designed to take one optional argument, *days*, representing a number of days forward or backward in time. If you supply a positive number for the argument, DATETEXT adds the number to the current date and returns a text representation of a date in the future, such as

Sunday, June 13, 1993

Conversely, a negative argument results in a date in the past. If you omit the argument, DATETEXT returns a text value representing today's date.

The DATETEXT function illustrates two tools that are essential for writing custom functions: ARGUMENT and RETURN. The ARGUMENT function defines an argument for a custom function. You write one ARGUMENT function for each argument that your custom function will require. The RETURN function defines the return value from a custom function.

Organizing Macros on a Macro Sheet

The DATETEXT example also illustrates a very useful way of presenting macros in a three-column format:

▲ The first column (column A in the example) shows names that are assigned to individual cells within the macro.

▲ The second column (column B) contains the formulas of the macro itself.

▲ The third column (column C) provides brief comments and explanations of individual formulas in the macro.

Because formulas in a macro can refer to other macro sheet cells by name, displaying the names in column A makes the macro easier to understand. This first column also simplifies the steps of setting up the macro: After entering names into the column, you can then use the Formula ➤ Create Names command to assign all the names in column A to the corresponding cells in column B. See NAMES for more information about this command.

Running Macros

The approach you take for running a macro depends upon whether the macro is defined as a command macro or a custom function macro.

To Run a Command Macro

1. Choose File ➤ Open to open the sheet that contains the macro, if it is not already open.

2. If necessary, activate the type of document that the macro is designed to work on. For example, if the macro performs an operation on a worksheet, make sure that a worksheet is active before you select the macro.

3. Choose Macro ➤ Run. The Run Macro dialog box shows a list of all the macros that are currently available for use.

4. Select a macro and click OK.

 **SHORTCUTS**

Press the ⌘-Option-*letter* combination that you originally assigned the macro in the Define Name dialog box (or ⌘-Option-Shift-*letter* if you assigned an uppercase shortcut key). Excel begins running the macro as soon as you press the shortcut key.

 **EXAMPLE**

Suppose you assign the lowercase letter *s* as the shortcut key for the PageSetup macro shown earlier in this entry. Once the macro sheet is open, the fastest way to run the macro is to press ⌘-Option-S on the keyboard. (Alternatively, you can press Control-S.)

NOTES

Excel provides several ways to make macros more convenient to use:

▲ You can save a macro sheet in the add-in format, and then choose Options ➤ Add-ins to add the sheet's name to the list of installed add-in macros. As a result, all of the macros on the sheet are available each time you start Excel. See ADD-IN MACROS for details.

▲ You can save a macro in the Global Macros sheet. This sheet is automatically opened as a hidden document whenever you start Excel, and all of its macros are available for use. See MACRO RECORDING for more information.

▲ You can assign a macro to a graphic object (see GRAPHIC OBJECTS) or to a custom tool on a toolbar (see TOOLBARS). After this assignment, you can perform the macro simply by clicking the graphic or the tool with the mouse. This feature is particularly useful for macros that are stored in the Global Macros sheet, because no additional macro sheet needs be opened to run the macro.

To Use a Custom Function

1. Open the macro sheet that contains the custom function.

2. Activate a worksheet (or macro sheet) and select the cell where you want to use the function.

3. Begin the entry by typing an equal sign (=). Then enter an external reference to the macro. The external reference consists of the name of the macro sheet, an exclamation point, and the name of the custom function.

4. Enter the function's arguments, if any, between parentheses after the macro name. (If the function takes no arguments, type a pair of empty parentheses.) Then press Enter.

SHORTCUTS

Click the Paste Function tool on the Macro toolbar, and select the custom function's name from the Paste Function dialog box.

EXAMPLE

Suppose the DATETEXT function shown earlier in this entry is stored in a macro sheet named Date Macros. You can enter a call to the function into a worksheet cell as follows:

    ='Date Macros'!DATETEXT(365)

Notice the single quotation marks around the macro sheet name; this punctuation is necessary when the name contains spaces or other special characters. In this example, a value of 365 is sent as the argument to the function. As a result, the function returns a text representation of the date 365 days from today.

Using the Global Macros Sheet

You can enter or copy a custom function macro to the Global Macros sheet. (Excel initially creates this sheet the first time you use the macro recorder and select the option to store the resulting command macro in the Global Macros sheet. See MACRO RECORDING for details.) To display the sheet, select Window ➤ Unhide and select Global Macros. Enter or copy the custom function macro. Then choose Window ➤ Hide to hide the macro sheet again. If you were to copy the DATETEXT function to the Global Macro sheet, a call to the function would appear as follows:

    ='Global Macros'!DATETEXT(365)

If a custom function is part of an installed add-in macro sheet, you do not need to enter the function name as an external reference. You can simply enter the name of the function itself, followed by any arguments in parentheses; for example:

=DATETEXT(365)

SEE ALSO

Add-in Macros, Customizing Excel, Date Entries, Graphic Objects, Links between Worksheets, Macro Debugging, Macro Recording, Names, Opening Files, Page Setup, References, Toolbars.

Mathematical Functions

Excel's library of mathematical functions include several categories of tools, including trigonometric, logarithmic, exponential, integer and rounding, random-number, summation, matrix, and miscellaneous calculation functions.

To Enter a Mathematical Function into a Worksheet

1. Select the cell or range where you want to enter the function.

2. Choose Formula ➤ Paste Function, and select the Math & Trig category. The Paste Function box shows the entire list of mathematical functions.

3. Select the name of a function and click OK.

4. Enter arguments for the function in the active formula bar, and press Enter.

SHORTCUTS

From the keyboard, enter an equal sign followed by the function's name, and then press Control-A to display names for the function's arguments in the formula bar.

NOTES

Here is a grouped list of the functions available in this category:

▲ Absolute value and sign (ABS, SIGN).

▲ Base conversion (BASE).

▲ Common divisor and multiple (GCD, LCM).

▲ Factorial (FACT, FACTDOUBLE).

▲ Integer and rounding (CEILING, EVEN, FLOOR, INT, MROUND, ODD, ROUND, TRUNC).

▲ Inverse trigonometric (ACOS, ACOSH, ASIN, ASINH, ATAN, ATAN2, ATANH).

▲ Logarithmic and exponential (EXP, LN, LOG, LOG10).

▲ Matrix (MDETERM, MINVERSE, MMULT).

▲ Products, quotients, and remainders (MOD, PRODUCT, QUOTIENT).

▲ Random number (RAND, RANDBETWEEN).

▲ Square roots (SQRT, SQRTPI).

▲ Summation (SERIESSUM, SUM, SUMPRODUCT, SUMSQ, SUMX2MY2, SUMX2PY2, SUMXMY2).

▲ Trigonometric (COS, COSH, PI, SIN, SINH, TAN, TANH).

▲ Miscellaneous (COMBIN, MULTINOM).

 **SEE ALSO**

Engineering Functions.

Moving Data

You can move data from one range of worksheet cells to another by using the familiar Cut and Paste commands, or by dragging the range with the mouse.

To Move Data Using Cut and Paste

1. Select the range of data you want to move.

2. Choose Edit ➤ Cut.

3. Select the upper-left corner of the location to which you want to move the data.

4. Choose Edit ➤ Paste.

SHORTCUTS

Press ⌘-X for the Cut command, and ⌘-V for Paste, or use the Cut and Paste tools. These tools are not initially part of a toolbar; see TOOLBARS for instructions on moving them to a toolbar.

NOTES

Proceed cautiously when you move formulas that contain references. If you move a formula alone—without moving the range of data that it refers to—the references remain fixed, and the result of the formula does not change. If you move a formula along with the entire range it refers to, Excel adjusts the references accordingly, but again the result of the formula remains the same. However, you should generally avoid moving a formula along with only part of the range of data it refers to.

To Move a Range by Dragging

1. Select the range that you want to move.

2. Position the mouse pointer along the border of the selection. The pointer becomes a black arrow.

3. Drag the selection to its new position in the worksheet. While you drag, an empty frame represents the selection that you are moving.

4. Release the mouse button. The entire selection moves to its new location.

NOTES

To insert the selection between existing blocks of data, hold down the Shift key while you drag. A horizontal or vertical line represents the position to which the data will be moved and inserted. Release the mouse button to complete the move.

SEE ALSO

Copying Data, Selecting a Range.

Names

A name is an identifier that you define to represent a cell or range on a worksheet or macro sheet. You can use either the Formula ➤ Define Name command or the Formula ➤ Create Names command to assign names to cells and ranges. Once you have defined the names, you can use them to clarify the meaning of formulas you write: A name takes the place of a cell or range reference, resulting in formulas that people can understand more readily. You can also define names to represent values or formulas that are not actually entered into worksheet cells.

To Create a Name Using the Define Name Command

1. Select the cell or range to which you want to assign a name, and choose Formula ➤ Define Name.

2. Enter a name into the Name box, and click OK.

SHORTCUTS

Press ⌘-L to display the Define Name dialog box.

NOTES

A name must begin with a letter or an underscore character, and may contain letters, digits, underscores, and periods. Spaces are not allowed. Instead of a space you can use an underscore character or capitalization to clarify the meaning of a name; for example:

>   Base_Usage
>   BaseUsage

Although you might choose to make use of capitalization in this way, alphabetic case in names is not significant to Excel. For example, Excel considers the names BaseUsage, BASEUSAGE, and baseusage to be the same. A name can be as long as 255 characters.

If you select a cell or range that contains a text entry—or is located below or to the right of a cell that contains a text entry—Excel suggests the text for the name when you choose Formula ➤ Define Name.

In the Refers to box of the Define Name dialog box, you can enter any cell or range reference, beginning with an equal sign (=). In practice, names typically represent absolute references, though Excel allows you to define a name for a relative or mixed reference. You can also enter a numeric or text value or an entire formula into the Refers to box; in this case, the name you define represents a value or formula that is not present on the worksheet itself.

The Names in Sheet box lists all the names that are already defined for the current worksheet or macro sheet. You can delete a name's definition by highlighting the name in the list and clicking the Delete button. When you do so, any formula that uses the deleted name results in a #NAME? error value.

EXAMPLE

The following worksheet contains a formula in cell B8 to calculate a monthly billing charge for electricity usage.

	A	B	C
1	*Electricity Bill*		
2			
3	Rate 1	$0.11	
4	Rate 2	$0.14	
5	Base for Rate 1	700	kwh
6			
7	Usage this month	1425	kwh
8	Amount charged	$178.50	
9			

The formula takes into account two different rates charged for usage: the first rate of $0.11 per kwh (kilowatt-hour) is for usage up to a base of 700 kwh per month; the second rate of $0.14 per kwh is for usage beyond the base. An IF function chooses between two possible formulas—one for a month's usage that exceeds the base, and another for usage that is within the base:

$$=IF(B7>B5, \; B5*B3+(B7-B5)*B4, \; B7*B3)$$

If the usage is greater than the base, the formula adds the charge for the base usage to the charge for the usage beyond the base. If the usage is within the base, the formula just multiplies the usage by the base rate. See LOGICAL FUNCTIONS for information about the IF function.

You can simplify and clarify the presentation of this formula by defining names for the cells that contain the rates, the base, and the month's usage: Assign the names Rate1 to B3, Rate2 to B4, Base to B5, and Usage to B7. When these names are applied to the formula, here is the result:

$$=IF(Usage>Base, \; Base*Rate1+(Usage-Base)* \\ Rate2, Usage*Rate1)$$

As you can see, the names make this detailed formula easier to decipher.

To Create Names from Text Entries

I. Select a range that includes text entries that you want to assign as names to corresponding cells, rows, or columns in the range selection. The text entries can appear on the top or bottom row and/or the left or right column of the selection.

2. Choose Formula ➤ Create Names.

3. In the Create Names dialog box, select any combination of the four check box options: Top Row, Left Column, Bottom Row, and Right Column. Then click OK. Excel assigns names from the indicated rows and columns to the corresponding adjacent cells in the range.

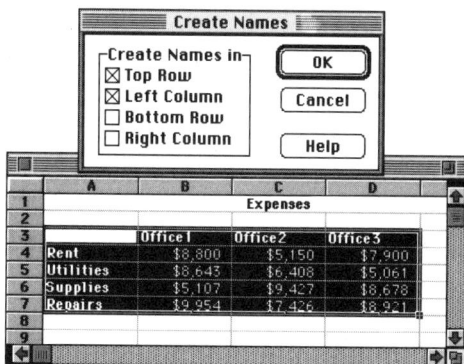

SHORTCUTS

Press ⌘–Shift-F3 to display the Create Names dialog box.

EXAMPLE

The following worksheet compares expenses incurred in three different offices of the same company. The text entries in column A represent the expense categories, and the entries in row 3 represent the offices.

183

	A	B	C	D	E
1			Expenses		
2					
3		Office1	Office2	Office3	Total
4	Rent	$8,800	$5,150	$7,900	$21,850
5	Utilities	$8,643	$6,408	$5,061	$20,112
6	Supplies	$5,107	$9,427	$8,678	$23,212
7	Repairs	$9,954	$7,426	$8,921	$26,301
8	Total	$32,504	$28,411	$30,560	$91,475
9					

To assign names from column A and row 3 to the ranges inside the expense table, select the range A3:D7 (not including the Total row and column) and choose Formula ➤ Create Names. Excel suggests the Top Row and Left Column options as appropriate choices for this selection. Click OK to accept these options. As a result, Excel assigns the names Rent, Utilities, Supplies, and Repairs to the four row ranges B4:D4, B5:D5, B6:D6, and B7:D7. Likewise, the names Office1, Office2, and Office3 are assigned to the column ranges B4:B7, C4:C7, and D4:D7. You can use these names in the SUM formulas that calculate the totals in row 8 and column E. For example, here is the formula to find the total expenses in Office1:

=SUM(Office1)

and this is the formula for the total rent expense for all three offices:

=SUM(Rent)

To Go To a Named Cell or Range

Choose Formula ➤ Goto, select a name from the list of defined names, and click OK.

SHORTCUTS

Press ⌘-G or F5 to display the Goto dialog box.

NOTES

When you select a named cell or all of a named range—for example, as a result of the Goto command—Excel displays the name itself at the left side of the formula bar.

Several Excel commands create special names on a worksheet to identify ranges for particular operations. For example, the Set Database, Set Criteria, and Set Extract commands in the Data menu; the Set Print Area command in the Options menu; and the Set Recorder command in the Macro menu. Choosing Formula ➤ Goto is one easy way to review the location of these range name definitions.

To Paste a Name into a Formula

Choose Formula ➤ Paste Name, select a name from the list of defined names, and click OK. Excel activates the formula bar (if you have not already begun a formula) and enters the name as an operand in the formula.

SHORTCUTS

To open the Paste Name dialog box, click the Paste Name tool on the Macro toolbar.

 **NOTES**

To create a two-column list of all the names defined on the current worksheet along with their corresponding ranges, select an empty location on the worksheet and choose Formula ➤ Paste Name. Click The Paste List button, and Excel enters the list onto the worksheet. For example, here is the name list created for the office expense worksheet you examined earlier in this entry.

	H	I	J	K
2				
3		Office1	= $B$4:$B$7	
4		Office2	= $C$4:$C$7	
5		Office3	= $D$4:$D$7	
6		Rent	= $B$4:$D$4	
7		Repairs	= $B$7:$D$7	
8		Supplies	= $B$6:$D$6	
9		Utilities	= $B$5:$D$5	
10				

To Apply Names to an Existing Formula

1. Select a cell or range containing formulas. The references in these formulas should be ones for which you have subsequently defined names.

2. Choose Formula ➤ Apply Names. In the Apply Names list, select all the names that you want to apply to the current formula. (To include or exclude a name from the multiple selection, hold down the ⌘ key and click the name.)

3. Click OK. Excel applies the names to the references in the currently selected formulas.

SEE ALSO

Databases SnapGuide, Database Operations, Dialog Editor, Formulas SnapGuide, Info Window, Links between Worksheets, Macros Snap-Guide, Macro Recording, Printing Worksheets, References, Selecting a Range, Summation.

Notes

A note is a text annotation that you attach to a cell in a worksheet or a macro sheet. On a Macintosh system that has the appropriate hardware and software, a note can also include a voice recording or other sound effect.

To Annotate a Cell

1. Select the cell and choose Formula ➤ Note. The Cell Note dialog box contains a scrollable text box, labeled Text Note, in which you can enter a note for the current cell.

2. Type a note for the current cell in the Text Note box. (When the Text Note box is active, a flashing vertical insertion point indicates the current position in the text box.)

3. Click OK to attach the note to the current cell.

 **NOTES**

Word wrap takes place automatically as you type a note into the Text Note box. To start a new paragraph, press Control-Enter to insert a carriage-return. Press Control-Tab to insert a tab. You can use all the familiar Macintosh editing features—including cut-and-paste and copy-and-paste—inside the Text Note box.

While the Cell Note dialog box is open, you can also attach notes to other cells in the active sheet: First click the Add button to attach the contents of the Text Note box to the current cell. Then activate the Cell box and click a different cell on the sheet or type a reference directly into the Cell box. Activate the Text Note box and type a new note or edit the current note. Finally, click the Add button to attach the note to the new cell. Repeat this process for each cell that you want to annotate.

A cell that contains a note has a special marker that is displayed at the upper-right corner of the cell. On a color monitor, the cell note indicator appears as a small red bullet.

To View or Edit the Notes Attached to Cells in the Active Sheet

1. Select any cell that displays a cell note indicator, and choose Formula ➤ Note. The Text Note box displays the note for the current cell.

```
┌──────────────────────── Cell Note ────────────────────────┐
│ Cell: [E8]         Text Note:                    ┌──────────┐ │
│                    ┌─────────────────────────┐   │    OK    │ │
│ Notes in Sheet:    │ This is the total expense │   └──────────┘ │
│ ┌─────────────────┐│ amount for all three offices│  ┌──────────┐ │
│ │A1: Expense sheet...⇧│ in all expense categories. │  │  Close   │ │
│ │E8: This is the tota...││                          │  └──────────┘ │
│ │                 ││                          │   ┌──────────┐ │
│ │                 ││                          │   │   Add    │ │
│ │                 ││                          │   └──────────┘ │
│ │                 ││                          │   ┌──────────┐ │
│ │                 ││                          │   │  Delete  │ │
│ │                 ││                          │   └──────────┘ │
│ │                 ││                          │   ┌──────────┐ │
│ │                 ││                          │   │   Help   │ │
│ │                 │└─────────────────────────┘   └──────────┘ │
│ │                 │┌─Sound Note────────────────────────────┐ │
│ │                ⇩││ [Record...]    [  Play  ]   [Import...] │ │
│ └─────────────────┘└────────────────────────────────────────┘ │
└────────────────────────────────────────────────────────────┘
```

		Expenses			
1					
2					
3		Office1	Office2	Office3	Total
4	Rent	$8,800	$5,150	$7,900	$21,850
5	Utilities	$8,643	$6,408	$5,061	$20,112
6	Supplies	$5,107	$9,427	$8,678	$23,212
7	Repairs	$9,954	$7,426	$8,921	$26,301
8	Total	$32,504	$28,411	$30,560	$91,475
9					
10					

2. Optionally, make changes in the note, or append text to the end of the note displayed in the box. Then click the Add button to attach the edited note to the cell.

3. To view the note for another cell, select any one of the cells listed in the Notes in Sheet box. Excel displays the selected note in the Text Note box.

4. Repeat steps 2 and 3 for as many notes as you want to view and/or edit.

5. Click the Close button to close the Cell Notes dialog box.

SHORTCUTS

To open the Cell Note dialog box and view the note for a cell, double-click any cell that displays a cell note indicator.

NOTES

While the Cell Note dialog box is open, you can delete the note from any individual cell: Select the cell in the Notes in Sheet list and click the Delete button. Excel displays a warning box with the message "Note will be permanently deleted." Click OK to delete the note. (Using the Edit ➤ Clear command you can delete an entire range of cell notes all at once. See the last section of this entry for details.)

To Copy Notes

1. Select the cell or range containing the notes you want to copy, and choose Edit ➤ Copy. A moving border appears around the selection.

2. Select the cell or the upper-left corner of the range to which you want to copy the notes.

3. Choose Edit ➤ Paste Special. In the Paste Special dialog box, select the Notes option, and click OK. Excel copies the note or notes from the source range to the destination.

NOTES

To copy notes along with the other contents of a cell or range, you can use any of the techniques available for copying data in a worksheet. See COPYING DATA for details.

To Print Notes

1. If you want the printed notes to be identified by cell location, choose File ➤ Page Setup and click the Row & Column Headings option. An X appears in the corresponding check box. Click OK.

2. Choose File ➤ Print. In the Print dialog box, click the Notes option if you want to print the notes alone, or click Both if you want to print the worksheet (or macro sheet) along with the notes.

3. Click OK to begin printing.

EXAMPLE

The following printout shows a short worksheet that contains notes. This figure illustrates the format that Excel uses for printing notes when you check the Row & Column Headings option in the Page Setup dialog box.

	A	B	C
1	*Electricity Bill*		
2			
3	Rate 1	$0.11	
4	Rate 2	$0.14	
5	Base for Rate 1	700	kwh
6			
7	Usage this month	1425	kwh
8	Amount charged	$178.50	
9			

Cell: B3
Note: This is the rate for monthly usage that does not exceed the base usage amount. Customers who exceed their base amount for a given month will be charged at the higher second rate.

Cell: B4
Note: The second rate is for usage in excess of the base amount.

Cell: B5
Note: The base usage level is calculated individually for business customers; it varies according to the type of business and other factors. For residential customers, the base varies according to the number of occupants and the square footage of the home.

The File ➤ Print command retains the Notes or Both setting until you change it again. Before you try to print a worksheet without notes, choose File ➤ Print and click the Sheet setting.

To Attach a Sound Note to a Cell

1. Select the cell and choose Formula ➤ Note.

2. In the Cell Note dialog box, click the Record button. (If this button is dimmed, your computer does not have the necessary hardware and software resources to record sound.)

3. Click the Record button in the resulting dialog box, and use the microphone attached to your system to record the sound. Click Stop to end the recording, and then click Save.

4. Back on the Cell Note dialog box, click Add to attach the recording to the cell. Then click OK to close the Cell Note dialog box.

NOTES

To listen to the sound note attached to a cell, double-click the cell. In response, Excel plays the recording. If the cell also has a text note, Excel opens the Cell Notes dialog box.

To Delete Notes from a Range of Cells

1. Select the range from which you want to delete notes.

2. Choose Edit ➤ Clear. On the Clear dialog box, click the Notes option to clear notes alone without deleting the other contents of the range.

3. Click OK.

NOTES

You can choose Edit ➤ Undo Clear (or press ⌘-Z) immediately after a deletion if you decide you want to restore the notes to the range of cells.

SEE ALSO

Clearing Data, Copying Data, Deleting, Info Window, Previewing, Printer Setup, Printing Worksheets, Undo.

Number Formats

You can use Excel's Format ➤ Number command to display numeric entries in a variety of built-in formats. The format categories include Number, Currency, Date, Time, Percentage, Fraction, and Scientific.

To Format Numeric Values in a Worksheet

1. Select the cell or range of values that you want to format, and choose Format ➤ Number.

2. In the Number Format dialog box, select the name of a format category in the Value Type box. The Format Codes box lists all the built-in codes available in the selected category.

3. Select a format code and click OK.

NUMBER FORMATS

SHORTCUTS

Point to the selected range and press the ⌘-Option keys while you click the mouse button; then choose the Number command from the resulting shortcut menu. Alternatively, hold down the Control-Shift combination and press one of the following keys to apply a selected format:

$	for currency with two decimal places.
!	for numeric with two decimal places.
%	for percentage with no decimal places.
^	for scientific notation.
~	for the General format.
@	for the h:mm time format.
#	for the dd-mm-yy date format.

In addition, the Formatting toolbar has five tools that apply numeric formats: The Currency, Percent, and Comma Style tools, which apply three of the most commonly used built-in styles; and the Increase Decimal and Decrease Decimal tools, which change the number of decimal places displayed for numeric values.

EXAMPLE

The worksheet below shows examples of all the built-in formats from the Format ➤ Number command. The first column in this worksheet shows the format codes, and the second and third columns show how the positive and negative numbers 23456.75 and −23456.75 appear with these formats applied.

All			
General	23456.75	-23456.75	
Number			
0	23457	-23457	
0.00	23456.75	-23456.75	
#,##0	23,457	-23,457	
#,##0.00	23,456.75	-23,456.75	
#,##0_);(#,##0)	23,457	(23,457)	
#,##0_);[Red](#,##0)	23,457	(23,457)	(red)
#,##0.00_);(#,##0.00)	23,456.75	(23,456.75)	
#,##0.00_);[Red](#,##0.00)	23,456.75	(23,456.75)	(red)
Currency			
$#,##0_);(#,##0)	$23,457	($23,457)	
$#,##0_);[Red](#,##0)	$23,457	($23,457)	(red)
$#,##0.00_);(#,##0.00)	$23,456.75	($23,456.75)	
$#,##0.00_);[Red](#,##0.00)	$23,456.75	($23,456.75)	(red)
Date			
m/d/yy	3/21/68		
d-mmm-yy	21-Mar-68		
d-mmm	21-Mar		
mmm-yy	Mar-68		
m/d/yy h:mm	3/21/68 18:00		
Time			
h:mm AM/PM	6:00 PM		
h:mm:ss AM/PM	6:00:00 PM		
h:mm	18:00		
h:mm:ss	18:00:00		
m/d/yy h:mm	3/21/68 18:00		
Percentage			
0%	2345675%	-2345675%	
0.00%	2345675.00%	-2345675.00%	
Fraction			
# ??	23456 3/4	-23456 3/4	
# ??/??	23456 3/4	-23456 3/4	
Scientific			
0.00E+00	2.35E+04	-2.35E+04	

NOTES

If you use one of the built-in date or time formats when you enter a date or time value in a cell, Excel recognizes the value as a chronological entry and automatically applies the appropriate format to the cell. The numeric value stored in the cell is a serial date or serial time value. See DATE ENTRIES and TIME ENTRIES for details.

You can use Excel's standard format codes to create custom formats use in a worksheet. See CUSTOM NUMBER FORMATS.

SEE ALSO

Autoformat, Copying Formats, Custom Number Formats, Date Entries, Formatting Worksheet Cells, Time Entries.

Object Linking and Embedding (OLE)

Object linking and embedding is a technique for sharing information and features between Excel and other Macintosh applications. Using the OLE approach, you can embed a document from a different application into an Excel worksheet. Inside the worksheet, the embedded document appears as a graphic object that you can move and resize in any way that suits your presentation. Likewise, you can embed an Excel chart or worksheet range into a document created in a different Macintosh application.

To Embed an Object into a Worksheet

I. Activate the worksheet and select the cell where you want to embed the object.

2. Choose Edit ➤ Insert Object. In the Insert Object dialog box, choose an application from the Object Type list, and click OK. Excel starts the selected application.

3. Develop the document that you want to embed into your worksheet. When your work is complete, choose the command that closes the document in the other application—for example, File ➤ Close. (If a message box displays a question such as "Save changes in Worksheet1?" click Yes.) Excel reappears, and the embedded object is now part of your worksheet.

NOTES

To select an embedded object, click it with the mouse; Excel displays selection handles around the perimeter of the object. You can resize the object by dragging a selection handle. Reposition the object by dragging its border. To deselect the object, click elsewhere on your worksheet.

Most of the features described in the GRAPHIC OBJECTS entry also apply to embedded objects. In particular, you can perform the following operations on embedded objects:

▲ Change the color, style, or pattern of the object's border and interior. (Select the object, and choose Format ➤ Patterns.)

▲ Specify the object's relation to its underlying cells. (Select the object, and choose Format ➤ Object Properties.)

▲ Attach a macro to the object. (Select the object, and choose Macro ➤ Assign to Object. If a macro is attached to an object, you can click the object to run the macro. To select the object, press the ⌘ key while you click it.)

See GRAPHIC OBJECTS for more information about all these operations. Also, note that a shortcut menu is also available for an embedded object. To view this menu, point to the object, hold down the ⌘-Option keys, and click the mouse button.

To Edit an Embedded Object

1. Double-click the object. In response, Excel reopens the source application and displays the object as a document in the application.

2. Use the features of the source application to complete any changes you want to make.

3. Close the document again. The edited document appears once again as an embedded object in your worksheet.

NOTES

If an embedded object has an attached macro, select the object first (press ⌘ and click the object), and then double-click the object to open its source application.

To Embed an Excel Object in Another Application

1. Select the worksheet range or the chart that you want to embed, and choose Edit ➤ Copy.

2. Start the other application, and open the document in which you want to embed the Excel object.

3. Choose Edit ➤ Paste Special and paste the object (or choose the command required by the host application to complete the OLE operation).

NOTES

To complete these steps successfully, you must select an application that supports OLE operations. You can double-click the Excel object to switch back to Excel and edit the original sheet or chart.

SEE ALSO

Borders, Charting SnapGuide, Dynamic Links between Applications, Graphic Objects, Macros SnapGuide, Patterns.

Opening Files

Use the File ➤ Open command to open Excel worksheets, charts, macro sheets, or workbooks from disk. Use File ➤ New to create new Excel documents in any of these same categories.

To Open an Excel Document from Disk

1. Choose File ➤ Open.

2. If necessary, use the folder and file lists to find the location for the file you want to open.

3. Select the document's name and click Open.

SHORTCUTS

If the file you want to open is among the four most recently opened files (listed at the bottom of the File menu), select the name directly from this list. Alternatively, click the Open File tool in the Standard toolbar. This tool displays the Open dialog box.

NOTES

If you want to examine a document but not change its contents, click the Read Only option on the Open dialog box. If you make changes in the file, Excel will allow you to save the file under a new name, but not to update the file under its existing name.

To Open a New Excel Document

1. Choose File ➤ New.

2. Select a document type from the New list, and click OK.

SHORTCUTS

Press ⌘-N to open the New dialog box. Click the New Worksheet tool in the Standard toolbar to open a new worksheet.

SEE ALSO

Add-in Macros, Charting SnapGuide, Exiting Excel, File Formats, Folders, Links between Worksheets, Macros SnapGuide, Passwords, Protecting Documents, Saving Files, Template Window Operations, Workbooks.

Outlines

You can create an outline in any worksheet that is organized in sections with rows or columns of subtotals and totals. To simplify your work with the outline, Excel displays outline level symbols, collapse symbols, and expand symbols just to the left and/or just above the outlined worksheet. Using these symbols, you can select levels of the outline to view and hide—that is, you can focus on the whole worksheet or on selected levels of subtotals and totals.

To Create an Outlined Worksheet

1. Develop a worksheet in which numeric data is divided into sections, with levels of subtotals and totals at the end of each section. The subtotals can be in rows, columns, or both.

2. Select the range of data that you want to outline, or select the cell at the upper-left corner of this range.

3. Choose Formula ➤ Outline. The Outline dialog box contains check boxes for selecting row or column outline organization. Initially both options are checked.

4. If the subtotals are in rows, check only the option labeled Summary rows below detail. If the subtotals are in columns, check only the option labeled Summary columns to the right of detail. Check both options if your worksheet contains both row and column subtotals.

5. Optionally, click the Automatic Styles option if you want Excel to apply predefined styles to different levels of the outline.

6. Click the Create button. At the left of the row headings and/or above the column headings, Excel displays outline level symbols and collapse symbols.

NOTES

Excel determines the levels of the outline from the way you have organized subtotals and totals (or other summary-type formulas) at the end of each section of your worksheet. The outline does not change the content of your worksheet in any way; rather, it gives you tools for temporarily hiding detail sections of your worksheet so you can focus on the subtotals and totals.

To Focus on Selected Levels of the Outlined Worksheet

Click one of the numbered outline level symbols that Excel displays for the row levels or the column levels. Excel temporarily hides all levels of the worksheet *after* the level that you click.

EXAMPLE

The worksheet below shows quarterly retail sales for a group of products carried in three different stores. The worksheet contains a section for each store. In a given section, the store's sales for each product appear in individual detail rows. Each store's total quarterly sales appear below the product data, in rows 8, 12, and 16. Finally, the last row of the worksheet shows the total sales in all three stores (row 17).

	A	B	C	D	E	F
1		Sales of Three Computer Models				
2		(in thousands of $)				
3						
4			Quarter 1	Quarter 2	Quarter 3	Quarter 4
5	L.A. Store	Home Model	$54	$83	$53	$95
6		Business Model	$86	$74	$93	$66
7		Super Tech Model	$61	$88	$50	$60
8		L.A. Total	$201	$245	$196	$221
9	S.F. Store	Home Model	$62	$65	$50	$53
10		Business Model	$89	$58	$81	$99
11		Super Tech Model	$87	$67	$55	$84
12		S.F. Total	$238	$190	$186	$236
13	N.Y. Store	Home Model	$61	$82	$75	$53
14		Business Model	$82	$86	$67	$67
15		Super Tech Model	$83	$83	$57	$80
16		N.Y. Total	$226	$251	$199	$200
17	*** Grand Total ***		$665	$686	$581	$657

To create an outline on this worksheet, select cell A5 (the upper-left corner of the outline area) and choose Formula ➤ Outline. In the Outline dialog box, remove the X from the Summary columns check box, and keep the X in the Summary rows check box. Then click the Create button. Excel creates an outline with three levels: The highest level (represented by level symbol 1) contains only the grand total for all three stores; the intermediate level (level symbol 2) contains the three store totals along with the grand total.; and the lowest level (level symbol 3) contains all the sales data and all the totals.

You can simply click a level symbol to view different levels of the outline. For example, click level symbol 2 to hide the sales data and view only the store totals and the grand total, as shown in the figure directly below. Click level symbol 1 to hide everything but the grand total, as in the next figure. To view the entire worksheet again, click level symbol 3.

	A	B	C	D	E	F
1		Sales of Three Computer Models				
2		(in thousands of $)				
3						
4			Quarter 1	Quarter 2	Quarter 3	Quarter 4
8		L.A. Total	$201	$245	$196	$221
12		S.F. Total	$238	$190	$186	$236
16		N.Y. Total	$226	$251	$199	$200
17	*** Grand Total ***		$665	$686	$581	$657

	A	B	C	D	E	F
1		Sales of Three Computer Models				
2		(in thousands of $)				
3						
4			Quarter 1	Quarter 2	Quarter 3	Quarter 4
17	*** Grand Total ***		$665	$686	$581	$657

NOTES

You can also collapse or expand individual sections of the outline by clicking the collapse symbol (a minus sign) or the expand symbol (a plus sign) for the section.

The Utility toolbar contains four important tools, discussed below, that relate to outlining. To view these tools, point to any open toolbar, press ⌘-Option while you click the mouse button, and choose Utility from the resulting shortcut menu:

Tool	Use
Promote	shifts a section of your worksheet to a higher level in the outline. To perform this operation, select the entire section of rows or columns that you want to promote, and click the Promote tool or press ⌘-Shift-J.

Tool	Use
Demote	shifts a section to a lower level in the outline. Select the section you want to demote, and click the Demote tool or press ⌘-Shift-K.
Show Outline Symbols	displays or hides the outline symbols above or to the left of your worksheet. The tool is a toggle: click it once (or press ⌘-8) to hide the symbols, and click it again to display them.
Select Visible Cells	creates a multiple range selection of only those rows or columns that are visible at a given outline level. To perform this operation, click an outline level symbol to view the level you want, select a range of the worksheet, and then click the Select Visible Cells tool. (Clicking this tool is equivalent to selecting the Visible Cells Only option in the Formula ➤ Select Special dialog box.) You might want to use this tool to select subtotal rows so you can create a chart, as shown in the figure below.

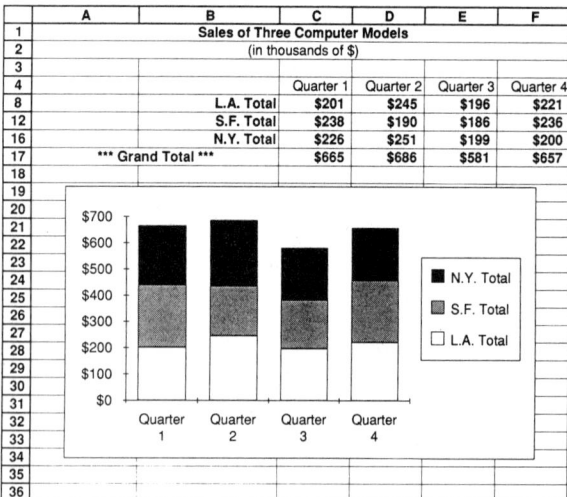

	A	B	C	D	E	F
1		Sales of Three Computer Models				
2		(in thousands of $)				
3						
4			Quarter 1	Quarter 2	Quarter 3	Quarter 4
8		L.A. Total	$201	$245	$196	$221
12		S.F. Total	$238	$190	$186	$236
16		N.Y. Total	$226	$251	$199	$200
17	*** Grand Total ***		$665	$686	$581	$657

To Delete an Outline

1. Select all the rows of the outline by dragging the mouse down the appropriate row headings at the left side of your worksheet.

2. Click the Promote tool on the Utility toolbar (or press ⌘-Shift-J) multiple times until all the outline symbols disappear from the left side of the worksheet.

3. Select all the columns of the outline by dragging the mouse across the appropriate column headings at the top of your worksheet, and repeat the process described in step 2.

SEE ALSO

Charting SnapGuide, Crosstab ReportWizard, Hiding, Selecting a Range, Summation.

Page Setup

The options of the File ➤ Page Setup command give you control over the layout of a worksheet, chart, or macro sheet on the printed page.

To Select Options for the Printed Page

Choose File ➤ Page Setup, and select any combination of options. (The available options may vary according to the features of the installed printer.)

▲ Under the Paper or Media heading, select an option for the type of paper, transparency, or envelope that you want to print on.

▲ In the Orientation group, select the portrait icon to print the document from the top to the bottom of the paper or the landscape icon to prit the document sideways.

▲ In the Margins box, enter measurements for the left, right, top, and bottom margins. To center the document on the page, click one or both of the Center check boxes, labeled Horizontally and Vertically.

▲ For worksheets and macro sheets, select the Row & Column Headings check box if you want to print the sheet's headings, and keep the X in the Cell Gridlines check box if you want to print the gridlines. Select the Black and White cells check box for black and white printing.

▲ If you want the page numbering to start at some point other than 1, enter the first page number in the Start Page No.'s At box. By default, page numbers are printed in the footer. See HEADERS AND FOOTERS for details.

▲ In the Page Order box, select one of the two options—Down, then Over; or Over, then Down—to specify how the pagination should be organized in a multi-page document.

▲ In the Reduce/Enlarge box, enter a value less than 100% to reduce the size of a printed document, or a value greater than 100% to enlarge the printed document. Alternatively, click the Fit to option button if you want Excel to scale the document automatically to fit on the printed page.

▲ If the active document is a chart, select one of the three options in the Chart Size box: Size on screen, Scale to fit page, or Use full page. See PRINTING CHARTS for details and examples.

NOTES

A column of command buttons appears on the right side of the Page Setup dialog box. Click the Header button or the Footer button to open the Header or Footer dialog box. See HEADERS AND FOOTERS for details. Click the Print button to open the Print dialog box and print the document.

SEE ALSO

Headers and Footers, Previewing, Printer Setup, Printing Charts, Printing Worksheets.

Panes

By dividing a worksheet or macro sheet into panes, you can view two or four different parts of the sheet at once.

To Divide a Sheet into Panes

Select the row, column, or cell at which you want to divide the sheet, and choose Window ➤ Split.

SHORTCUTS

Drag the vertical split bar to the right, across the horizontal scroll bar; or drag the horizontal split bar down the vertical scroll bar. (The split bars are small black rectangles, initially located at the left end of the horizontal scroll bar and at the top of the vertical scroll bar.) Alternatively, double-click a split bar to create two panes that are approximately the same size.

NOTES

The Window ➤ Split command creates two or four panes, depending on the range or cell selection at the time you choose the command:

▲ To create two panes that are split vertically, select an entire column or a single cell in row 1 (other than cell A1).

▲ To create two panes split horizontally, select an entire row or a single cell in column A (other than cell A1).

▲ To create four panes, select any cell except in row 1 or column A.

▲ To create four panes of approximately equal size, select cell A1.

Scrolling is synchronized in the panes of a split sheet: With a horizontal split, the two panes stay together during horizontal scrolling; and with a vertical split, the two panes stay together during vertical scrolling.

To Freeze the Panes

Choose Window ➤ Freeze Panes.

NOTES

This command prevents the top pane from scrolling vertically, or the left pane from scrolling horizontally. It may be useful if the left or top pane contains labels or other data that you want to keep in view, even while you scroll in the other panes.

Choose Window ➤ Unfreeze Panes to return the panes to their original scrolling capabilities.

To Remove Panes from a Sheet

Activate the sheet and choose Window ➤ Remove Split.

SHORTCUTS

Double-click a split bar to send it back to its initial position.

SEE ALSO

Window Operations.

Parsing

Parsing is the process of separating long lines of text into individual data items, and entering each item into a separate cell on a worksheet. You may need to parse data that you have copied into Excel from another application.

To Parse Lines of Text in a Worksheet

1. Select a column range (one column wide) in which each cell contains a similarly formatted line of text.

2. Choose Data ➤ Parse. In the Parse dialog box, the Parse Line displays the first line of text in the selection. Within this line, pairs of brackets indicate the positions where Excel expects to separate the line into data values.

3. If Excel's initial guess is inaccurate, activate the line and change the positions of the brackets. (Click the Clear button to remove all brackets from the line. Click Guess to restore Excel's initial guess.)

4. Click OK to parse the lines of data.

NOTES

Excel uses the same pattern to parse every line in the selected column range. In a successful parse, Excel recognizes the data types of individual values in the parsed lines, and enters the data into cells accordingly. This applies to formatted numbers as well as dates.

PARSING

Parsing is sometimes a process of trial-and-error. If the first parse operation does not produce the result you want, choose Edit ➤ Undo Parse. Then choose Data ➤ Parse again and try placing the brackets at different positions.

EXAMPLE

The worksheet below shows some lines of data that were copied to Excel via the Clipboard from another Macintosh application. In its current form, the information consists of single lines of text stored entirely in column A. Within each line, data items are separated by spaces.

	A	B	C	D	E
1	1/10/92		Postage	$15.72	
2	1/12/92		Supplies	$19.88	
3	1/13/92		Delivery	$15.25	
4	1/15/92		Supplies	$22.95	
5	1/17/92		Supplies	$14.32	
6					

To separate these lines into individual data entries, select the range A1:A5 and choose Data ➤ Parse. Excel uses brackets to suggest the following pattern for separating the lines into data items:

[1/10/92   ][Postage   ][$15.72]

This pattern seems correct, so click the OK button in the Parse dialog box. Excel separates the lines into three columns of data, as shown in this figure:

	A	B	C	D	E
1	1/10/92	Postage	$15.72		
2	1/12/92	Supplies	$19.88		
3	1/13/92	Delivery	$15.25		
4	1/15/92	Supplies	$22.95		
5	1/17/92	Supplies	$14.32		
6					

Notice that the first column contains date entries (that is, serial numbers formatted as dates), and the third column contains currency-formatted numeric values. Even though the original unparsed lines were text entries, Excel has recognized the correct data types of the values in the lines.

SEE ALSO

Clipboard, Copying Data, Date Entries, File Formats.

Passwords

You can use a password to restrict access to an Excel file that is saved on disk. (In addition, passwords are an optional part of the scheme for protecting the contents of a worksheet. See PROTECTING CELLS and PROTECTING DOCUMENTS for details.)

To Save a File with a Password

1. Activate the file you want to save, and choose File ➤ Save As.

2. In the Save Worksheet as box, enter a name for the file. Then click the Options button.

3. In the Save Options dialog box, enter a password in the text box labeled Protection Password. In the Password text box, Excel displays a bullet for each character you type. (You can press the Backspace key to erase any character that you want to retype.) Click OK when you complete the password entry. The Confirm Password dialog box appears.

4. Type the same password again, and click OK. Finally, click Save to save the file to disk.

NOTES

A password that you enter into the Save Options dialog box may be up to 15 characters long, and alphabetic case is significant. If the passwords you type into the Save Options and Confirm Password dialog boxes are not identical, Excel displays a warning box with the message "Confirmation password is not identical." You are then returned to the Save Options dialog box to try again.

To Open a Password-Protected Document

1. Choose File ➤ Open and select the name of the file you want to open. When you click OK, Excel displays the Password dialog box on the screen.

2. Enter the password and click OK. If your password is correct, Excel opens the file.

NOTES

If the password you enter is not correct, Excel displays a warning box with the message "Incorrect password." You cannot open the file without the correct password.

To Save a File without its Password

1. Open a password-protected file, and then choose File ➤ Save As to save it again.

2. On the resulting dialog box, click the Options button. In the Save Options dialog box, delete the bullets that represent the password, and then click OK.

3. Complete the save operation. The file can now be opened without a password.

SEE ALSO

Opening Files, Protecting Cells, Protecting Documents, Saving Files.

Patterns

With the Format ➤ Patterns command, you can apply shading to a
range of cells on a worksheet, or select a border style and a fill
color for a graphic object. (When a chart window is active, you
can use the same command to change the color and appearance of
individual elements of the chart, including the series, the individual data markers, the legend, the chart area, the plot area, and
the axes. See PRINTING CHARTS for instructions and examples.) The
options available on the Patterns dialog box depend on the type of
selection you have made.

To Apply Shading to a Range of Cells

1. Select the range, and choose Format ➤ Patterns. The Patterns dialog box contains three pull-down lists, labeled Pattern, Foreground, and Background.

2. Select a shading pattern from the Pattern list.

3. Select a combination of colors for the shading from the
   Foreground and Background lists. Note the result of your
   selections in the Sample box.

4. Click OK.

SHORTCUTS

Point to the selected range, press ⌘-Option while you click the
right mouse button, and choose the Patterns command from the
shortcut menu.

To Change the Fill Pattern and Border of a Graphic Object

1. Select the object, and choose Format ➤ Patterns.

2. Make selections from the Pattern, Foreground, and Background lists in the Fill group.

3. In the Border group, select a border style (solid, broken, dotted, or patterned) from the Style list. Then make selections from the Color and Weight lists.

4. Click the Shadow check box if you want a black shadow to appear behind the object.

5. Click the Rounded Corners check box if you want round rather than square corners. (This option is available only for objects that start out with square corners.)

6. Click OK to apply the patterns.

 **SHORTCUTS**

Choose the Patterns command from the object's shortcut menu.

 **SEE ALSO**

Borders, Charting SnapGuide, Colors, Formatting Worksheet Cells, Graphic Objects, Printing Charts, Shading.

Point Size

The size of the type in a given font is measured in points, where one inch is equivalent to 72 points. You can choose from a range of point sizes in a selected font.

To Change the Font Size in a Range of Cells

1. Select the range and choose Format ➤ Font. The Font dialog box appears.

2. Select a size in the scrollable Size list, or enter a size value directly into the Size text box. Then click OK.

SHORTCUTS

Because you may want to use a variety of type sizes in the same worksheet, Excel gives you two quick ways to change the size in a selected range:

▲ Click the Increase Font Size tool or the Decrease Font Size tool on the Standard toolbar. Each time you click one of these tools, the size changes to the next higher or lower available measurement. When no more standard sizes are available, you'll hear a beep.

▲ Select or enter a size in the Font Size box in the Formatting toolbar.

EXAMPLE

The worksheet below shows a range of sizes for the font known as Times. The sizes shown range from 8 points to 72 points.

	A	B	C	D	E
1	Excel				
2	Excel				
3	Excel				
4	Excel				
5	Excel				
6	Excel				
7	Excel				
8	Excel				
9	Excel				
10	Excel				
11	Excel				
12	Excel				
13	Excel				
14	Excel				
15	Excel				

NOTES

When you change the point size in a range of cells on a worksheet, Excel automatically adjusts the row height to accommodate the new size.

You can also use the Format ➤ Font command—or any of the equivalent shortcuts—to change the font of any text displayed in a chart, including titles, legend text, labels displayed along axes, and unattached text.

SEE ALSO

Charting SnapGuide, Fonts, Formatting Worksheet Cells, Row Height.

Previewing

The File ➤ Print Preview command displays a preview window in which you can see how a worksheet, chart, or macro sheet will look on the printed page. This window gives you the opportunity to examine the document's page layout, formatting, and content before you actually print it.

To Preview a Document Before You Print It

Activate the document that you want to preview, and choose File ➤ Print Preview. The preview window displays a full-page picture of the active document. Across the top of the window you'll find a variety of tools you can use to study or modify the printed document:

▲ Click the Next or Previous tool to scroll to the next or previous page in the document.

▲ Click the Zoom button (or point to the document picture itself and click the mouse button when you see the magnifying glass pointer) to enlarge the view of the printed document. In the Zoom mode, use the scroll bars to move up, down, or across the document. To return to the regular page preview display, click the mouse anywhere on the zoomed document.

▲ Click the Print button to open the print dialog box, or the Setup button to open the Page Setup dialog box.

▲ Click the Margins button if you want to adjust margins in your document. Excel displays margin lines and handles that you can drag to make visual adjustments in the top, bottom, left, or right margins. For a worksheet or macro sheet, Excel also displays handles to represent the current column widths; you can drag any of these handles to increase or decrease the width of a column. Click the Margin button again to remove the margin handles from the window.

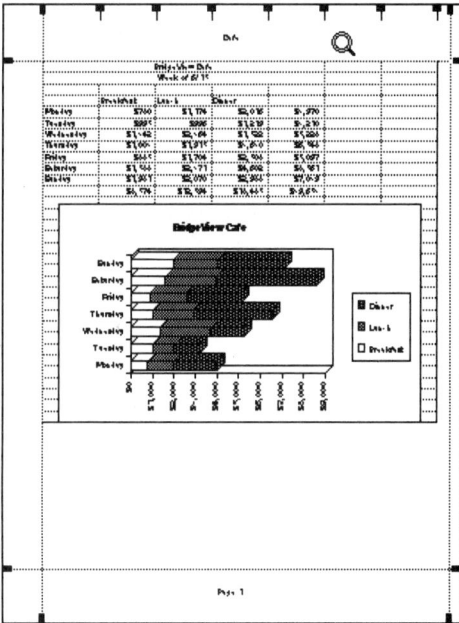

▲ Click Close to return to your document in the Excel application window.

SHORTCUTS

Click the Print Preview tool to open the preview window. This tool is not initially part of any toolbar; see TOOLBARS to learn how to display it in a toolbar. Alternatively, if the Print Preview tool is not available, hold down the Shift key and click the Print tool on the Standard toolbar.

SEE ALSO

Column Widths, Page Setup, Printing Charts, Printing Worksheets.

Printer Setup

You use the Chooser to select a printer on the Macintosh. For some selections, the File ➤ Page Setup command may also display special options for changing the operational settings of the printer.

To Change the Printer Settings

1. Pull down the Apple menu and start the Chooser.

2. On the Chooser dialog box, click the icon for the printer you want to use.

3. Select a printer port, and then close the Chooser.

4. Back in Excel, choose File ➤ Page Setup to see if there are any special options for the selected printer. (For example, you may find an Options button; click it to view printer-specific options.)

SEE ALSO

Page Setup, Printing Charts, Printing Worksheets.

Printing Charts

To print a chart without its source worksheet, you must display the chart in a window of its own, not as an embedded object in the worksheet. Using the Page Setup command, you can specify how you want the chart to appear on the printed page.

To Print a Chart

1. If the chart is embedded in its source worksheet, double-click the chart to open a chart window. Resize the chart window (by dragging the window's size box with the mouse) to produce the height-to-width ratio that you want to see in the chart.

2. Choose File ➤ Page Setup. In the Page Setup dialog box, select one of the three option buttons in the Chart Size group:

   ▲ Size On Screen prints the chart in the same size as the actual chart window you have produced.

   ▲ Scale to Fit Page fills as much of the printed page as possible, while maintaining the height-to-width ratio that you have established in the chart window.

   ▲ Use Full Page stretches the chart over the length and width of the page, ignoring the chart window's height-to-width ratio.

3. Click OK. Then choose File ➤ Print to open the Print dialog box. Enter a new value in the Copies text box if you want to print more than one copy of the chart. Click OK to begin printing.

SHORTCUTS

Click the Print tool on the Standard toolbar to print the chart. This tool bypasses the Print dialog box and begins printing immediately.

EXAMPLE

The figures below show two copies of the same chart, the first printed under the Scale to Fit Page option and the second under the Use Full Page option:

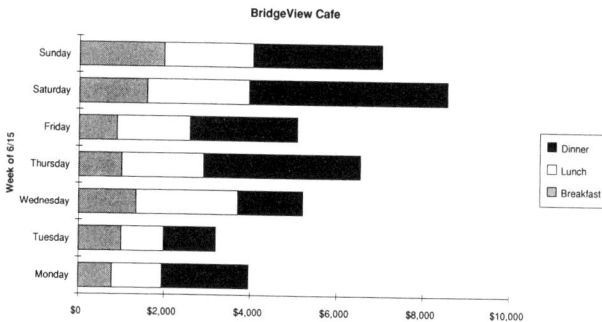

BridgeView Cafe

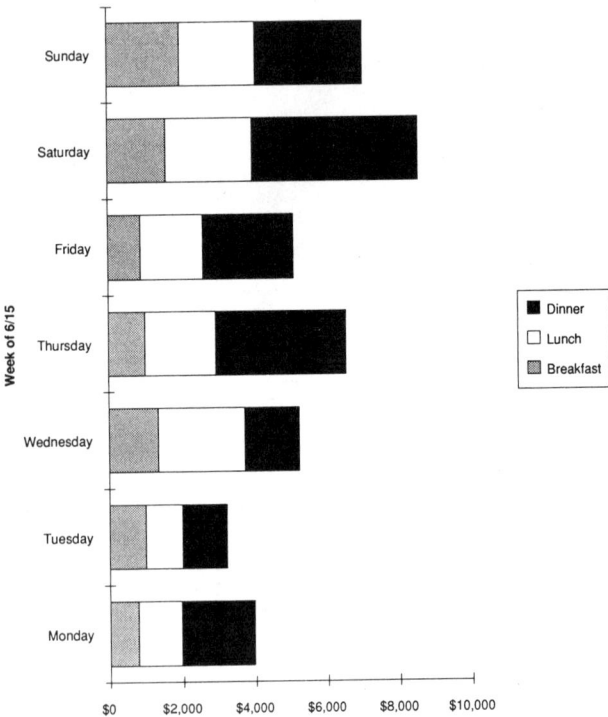

BridgeView Cafe

NOTES

When you print a full-color screen chart on a black-and-white printer, Excel selects shades of gray along with black and white to substitute for the colors. (Using the Format ➤ Patterns command, you can select gray shades yourself if you prefer; see the next section of this entry for details.) Depending on your printer, you may be able to modify the "texture" of the gray shades by selecting an option in the Quality group in the print dialog box. Experiment with the options available in this list and decide which effect you like the best.

To Create a Black-and-White Chart on the Screen

1. Select a series in the chart, and choose Format ➤ Patterns. The Patterns dialog box appears.

2. In the Foreground list, select black.

3. In the Pattern list, select the gray pattern that you want to apply to the current series on the chart. Then click OK.

4. Repeat steps 1, 2, and 3 for each series in the chart.

5. Choose File ➤ Print and click OK (or click the Print tool in the Standard toolbar) to print the chart. The printed chart will be the same as the black-and-white chart on the screen.

EXAMPLE

This figure shows a chart in which black-and-white patterns have been applied to each series:

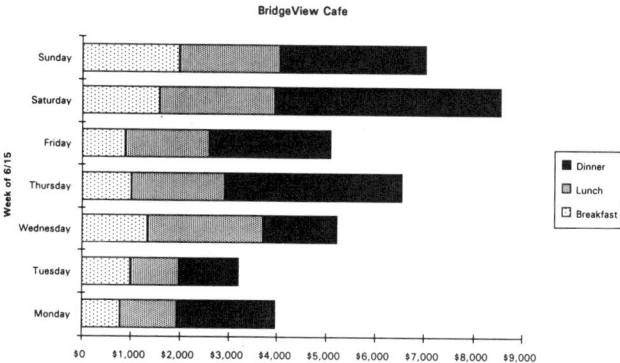

SEE ALSO

Charting SnapGuide, ChartWizard, Colors, Patterns, Previewing, Printer Setup.

Printing Worksheets

Before you print a worksheet (or a macro sheet), you can define print titles, page breaks, and the print area.

To Print a Worksheet (or a Macro Sheet)

1. Activate the sheet that you want to print, and optionally set the print area, the print titles, and manual page breaks. (See the upcoming sections of this entry for details.)

2. If you want to change any aspect of the page layout, choose File ➤ Page Setup and select a combination of options on the resulting dialog box. (See Page Setup for details.) Click OK to confirm the options you select.

3. Choose File ➤ Print. The Print dialog box appears. The options on this dialog box may vary according to the current printer selection. See PRINTER SETUP.

4. In the Print Range group (or the Pages group), enter a range of page numbers in the From and To boxes if you want to print less than the entire document.

5. If your worksheet includes notes, select an option in the Print group: Sheet to print only the worksheet; Notes to print only the notes; or Both to print the sheet and the notes.

6. In the Copies box, enter the number of copies if you want more than one.

7. Select any other appropriate options. Then click OK to begin printing.

SHORTCUTS

Click the Print tool on the Standard toolbar to print the document immediately without viewing the Print dialog box.

To Define a Print Area before Printing

Select the range of cells you want to print and choose Options ➤ Set Print Area.

SHORTCUTS

Click the Set Print Area tool on the Utility toolbar.

NOTES

If the print area is a single contiguous range, Excel marks off the area with vertical and horizontal lines of dashes. (Alternatively, you can select multiple ranges for the print area; when you print the sheet, each range appears on a separate page.) Excel defines the name Print_Area for the selected range.

The default print area is the entire range that contains any entries. For example, if the last entry in the active worksheet is in cell X27, the default print area is A1:X27. However, the name Print_Area is not defined unless you select the Options ➤ Set Print Area command.

To Define Print Titles before Printing

I. Select a row of entries that you want to appear at the top of each printed page, and/or select a column of entries that you want to appear at the left side of each page. (To select both, click the row heading, then hold down the ⌘ key and click the the column heading.)

2. Choose Options ➤ Set Print Titles. In the Set Print Titles dialog box, make sure the Titles for Columns and the Titles for Rows boxes contain the correct references, and click OK.

NOTES

Excel assigns the name Print_Titles to the range of titles.

Print titles are useful for clearly identifying data in a multipage document. Without a title setting, you might see column titles or row titles only on the first page of the printed document.

To Set a Manual Page Break

Select a column for a vertical page break, a row for a horizontal page break, or a single cell for both. Then choose Options ➤ Set Page Break.

NOTES

Manual page breaks appear just above a selected row, just to the left of a selected column, or just above and to the left of a selected cell. Excel marks manual page breaks with a line of dashes, slightly darker than the line for automatic page breaks. If you do not set manual page breaks, Excel calculates automatic page breaks appropriate for the page size and the margin settings.

To Remove Settings for Print Area, Print Titles, or Page Breaks

1. Click the Select All button to select the entire sheet. (This button is located at the intersection of the column headings and the row headings, at the upper-left corner of the worksheet.)

2. Choose Options ➤ Remove Print Area to delete the print area setting.

3. Choose Options ➤ Remove Print Titles to delete the titles setting.

4. Choose Options ➤ Remove Page Break to delete all manual page break settings.

SHORTCUTS

Press ⌘–A or ⌘–Shift-spacebar to select the entire worksheet.

NOTES

The three Remove commands are available in the Options menu only when the entire worksheet is selected.

An alternative way to delete the print area or titles setting is to choose Formula ➤ Define Name, select the Print_Area or Print_Titles name, and click the Delete button. Deleting the name is the same as removing the setting.

SEE ALSO

Notes, Page Setup, Previewing, Printer Setup, Selecting a Range.

Protecting Cells

By applying cell protection to a worksheet, you can prevent any changes to the entries in the cells, and you can hide the formulas in the cells. Cell protection is a two-step process: First you select a combination of protection options from the Format ➤ Cell Protection command, and then you activate the protection by choosing the Options ➤ Protect Document command. You can also create a password to prevent others from removing the protection.

To Protect a Range of Cells on a Worksheet

I. Select a range in which you want to change the protection options, and choose Format ➤ Cell Protection. The Cell Protection dialog box has two check box options: The Locked option prevents changes to entries in the cells, and

227

the Hidden option hides the formulas in the cells. (By default, the Locked option is checked for all cells in a worksheet.)

2. Check the combination of options that you want to apply to the current range, and click OK.

3. If you want to select different protection options for different ranges on the worksheet, repeat steps 1 and 2 for each range you want to change.

4. Choose Options ➤ Protect Document. The Protect Document dialog box has three check box options: Cells, Objects, and Windows. Only the Cells option needs to be checked to activate cell protection. (Uncheck the other options if you wish; see PROTECTING DOCUMENTS for information about these options.)

5. If you want to use a password to enforce protection, enter a word into the Password text box. Excel displays a bullet for each character you type.

6. Click OK. If you are using a password, the Confirm Password dialog box appears. Enter the password again and click OK to confirm. Cell protection is now active in the selected range.

SHORTCUTS

Before choosing the Options ➤ Protect Document command, you can click the Lock Cell tool on the Utility toolbar to change the Locked status of a range of cells. This tool is a toggle: Click it once to remove the Locked status (because Locked is checked by default for all cells), and click it again to reapply the status.

NOTES

To lock the cells only in a selected range of a worksheet, begin by selecting the entire worksheet (click the Select All button) and clicking the Lock Cell tool on the Utility toolbar to uncheck the

Locked option for the worksheet. Then select the range you want to lock, and click the Lock Cell tool again to apply the Locked option to the range. Finally, choose Options ➤ Protect Document to activate the selected protection options.

Once you choose Options ➤ Protect Document, no changes are allowed in the contents of locked cells. If you try to enter a new value or formula into a locked cell, a warning box appears with the message "Locked cells cannot be changed." Excel also dims menu commands that would result in changes to the protected worksheet. If you have selected the Hidden option as well, no formula or other entry appears in the formula bar when you select a cell in the protected range.

Formulas in locked cells can still be recalculated. For example, if you change a value in an unlocked cell that affects a formula in a locked cell, Excel recalculates the formula and displays the new result.

You can copy a protected range of cells. Select the range and choose Edit ➤ Copy; then choose an unlocked range on the current worksheet—or activate an unprotected worksheet—and choose Edit ➤ Paste. If the Hidden option is checked for the source worksheet range, Excel copies only values—not formulas—to the destination (any formulas in the source are converted to their current values in the destination).

You can also apply a protection scheme to a macro sheet. But keep in mind that a macro sheet displays formulas by default. If you apply the Hidden option in this case, the macro sheet will appear to be empty.

To Remove Cell Protection

Choose the Options ➤ Unprotect Document command. If you used a password to protect the cells, you must now re-enter the password to remove protection. If there is no password, Excel removes protection immediately.

SEE ALSO

Copying Data, Formatting Worksheet Cells, Formula Bar, Formulas SnapGuide, Hiding, Passwords, Protecting Documents, Recalculating.

Protecting Documents

Excel provides several commands for protecting documents and their contents from changes. The Options ➤ Protect Document command activates protection for the entries in cells, for graphic objects in a worksheet, and for the properties of the worksheet window. For an unembedded chart window, the Chart ➤ Protect Document command protects the chart itself and the properties of the window.

To Protect a Worksheet and its Contents from Changes

1. Select a range of cells for which you want to select protection options, and choose Format ➤ Cell Protection. Check the options you want to activate and click OK. The Locked option is checked by default for all cells of a worksheet; see PROTECTING CELLS for details.

2. Select an embedded graphic object on the worksheet, and choose Format ➤ Object Protection. Note that the Locked option is checked by default for all objects. Click Locked to uncheck the option if you do not want to protect the object. Then click OK.

3. Repeat steps 1 or 2 to change the protection options for any·other ranges or objects on the worksheet.

4. Choose Options ➤ Protect Document. The Protect Document dialog box has three check box options, labeled

Cells, Objects, and Windows. Check any combination of these options in the dialog box:

▲ The Cells option activates the protection options you have selected in the Format ➤ Cell Protection command.

▲ The Objects option prevents locked objects from being moved, resized, or edited.

▲ The Windows option prevents changes in the size, shape, and position of the active window.

5. If you want to use a password to prevent others from removing protection, enter a word into the Password dialog box. (Excel displays a bullet for each character you type.)

6. Click OK. If you are using a password, the Confirm Password dialog box appears. Enter your password a second time, and then click OK. The protection options are now active.

SHORTCUTS

Before you choose Options ➤ Protect Document, click the Lock Cell tool on the Utility toolbar to check or uncheck the Locked option for a range of cells or an object.

NOTES

For a selected text box, the Object Proection dialog box has two check box options: The Locked option protects the object from being moved or resized, and the Lock Text option prevents changes in the object's text contents. See TEXT BOX for more information about this type of object.

The password you enter into the Protect Document dialog box can be as long as 255 characters. Alphabetic case is significant. (In contrast, a password in the Save Options dialog box can contain a maximum of 15 characters. See PASSWORDS for more information.)

The Options ➤ Protect Document command is also available for a macro sheet.

To Remove Document Protection

Choose the Options ➤ Unprotect Document command. If you used a password to protect the cells, you must now re-enter the password to remove protection. If there is no password, Excel removes protection immediately.

To Protect an Unembedded Chart Window

1. Activate the chart window and choose Chart ➤ Protect Document.

2. Check the Chart option to protect the contents of the chart window from changes. Check the Windows option to prevent changes in the size, shape, or position of the window itself.

3. Optionally, enter a password.

4. Click OK. If you are using a password, enter it again in the Confirm Password dialog box. Then click OK.

NOTES

The Chart ➤ Protect Document command is available only for chart windows that you create by choosing the File ➤ New command (not for windows that you open by double-clicking a chart object that is embedded in a worksheet).

When you protect a chart, Excel dims all commands in the Edit, Gallery, Chart, and Format menus that would result in changes in the chart itself. To unprotect a chart document, choose Chart ➤ Unprotect Document.

SEE ALSO

Charting SnapGuide, Graphic Objects, Macros SnapGuide, Passwords, Protecting Cells, Text Box, Window Operations.

Queries on External Databases

The Data Access Macro provides tools for performing queries on an external database. If your Macintosh is connected to a network, you can use this add-in macro to extract records from a shared database and paste the records into an Excel worksheet.

To Open the Data Access Macro

1. Activate the worksheet from which you want to perform database queries.

2. Choose File ➤ Open. Open the Macro Library folder, which is located in the folder where Excel is installed, and select Data Access Macro in the file list.

3. Click the Open button to open the macro.

NOTES

When the Data Access Macro is open, you can use commands in the Data menu to access data both from worksheet-based databases in Excel and from external databases:

▲ The Data ➤ Set Database command gives you a choice between defining a worksheet database or connecting to an external database.

▲ The Data ➤ Paste Fieldnames command reads the field names from a connected external database and copies the names to the active worksheet. (You can then use Data ➤ Set Criteria to create a criteria range for selecting records from the external database; and Data ➤ Set Extract to create an extract range for pasting records from the database.)

▲ The Data ➤ SQL Query and Data ➤ Query Assistant commands provide alternative ways to build queries and to extract data from a connected external database.

SEE ALSO

Add-in Macros, Database SnapGuide, Database Criteria, Database Operations.

Recalculation

By default, recalculation is automatic in Excel. This means that Excel recalculates dependent formulas whenever you change an entry on a worksheet. In some circumstances—notably when you are dealing with a detailed worksheet containing complex formulas—you may want to switch to manual recalculation. Under this setting, Excel recalculates open worksheets only on command.

To Switch to Manual Recalculation

1. Choose Options – Calculation. The Calculations Options dialog appears.

2. In the Calculation group, select the Manual option button, and then click OK.

NOTES

Under the Manual recalculation setting, the status bar displays the work "Calculate" whenever a change takes place that would affect

the result of a dependent formula. In other words, when you
see the word "Calculate," you know that one or more formulas
need to be recalculated.

To Recalculate Manually

1. Choose Options ➤ Calculation.

2. On the Calculation Options dialog box, click the Calc Now
button to recalculate all open worksheets.

 **SHORTCUTS**

▲ Press ⌘–=.

▲ Click the Recalculate tool on the Utility toolbar.

▲ Press the F9 function key.

 **NOTES**

When you use any of these techniques to recalculate, Excel recalculates the dependent formulas on all open worksheets. The word "Calculate" disappears from the status bar as soon as you recalculate.

To recalculate only the active worksheet, click the Calc Document
button on the Calculation Options dialog box, or press ⌘–Shift–+
or Shift-F9.

To switch back to automatic recalculation, choose Options ➤
Calculation, click the Automatic option button, and click OK.

 **SEE ALSO**

Formula Bar, Formulas SnapGuide, Info Window, Iteration.

References

A reference identifies a cell or a range of cells by position on a worksheet. In a formula, a reference stands for the value stored in a cell or the values stored in a range. For the purposes of copying a formula, you can write a reference in any of three types—relative, absolute, or mixed—depending on how you want the reference to appear in copies of the formula. Excel also has two different reference styles, known as the A1 and R1C1 styles; each style has its own way of denoting relative, absolute, and mixed references. An external reference identifies a cell or range on another worksheet, and creates a link between two worksheets.

To Change a Reference Type in the Formula Bar

Position the insertion point just after the reference in the active formula bar, or highlight the entire reference in the case of a range. Then choose Formula ➤ Reference one or more times to change the reference from relative to absolute to mixed.

SHORTCUTS

Press ⌘-T repeatedly to step through the possible reference types.

NOTES

In the default A1 reference style, Excel uses dollar signs to denote absolute or mixed references. For example:

▲ $E$9 is an absolute reference. When you copy a formula containing this $E$9 as an operand, the reference is copied unchanged and always refers to cell E9.

▲ E$9 is a mixed reference, where the column reference (E) is relative and the row reference ($9) is absolute. When you copy a formula containing E$9 as an operand, the reference to row 9 remains fixed, but the reference to column E can change relative to the column of the copied formula.

▲ $E9 is a mixed reference, where the the column reference ($E) is absolute and the row reference (9) is relative. When you copy a formula containing $E9 as an operand, the reference to column E remains fixed, but the reference to row 9 can change relative to the row of the copied formula.

▲ E9 is a relative reference, where both the column and the row are relative. When you copy a formula containing E9 as an operand, both the column and the row can change relative to the position of the copied formula.

See COPYING FORMULAS for more information and examples.

The Formula ➤ Reference command is available only when the formula bar is active. Choose the command four times—or press ⌘-T four times—to step through the complete cycle of reference types and back to the original reference.

Excel has an alternate reference style, known as R1C1, in which columns and rows are both numbered on the worksheet.

To Change to the R1C1 Reference Style

1. Choose Options ➤ Workspace. The Workspace Options dialog box appears on the screen.

2. In the display group, click the R1C1 option. An X appears in the corresponding check box.

3. Click OK.

NOTES

When you make this change, the letter column headings are replaced with numbers on all worksheets. Columns are numbered from 1 to 256. For example, the A1-style reference E9 becomes R9C5 in the R1C1 style.

A relative reference in the R1C1 style is denoted with brackets around the relative portions of the reference. For example:

▲ R[9]C[5] is a relative reference to the cell that is nine rows down and five columns to the right from the current cell. R[−9]C[−5] is a reference to the cell that is nine rows up and five columns to the left from the current cell.

▲ R9C[5] is a mixed reference to the cell in row 9 that is five columns to the right of the current cell.

▲ R[9]C5 is a mixed reference to the cell in column 5 that is nine rows down from the current cell.

▲ R9C5 is an absolute reference to the cell at the intersection of row 9 and column 5—in other words, cell E9 in the A1 reference style.

NOTES

To switch back to A1-style references, choose Options ➤ Workspace, remove the X from the R1C1 check box, and click OK.

To Create an External Reference

1. Select the cell in which you want to create an external reference.

2. Enter an equal sign (=) to begin a formula and to activate the formula bar. Then type the name of another worksheet followed by an exclamation point.

3. After the exclamation point, type a reference to a cell on the other worksheet, and then press Enter.

SHORTCUTS

If both worksheets are open, you can use the pointing technique to enter an external reference: Select a cell on the current worksheet,

enter an equal sign, and then point to the target cell on the other
worksheet.

NOTES

If the name of the other worksheet includes spaces or a disk or
folder name, enclose the name in single quotation marks; for
example:

='MacintoshHD:Excel Files:Sales 1991'!B2

If you enter an external reference in this complete form, the
other worksheet need not be open to create a link with the active
worksheet.

You can also use the Edit ➤ Copy and Edit ➤ Paste Link commands to enter an external reference and create a link between
worksheets. See LINKS BETWEEN WORKSHEETS for details.

SEE ALSO

Array Formulas, Copying Formulas, Formula Bar, Formulas Snap-
Guide, Info Window, Links between Worksheets, Macro Recording,
Names, Selecting a Range, Summation.

Repeating Commands

The Edit ➤ Repeat command gives you a quick way to repeat the
last operation you performed in Excel.

To Repeat the Previous Command

Pull down the Edit menu and choose the Repeat command.

SHORTCUTS

Click the Repeat tool on the Utility toolbar, or press ⌘-Y.

NOTES

If the previous command cannot be repeated, Repeat is dimmed in the Edit menu, or the command is displayed as Can't Repeat.

You can perform an operation on one worksheet—such as a formatting command or File ➤ Page Setup—and then repeat the same operation on another worksheet. After completing the operation on the first worksheet, select the name of the second worksheet from the Window menu and then choose Edit ➤ Repeat.

SEE ALSO

Group Editing, Undo.

Replacing Worksheet Data

The Formula ➤ Replace command searches for an entry or part of an entry in a worksheet or macro sheet and replaces it with another entry.

To Replace Data in a Worksheet or Macro Sheet

1. Activate the document in which you want to replace data, and choose Formula ➤ Replace. The Replace dialog box appears on the screen.

2. In the Find What box, enter the text that you want to replace.

3. In the Replace With box, enter the replacement text.

4. In the Look at group, select the Whole option if the text you have entered in the Find What box represents an entire cell entry; or select Part if you want to search for the text as a portion of a cell entry.

5. In the Look by group, select Rows to search from the top to the bottom of your worksheet, or Columns to search from left to right.

6. Click the Match Case option, placing an X in its check box, if you want Excel to search for the text in the exact upper-case and lowercase combinations you have entered into the Find What box. Leave this option unchecked if you want to perform the search without regard for alphabetic case.

7. To begin the search-and-replace operation, use any sequence of the following command buttons:

▲ Click Find Next to find the next occurrence of the Find What text, or hold down the Shift key and click Find Next to find the previous occurrence.

▲ Click Replace to replace the target text in the current cell and then find the next occurrence.

▲ Click Replace All to replace all the remaining occurrences of the target text and close the Replace dialog box.

▲ Click Close to close the Replace dialog box without changing any additional entries.

NOTES

If Excel does not find the target text in your worksheet, a dialog box appears on the screen with the message "Could not find matching data to replace." If the search is unsuccessful, but you believe the text does exist in your worksheet, reopen the Replace dialog box and make sure you have selected the appropriate option in the Look at box, and the correct setting for the Match Case option.

You can use wildcard characters in the search text: ? stands for a single unspecified character, and * stands for a string of unspecified characters.

To restrict the search-and-replace operation to a specific range of cells on your worksheet, select the range before choosing the Replace command. Otherwise, Excel searches through the entire worksheet for the target text.

The Formula ➤ Replace command does not change the contents of notes in a worksheet or macro sheet.

EXAMPLE

You can use Formula ➤ Replace to edit formulas on a worksheet. For example, to change all the SUM functions on a worksheet to AVERAGE functions, follow these steps:

1. Activate the worksheet and choose Formula ➤ Replace.

2. Enter SUM in the Find What box and AVERAGE in the Replace With box.

3. Click the Part option in the Look at group.

4. Click the Replace All button.

Excel replaces the functions as instructed, and immediately recalculates the edited formulas.

SEE ALSO

Database Operations, Finding Worksheet Data, Formulas Snap-Guide, Notes.

Reports

A report is a printed sequence of scenarios and views that you have defined for a worksheet. The Report Manager is an add-in macro that prints reports from the definitions you create using two other Excel features:

▲ The View Manager (Window ➤ View) lets you define different ways of displaying and printing the information in a worksheet.

▲ The Scenario Manager (Formula ➤ Scenario Manager) lets you define sets of input values for a variety of different "what-if" scenarios on a worksheet.

Given these two kinds of definitions, the Report Manager combines scenarios and views in any way you choose, and prints the resulting report.

To Create and Print a Report

1. Activate a worksheet containing data from which you want to create a report.

2. Choose Formula ➤ Scenario Manager and create the scenarios you want in your report. See SCENARIOS for steps and examples.

3. Choose Window ➤ View and create the views you want to use in your report. See VIEWS for details.

4. Choose File ➤ Print Report. The Print Report dialog box appears. If this is the first time you have used the Report Manager for this worksheet, the list box labeled Reports is empty. A column of command buttons appears at the right side of the dialog box.

5. Click the Add button to create a report and assign it a name. The Add Report dialog box appears on the screen.

6. In the Report Name box, enter a name to identify the report you are about to create, and then read the instructions displayed beneath the text box. As you can see, a report consists of sections, where each section is characterized by a view and/or a scenario that you select.

7. Pull down the View list and select a view for the current section of the report.

8. Pull down the Scenario list and select a scenario for the current section.

9. Click the Add button. Excel displays a description of the section in the Current Sections list.

10. Repeat steps 7, 8, and 9 for each section that you want to include in your report. Then click OK when you have defined all the sections.

```
┌─────────────── Add Report ───────────────┐
│                                           │
│  Report Name:   Home Tables      ┌──────┐ │
│                                  │  OK  │ │
│  A report is made up of multiple └──────┘ │
│  sections. Each section can have ┌──────┐ │
│  a different view, or scenario,  │Cancel│ │
│  or both. To create a section,   └──────┘ │
│  choose a View and/or Scenario            │
│  and choose Add.                          │
│  ┌─Report Section────────────┐  ┌──────┐ │
│  │ View:    Terms and Table  │  │ Add  │ │
│  │ Scenario: Home 3          │  └──────┘ │
│  └───────────────────────────┘           │
│  Current Sections:             ┌────────┐ │
│  Terms and Table, Home 1       │Move Up │ │
│  Terms and Table, Home 2       ├────────┤ │
│  Terms and Table, Home 3       │MoveDown│ │
│                                ├────────┤ │
│                                │ Delete │ │
│  □ Continuous Page Numbers     ├────────┤ │
│                                │  Help  │ │
│                                └────────┘ │
└───────────────────────────────────────────┘
```

11. Back in the Print Report dialog box, select the name of the report you want to print from the Reports list. Then click Print.

12. In the Print dialog box, enter the number of copies you want to print of your report, and click OK. Excel begins printing your report.

NOTES

You can define multiple reports in the Report Manager, and assign a name to each one. When you save your worksheet, Excel saves the report definitions as well as the scenarios and views. To print another defined report, choose File ➤ Print Report, select the name of the report you want to print, and click Print.

The Report Manager, the Scenario Manager, and the View Manager are all add-in macros. As you begin using these three macros, you may begin to think of them as three parts of the same feature, the goal of which is to print multi-section reports from detailed worksheet scenarios.

SEE ALSO

Scenarios, Views.

Row Height

Adjusting the height of a row allows you to display multiple lines of text within a single cell, or to display large or small font sizes within the row.

To Change the Height of a Single Row

1. Select a cell in the row, or click the row heading to select the entire row.

2. Choose Format ➤ Row Height.

3. Enter a new value in the Row Height text box, and then click OK.

SHORTCUTS

Position the mouse pointer over the line located just under the row's heading, and drag the line down (for a greater height) or up (for a smaller height). Double-click the line to adjust the row height to the best fit for the current contents. Alternatively, point to the row heading, press ⌘-Option while you hold down the mouse button, and choose Row Height from the resulting short-cut menu.

EXAMPLE

In the worksheet shown below, cell A1 contains a three-line text entry that is displayed in a larger font size than the rest of the worksheet. The height of row 1 has been increased accordingly.

	A	B	C
1	XYZ Corp. Product Sales 1993		
2			
3		Q1	Q2
4	Product 1	$5,447	$8,369
5	Product 2	$8,635	$7,488
6	Product 3	$6,122	$8,897

To enter a multiline title in a cell, follow these general steps:

1. Select the cell, and type a line of text. Then press ⌘-Option-Enter to insert a carriage return into the entry. The height of the formula bar increases to accommodate the next line of the entry.

2. Repeat step 1 for each line of text that you want to include in the entry.

3. Press Enter to complete the entry.

4. While the cell is still selected, choose Format ➤ Alignment. In the Alignment dialog box, click the Wrap Text option, placing an X in the corresponding check box. Then click OK. Excel increases the row height to allow for multiple lines of wrapped text.

5. If the column is too narrow to display the lines of text in the way you entered them, increase the column width and then adjust the row height to produce the effect you want.

NOTES

To change the heights of a group of rows, select the rows and choose the Format ➤ Row Height command.

The standard row height row is the best fit for the largest font displayed in the row. Excel automatically adjusts the height of a row when you change the font of an entry in the row.

SEE ALSO

Alignment, Column Width, Fonts, Hiding, Point Size.

Saving Files

Use the File ➤ Save As command to save a worksheet, chart, or macro sheet to disk for the first time. Use File ➤ Save to update a file after you have made changes in a document.

To Save an Excel Document to Disk for the First Time

1. Choose File ➤ Save As.

2. If necessary, use the disk and folder list boxes to specify where you want to save the file.

3. Enter a name for the document in the Save Worksheet as box.

4. If you want to save the file in a format other than Excel's Normal format, click the Options button and make a selection from the File Format list in the Save Options dialog box. Then click OK.

5. Click Save to save the file.

 **SHORTCUTS**

Press ⌘-Shift-S or F12 to open the Save As dialog box. Or, click the Save tool on the Standard toolbar for a file that you have not saved before; Excel recognizes that you are saving the file for the first time, and opens the Save As dialog box.

 **NOTES**

Click the Options button on the Save As dialog box if you want to create a password for restricting access to the current file. See PASSWORDS for details. In addition, the Save Options dialog box has a check box labeled Create Backup File. If you check this option, Excel automatically maintains a backup copy (named Backup of FileName) each time you save the file.

To Update a File after Making Changes in a Document

Activate the file and choose File ➤ Save.

 **SHORTCUTS**

Click the Save tool on the Standard toolbar, or press ⌘-S.

 **NOTES**

If the active worksheet is an unbound document in a workbook, the File ➤ Save command saves only the worksheet. Use the File ➤ Save Workbook command to save the workbook and its documents. See WORKBOOKS for details.

Add-in Macros, Charting SnapGuide, Exiting Excel, File Formats, Folders, Links between Worksheets, Macros SnapGuide, Opening Files, Passwords, Protecting Documents, Window Operations, Workbooks.

Scenarios

Using the Scenario Manager, you can define and save sets of input data for exploring "what-if" scenarios on a worksheet. The Scenario Manager is especially useful on a worksheet that is organized into distinct "input" and "output" areas. In this context, the input area displays the values that serve as parameters for calculations performed in the output area. When you select a scenario, Excel enters the input values into specified cells and recalculates the worksheet accordingly.

To Define and View Scenarios on a Worksheet

1. Develop a worksheet that uses a range of input values to calculate data in an output area.

2. Use Formula ➤ Create Names or Formula ➤ Define Name to asssign names to the cells containing the input values. (These names are optional, but they make the Scenario Manager easier to use, as you'll see shortly.)

3. Choose Formula ➤ Scenario Manager. The Scenario Manager dialog box contains a text box labeled Changing Cells, along with a column of command buttons. The Changing Cells box is active initially.

4. On the active worksheet, point to the range of cells that contains the input values. If values are displayed in a noncontiguous range, hold down the ⌘ key while you point

to multiple ranges. As you do so, Excel enters the appropriate references into the Changing Cells box.

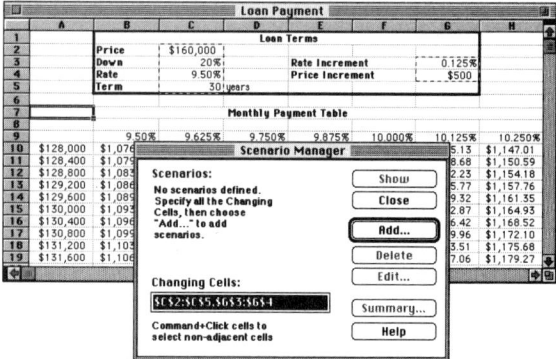

5. Click the Add button. The Add Scenario dialog box appears next. It contains a column of text boxes. The first one, labeled Name, is for identifying the current scenario. Subsequent text boxes are labeled with the names you assigned to the selected input cells on your worksheet, and the text boxes themselves contain the current data from those input cells. (If you did not assign names to the input cells, these text boxes are instead labeled with absolute references to the input cell locations.)

6. Enter a name for the current scenario in the Name text box. This name should be short and clearly identify the current scenario's input data. The name can contain spaces and special characters in addition to letters and digits.

7. Enter or edit values in the input cell text boxes. (For the first scenario you define, you may want to keep the current data, copied directly from your worksheet.) Then click the Add button.

8. Repeat steps 6 and 7 for each scenario you want to define. Each scenario can contain a different set of input values to be used in calculating formulas on the worksheet.

9. After defining your final scenario, click OK. The Scenario Manager dialog box returns to the screen, and a list box labeled Scenarios displays the names of all the scenarios you have defined.

10. To view one of the scenarios, highlight its name in the Scenarios list and then click the Show button. Excel replaces the entries in the input cells with the values of the selected scenario, and recalculates the worksheet accordingly.

11. Repeat step 10 for all the scenarios you want to view, and then click the Close button.

NOTES

When you save your worksheet, Excel saves all the scenario definitions along with it. To review a particular scenario, open the worksheet and choose the Formula ➤ Scenario Manager command. To print a sequence of scenarios, activate the worksheet on which you have defined scenarios and choose the File ➤ Print Report command. See REPORTS for further details.

To Create a Scenario Summary

I. Activate the worksheet on which you have defined the scenarios, and choose Formula ➤ Scenario Manager.

2. Click the Summary button. The Scenario Summary dialog box appears on the screen.

3. If you want to include formula results in the summary, enter a reference to the appropriate cell or range in the Result Cells box. (To enter a reference in this box you can point to the cell or range on the active worksheet, or you can type the reference directly from the keyboard.)

4. Click OK to create the scenario summary.

NOTES

Excel opens a new worksheet for the summary, and creates an outline to present the summary information. The worksheet includes a column of input data for each scenario you have defined, along with the corresponding result cells if you chose to include them in the summary.

EXAMPLE

The following worksheets illustrate the kind of organization that is best suited to the features of the Scenario Manager. This example uses a group of six input values to generate an output table of monthly mortgage payment calculations. The input values include:

▲ The table's initial house price (in cell C2, which is named Price).

▲ The percent down payment (in C3, named Down).

▲ The table's initial interest rate for the loan (in C4, named Rate).

▲ The term of the loan in years (in C5, named Term).

▲ The table's increment values for the interest rate (in G3, named RateIncr) and the price (in G4, named PriceIncr).

The output (in the range A9:H19) is a lookup table in which you can find the monthly payment corresponding to a particular home price and interest rate. Because each value in the output table is the result of a formula, changing one of the input values results in a completely new table.

	A	B	C	D	E	F	G	H
1					Loan Terms			
2		Price	$180,000					
3		Down	20%		Rate Increment		0.125%	
4		Rate	9.50%		Price Increment		$500	
5		Term	30 years					
6								
7					Monthly Payment Table			
8								
9			9.500%	9.625%	9.750%	9.875%	10.000%	10.125%	10.250%
10	$128,000	$1,076.29	$1,087.99	$1,099.72	$1,111.49	$1,123.29	$1,135.13	$1,147.01
11	$128,400	$1,079.66	$1,091.39	$1,103.15	$1,114.96	$1,126.80	$1,138.68	$1,150.59
12	$128,800	$1,083.02	$1,094.79	$1,106.59	$1,118.43	$1,130.31	$1,142.23	$1,154.18
13	$129,200	$1,086.38	$1,098.19	$1,110.03	$1,121.91	$1,133.82	$1,145.77	$1,157.76
14	$129,600	$1,089.75	$1,101.59	$1,113.46	$1,125.38	$1,137.33	$1,149.32	$1,161.35
15	$130,000	$1,093.11	$1,104.99	$1,116.90	$1,128.85	$1,140.84	$1,152.87	$1,164.93
16	$130,400	$1,096.47	$1,108.39	$1,120.34	$1,132.33	$1,144.35	$1,156.42	$1,168.52
17	$130,800	$1,099.84	$1,111.79	$1,123.77	$1,135.80	$1,147.86	$1,159.96	$1,172.10
18	$131,200	$1,103.20	$1,115.19	$1,127.21	$1,139.27	$1,151.37	$1,163.51	$1,175.68
19	$131,600	$1,106.56	$1,118.59	$1,130.65	$1,142.75	$1,154.88	$1,167.06	$1,179.27

	A	B	C	D	E	F	G	H
1					Loan Terms			
2		Price	$320,000					
3		Down	15%		Rate Increment		0.250%	
4		Rate	10.50%		Price Increment		$1,000	
5		Term	30 years					
6								
7					Monthly Payment Table			
8								
9			10.500%	10.750%	11.000%	11.250%	11.500%	11.750%	12.000%
10	$272,000	$2,488.09	$2,539.07	$2,590.32	$2,641.83	$2,693.59	$2,745.59	$2,797.83
11	$272,850	$2,495.87	$2,547.00	$2,598.41	$2,650.09	$2,702.01	$2,754.17	$2,806.57
12	$273,700	$2,503.64	$2,554.94	$2,606.51	$2,658.34	$2,710.43	$2,762.75	$2,815.31
13	$274,550	$2,511.42	$2,562.87	$2,614.60	$2,666.60	$2,718.85	$2,771.33	$2,824.06
14	$275,400	$2,519.19	$2,570.81	$2,622.70	$2,674.85	$2,727.26	$2,779.91	$2,832.80
15	$276,250	$2,526.97	$2,578.74	$2,630.79	$2,683.11	$2,735.68	$2,788.49	$2,841.54
16	$277,100	$2,534.74	$2,586.68	$2,638.89	$2,691.37	$2,744.10	$2,797.07	$2,850.29
17	$277,950	$2,542.52	$2,594.61	$2,646.98	$2,699.62	$2,752.52	$2,805.65	$2,859.03
18	$278,800	$2,550.29	$2,602.55	$2,655.08	$2,707.88	$2,760.93	$2,814.23	$2,867.77
19	$279,650	$2,558.07	$2,610.48	$2,663.17	$2,716.13	$2,769.35	$2,822.81	$2,876.52

	A	B	C	D	E	F	G	H
1					Loan Terms			
2		Price	$450,000					
3		Down	10%		Rate Increment		0.500%	
4		Rate	11.00%		Price Increment		$2,000	
5		Term	30	years				
6								
7					Monthly Payment Table			
8								
9			11.000%	11.500%	12.000%	12.500%	13.000%	13.500%	14.000%
10	$405,000	$3,856.91	$4,010.68	$4,165.88	$4,322.39	$4,480.11	$4,638.92	$4,798.73
11	$406,800	$3,874.05	$4,028.51	$4,184.40	$4,341.60	$4,500.02	$4,659.54	$4,820.06
12	$408,600	$3,891.19	$4,046.33	$4,202.91	$4,360.82	$4,519.93	$4,680.15	$4,841.39
13	$410,400	$3,908.34	$4,064.16	$4,221.43	$4,380.03	$4,539.84	$4,700.77	$4,862.71
14	$412,200	$3,925.48	$4,081.98	$4,239.94	$4,399.24	$4,559.75	$4,721.39	$4,884.04
15	$414,000	$3,942.62	$4,099.81	$4,258.46	$4,418.45	$4,579.67	$4,742.01	$4,905.37
16	$415,800	$3,959.76	$4,117.63	$4,276.97	$4,437.66	$4,599.58	$4,762.62	$4,926.70
17	$417,600	$3,976.90	$4,135.46	$4,295.49	$4,456.87	$4,619.49	$4,783.24	$4,948.02
18	$419,400	$3,994.04	$4,153.28	$4,314.00	$4,476.08	$4,639.40	$4,803.86	$4,969.35
19	$421,200	$4,011.19	$4,171.11	$4,332.52	$4,495.29	$4,659.31	$4,824.48	$4,990.68

To create the three scenarios, begin by developing the initial worksheet, and then choose Formula ➤ Scenario Manager. Select the ranges C2:C5 and G3:G4 as the entries in the Changing Cells box, and then define three scenarios, named Home 1, Home 2, and Home 3. The following Scenario Summary Report shows the input values for these three scenario definitions:

	A	B	C	D	E	F
1						
2		**Scenario Summary Report**				
3				Home 1	Home 2	Home 3
6		Changing Cells:				
7			Price	$160,000	$320,000	$450,000
8			Down	20%	15%	10%
9			Rate	9.50%	10.50%	11.00%
10			Term	30	30	30
11			RateIncr	0.125%	0.250%	0.500%
12			PriceIncr	$500	$1,000	$2,000
13		Result Cells:				
14			FirstPmtCalc	$1,076.29	$2,488.09	$3,856.91

Once you have defined the scenarios, you can quickly view any one of them by selecting a scenario name and clicking the Show button on the Scenario Manager dialog box.

SEE ALSO

Reports, Views.

Selecting a Range

Excel provides a variety of mouse and keyboard techniques for selecting a cell, a range of cells, or a group of noncontiguous ranges on a worksheet.

To Select a Cell

Click the cell with the mouse, or move the cell pointer by pressing any combination of arrow keys, $\rightarrow$, $\leftarrow$, $\downarrow$, or $\uparrow$.

NOTES

To move quickly to the beginning or end of a block of data in a worksheet, hold down the ⌘ key or the Control key and press an arrow key in the direction you want to move. Alternatively, press the End key and then press an arrow key. (The notation END appears on the status bar when you press End.)

To Select a Range

Drag the mouse over the range, or hold down the Shift key and press any combination of arrow keys.

NOTES

Another keyboard technique for selecting a range is to press the F8 function key to toggle into Extend mode, and then press any combination of arrow keys to select the range. The notation EXT appears on the status bar. Press Esc or F8 again to toggle out of Extend mode.

To Select Noncontiguous Ranges

Select the first range, and then hold down the ⌘ key or the
Control key while you select additional ranges.

NOTES

The notation for noncontiguous ranges is a list of range references
separated by commas.

To Select a Row or Column

Click the row heading or column heading with the mouse, or
press Shift-spacebar for a row or ⌘-spacebar for a column.

To Select an Entire Worksheet

Click the Select All button located at the intersection of the row
and column headings, or press ⌘-A or ⌘-Shift-spacebar.

SEE ALSO

Array Formulas, AutoFill, Copying Data, Filling Ranges, Formula
Bar, Formulas SnapGuide, Group Editing, Hiding, References,
Transposing Ranges.

Series

The Data ➤ Series command is a versatile tool for entering series
of numeric and date values in the rows or columns of a worksheet.
(In this context, a series is a sequence of values in which the
entries are calculated from a linear or exponential formula.) In
addition to a choice of series types, the Series command gives you
control over the step and stop values in a series. The start value is
always an existing entry in the worksheet range where you create

the series. You can also use this command to produce trend series, for which Excel calculates the linear or exponential "best fit" and modifies the data accordingly.

To Create a Series

1. In the first cell of a row or column range on the active worksheet, enter the initial value for the series you want to create. Then select the range for the series.

2. Choose Data ➤ Series. The Series dialog box displays three groups of option buttons, labeled Series in, Type, and Date Unit. For the Series in option, Excel automatically selects Rows or Columns according to the range you have already selected on the worksheet.

3. In the Type group, select the type of data series you want to create. If you select Date, Excel activates the Date Unit group. Select one of the unit options in the this group.

4. Optionally, enter a value in the Step Value box. (The default is 1.)

5. Optionally, enter a value in the Stop Value box.

6. Click OK to create the series.

 **SHORTCUTS**

You can use Excel's AutoFill feature to create some types of series on a worksheet. See AUTOFILL for details.

 **NOTES**

Excel's use of the Step Value depends on the type of series you select:

▲ For a linear series, the step value is added to each value to produce the next value in the series.

▲ For a growth series, each value is multiplied by the step value to produce the next value in the series.

▲ For a date series, the step value represents the number of days between one entry and the next in the series. (You can further refine the steps of a date series by selecting an option in the Date Unit group.)

The end of a series is determined either by the number you supply as the Stop Value, or by the end of the selected range, whichever comes first.

EXAMPLE

Columns A through D in the following worksheet show examples of date, linear, and growth series:

▲ The date series in column A is a weekday series—that is, a sequence of dates in which Saturdays and Sundays are omitted. To create a series like this one, enter the first date and select the range for the series. Then choose Data ➤ Series and select the Date and Weekday options. (In the illustration, the series is formatted by the ddd, m/d/yy custom format code; see CUSTOM NUMBER FORMATS for more information.)

▲ The date series in column B contains entries that are one month apart. To create this series, select the Date and Month options in the Series dialog box.

▲ The numeric series in column C is a linear series where the step value from one entry to the next is 0.25. To create this series, select the Linear option in the Series dialog box, and enter 0.25 in the Step Value box.

▲ The numeric series in column D is a growth series where each value is multiplied by 1.125 to calculate the next value. To create this series, select the Growth option in the Series dialog box, and enter 1.125 in the Step Value box.

	A	B	C	D	E	F	G	H
1				Series Examples				
2								
3	Date	Date	Linear	Growth		Linear		Growth
4	(weekday)	(month)	(step = .25)	(step = 1.125)		(Trend)		(Trend)
5	Mon, 6/22/92	6/22/92	-1	1000.00	1	1.17	1	1.14
6	Tue, 6/23/92	7/22/92	-0.75	1125.00	3	2.67	3	2.29
7	Wed, 6/24/92	8/22/92	-0.5	1265.63	4	4.17	4	4.58
8	Thu, 6/25/92	9/22/92	-0.25	1423.83		5.67		9.16
9	Fri, 6/26/92	10/22/92	0	1601.81		7.17		18.32
10	Mon, 6/29/92	11/22/92	0.25	1802.03		8.67		36.63
11	Tue, 6/30/92	12/22/92	0.5	2027.29		10.17		73.26
12	Wed, 7/1/92	1/22/93	0.75	2280.70		11.67		146.52
13	Thu, 7/2/92	2/22/93	1	2565.78		13.17		293.05
14	Fri, 7/3/92	3/22/93	1.25	2886.51		14.67		586.09
15								

To Create a Trend Series

1. In a row or column range, enter two or more tentative values for the trend series, and then select the entire range in which you want to create the series.

2. Choose Data ➤ Series. In the Series dialog box, click the Trend option, placing an X in the corresponding check box.

3. Select either Linear or Growth in the Type group, and click OK.

 **NOTES**

To create a trend series, Excel determines the "best fit" formula for the series—that is, the linear or exponential equation that best describes the tentative sequence of entries you have already entered into the series range. In the resulting series, Excel supplies new values in the series and adjusts the existing values to make them fit the formula.

When you create a trend series, make sure that you apply a format with one or more decimal places to the numeric entries in the series. If the series entries are formatted as integers you may not be able to see exactly how the series has been formed.

 **EXAMPLE**

In the worksheet example shown earlier in this entry, columns F and H contain examples of trend series. As displayed in columns E and G, the tentative entries for both of these series were 1, 3, and 4. For the linear series in column F, Excel calculates a step value of 1.5. To produce the growth series in column H, Excel uses a step multiplier of 2. Notice that Excel has adjusted the first three tentative values in both series.

 **SEE ALSO**

AutoFill, Filling Ranges, Formulas SnapGuide.

Shading

You can use background shading to highlight ranges of data on a worksheet.

To Apply Background Shading to a Worksheet Range

1. Select the range and choose Format ➤ Patterns.

2. Click the arrow next to the Pattern box, and select a shading pattern from the drop-down list.

3. For shading in color, choose colors from the Foreground and Background lists.

4. Click OK to apply the shading.

 **SHORTCUTS**

Select a range and click the Light Shading tool on the Formatting toolbar, or click the Dark Shading tool. (Dark Shading is not initially part of any toolbar. See TOOLBARS for instructions on displaying a tool in a toolbar.)

 **EXAMPLE**

The following worksheet illustrates the use of light shading to highlight selected ranges of values.

	A	B	C	D	E
1		Q1	Q2	Q3	Q4
2	Product 1	$8,557	$5,769	$8,111	$9,156
3	Product 2	$6,693	$9,044	$7,713	$6,771
4	Product 3	$7,532	$8,580	$5,006	$6,122
5	Product 4	$8,811	$9,731	$9,552	$9,475
6	Product 5	$9,632	$7,358	$7,466	$6,383
7	Product 6	$5,225	$6,507	$7,459	$5,895
8	Product 7	$5,337	$9,282	$9,212	$7,096
9	Product 8	$9,204	$7,213	$7,048	$6,026
10	Product 9	$5,548	$6,318	$8,016	$7,776
11	Product 10	$5,484	$7,398	$7,989	$9,974

 **SEE ALSO**

Colors, Patterns.

Shortcut Menus

The shortcut menus are designed to give you quick access to Excel's most commonly used menu commands. Shortcut menus are available for almost any item you work with in the Excel application window.

To Choose a Command from a Shortcut Menu

Point to an item in the Excel window and press ⌘-Option at the keyboard while you click the mouse button. Then choose a command in the menu that appears on the screen.

 **NOTES**

Most shortcut menus contain a selection of commands from Excel's Edit and Format menus. In addition, some shortcut menus contain special-purpose commands that apply to the specific item you are pointing to. Here are the items for which Excel supplies shortcut menus:

▲ Cell, range, column, or row selections on a worksheet. The shortcut menu contains commands for cut-and-paste, copy-and-paste, deletions, and insertions, along with a selection of formatting commands.

▲ Graphic objects in a worksheet, including buttons, drawn objects, text boxes, embedded charts, and other embedded objects. The shortcut menu for these objects contains commands from the Edit, Format, and Macro menus.

▲ Selected items or areas in a chart window. The shortcut menus for chart items include commands from the Edit, Gallery, Chart, and Format menus.

▲ Toolbars. When you press ⌘-Option and click a toolbar, Excel displays a list of all the available toolbars. To open a toolbar, choose a name from this list. In addition, the toolbar shortcut menu contains the Toolbars command from the Options menu; and the Customize command, which is otherwise accessible only by clicking a command button on the Toolbars dialog box. (See TOOLBARS for details.)

▲ Workbooks. There are two shortcut menus that apply to workbook items. When you press ⌘-Option and click a document icon with the mouse button, the shortcut menu contains a selection of commands from the Edit menu. When you click one of the three paging buttons (located at the lower-right corner of the workbook window), the shortcut menu contains selections for activating the workbook or any sheet in it, along with two commands: New and Group Edit.

SEE ALSO

Alignment, Borders, Charting SnapGuide, Clipboard, Column Width, Copying Data, Deleting, Excel Window, Fonts, Formatting Worksheet Cells, Graphic Objects, Group Editing, Inserting, Macros SnapGuide, Moving Data, Number Formats, Object Linking and Embedding, Patterns, Point Size, Row Height, Selecting a Range, Shading, Text Box, Toolbars, Workbooks.

Solver

In a worksheet containing a range of interrelated formulas, you can use Solver to find the best solution to a problem involving various combinations of input data. To find an optimum value, Solver adjusts specified data values within expressed constraints. Solver is an add-in macro that you open and run by choosing the Formula ➤ Solver command.

To Use the Solver

1. Set up a worksheet that includes

   ▲ A formula whose result you want to optimize by finding its maximum, minimum, or best value.

   ▲ One or more data entries that can be adjusted in order to find the optimal solution.

2. Select the cell that contains the formula whose value you want to optimize, and then choose the Formula ➤ Solver command. The Solver Parameters dialog box appears on the screen. The Set Cell box contains a reference to the selected cell.

3. Click one of the three option buttons in the Equal to group: Max to find the maximum result from the formula, Min to find the minimum result, or Value to find a specified result. If you choose Value, enter the result you want to achieve in the text box labeled Value of.

4. Activate the By Changing Cells box. On the worksheet, select the cell or cells containing the data values that you want to adjust in order to find the optimum solution. If you want to include more than one cell reference in this box, hold down the ⌘ key while you make multiple selections on the worksheet. (Move the Solver Parameters dialog box to any convenient location on the screen if it is covering a cell or range that you want to select.)

5. Click the Add button. The Add Constraint dialog box appears on the screen. In the Cell Reference box, enter a reference to a cell for which you want to express a constraint. (You can enter the reference directly from the keyboard, or you can click the cell on the worksheet.)

6. Click the down-arrow next to the operation list box, and select one of the three relational operators (<=, =, or >=); or select int if you want the constraint cell to remain an integer.

7. In the Constraint box, enter a value or formula (starting with an equal sign, =) that expresses the constraint you want to impose on the value in the selected cell. Then click OK. Back on the Solver Parameters dialog box, the constraint appears in the list box labeled Subject to the Constraints.

8. Repeat steps 5, 6, and 7 for any additional constraints you want to express. (You can use the Change button to edit an existing constraint, or the Delete button to remove a constraint from the list.)

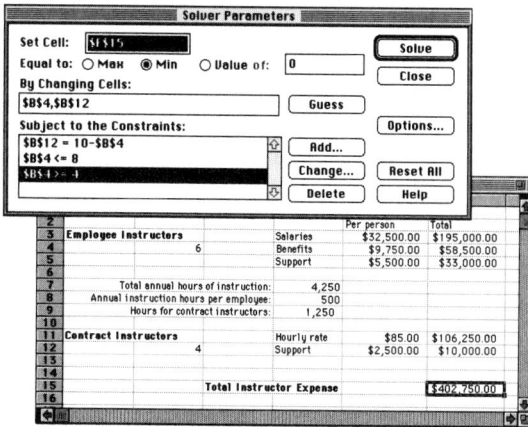

9. Click the Solve button to attempt a solution. When Solver completes its analysis, the Solver dialog box appears on the screen. If a solution has been found, the result is now shown on your worksheet.

10. Select the Keep Solver Solution option if you want to retain this new version of your worksheet data, or select Restore Original Values to revert to the previous version. If you want to generate reports from the Solver analysis, select any of the report titles listed in the Reports box. (To select more than one report, hold down the ⌘ key while you select the titles.) Then click OK.

EXAMPLE

The worksheet below illustrates a problem that is ideal for Solver analysis. The situation of this worksheet is this: A training company uses a combination of staff instructors who are full-time employees, and contract instructors who are called upon to work when they are needed. The worksheet shows the expenses related to each group of instructors. In addition, the range D7:D9 shows the total number of instruction hours per year, the number of instruction hours required from each employee instructor, and the number of remaining hours that must be covered by contract instructors.

	A	B	C	D	E	F
1	Best Mix of Employee and Contract Instructors					
2					Per person	Total
3	Employee Instructors			Salaries	$32,500.00	$195,000.00
4		6		Benefits	$9,750.00	$58,500.00
5				Support	$5,500.00	$33,000.00
6						
7			Total annual hours of instruction:	4,250		
8			Annual instruction hours per employee:	500		
9			Hours for contract instructors:	1,250		
10						
11	Contract Instructors			Hourly rate	$85.00	$106,250.00
12		4		Support	$2,500.00	$10,000.00
13						
14						
15			Total Instructor Expense			$402,750.00
16						

Because some of the current employees have expressed interest in working instead on a contract basis, the company wants to analyze the worksheet to find the best mix of employee and contract instructors. Here are the steps for using the Solver to perform this analysis:

1. Select cell F15, which contains the formula for total instructor expense.

2. Choose Formula ➤ Solver. The reference $F$15 appears in the Set Cell box.

3. Click the Min option to minimize the result of the expense formula.

4. Activate the By Changing Cells box. Hold down the ⌘ key and click cells B4 and B12. These cells, containing the number of employees in each category, are the values that will be adjusted during the Solver analysis.

5. Click the Add button. The company wants a minimum of four employee instructors and a maximum of eight. In addition, ten instructors are needed in all to satisfy scheduling requirements. To express these conditions, enter the following three constraints:

$$\$B\$12 = 10{-}\$B\$4$$
$$\$B\$4 <= 8$$
$$\$B\$4 >= 4$$

6. Back on the Solver Parameters dialog box, click Solve.

The following worksheet shows the new mix of employee and contract instructors that Solver suggests as the best solution for this problem:

	A	B	C	D	E	F
1	Best Mix of Employee and Contract Instructors					
2					Per person	Total
3	Employee Instructors			Salaries	$32,500.00	$130,000.00
4		4		Benefits	$9,750.00	$39,000.00
5				Support	$5,500.00	$22,000.00
6						
7			Total annual hours of instruction:	4,250		
8			Annual instruction hours per employee:	500		
9			Hours for contract instructors:	2,250		
10						
11	Contract Instructors			Hourly rate	$85.00	$191,250.00
12		6		Support	$2,500.00	$15,000.00
13						
14						
15			Total Instructor Expense			$397,250.00
16						

NOTES

Click the Options button on the Solver Parameters dialog box to adjust the way Solver performs its analysis. The Solver Options dialog box includes boxes for the maximum amount of time spent on the analysis, the number of trial solutions (iterations), the precision required for satisfying constraints, and other options.

When Solver completes its solution, the Solver dialog box lists the three reports that can be generated from the analysis:

▲ The Answer report shows the original data values alongside the new values produced for the Solver solution.

▲ The Limits report describes the upper- and lower-limit values of the adjustable cells and the formula result.

▲ The Sensitivity report gives information about the sensitivity of the solution to adjustments in constraints.

Excel opens a new worksheet to create each of the reports that you select on the Solver dialog box.

Finally, the Solver dialog box also has a Save Scenario button. By clicking this button you can supply a name for the solution and save it as a scenario. You can then choose Formula ➤ Scenario Manager whenever you want to review the solution.

SEE ALSO

Goal Seek, Scenarios.

Sorting

The Data ➤ Sort command rearranges a range of worksheet data in alphabetical, numeric, or chronological order. You can sort by rows or columns, using one, two, or three sorting keys. By choosing the Sort command more than once, you can also arrange to sort by more than three keys.

To Sort a Range of Data on a Worksheet

1. Select the range and choose Data ➤ Sort. The Sort dialog box contains groups of options labeled Sort by, 1st Key, 2nd Key, and 3rd Key.

2. Click the Rows or Columns option in the Sort by group to specify whether you want to rearrange rows (using a column as the sort key), or columns (using a row as the sort key).

3. Activate the 1st Key box, and enter a reference to any cell in the row or column that will serve as the first sort key. (You can enter the reference directly from the keyboard, or you can click a cell on the worksheet to identify the location of the key.) Click Ascending or Descending to specify the direction of the sort for this key.

4. Optionally, repeat the actions of step 3 to provide instructions for the 2nd Key and 3rd Key boxes.

5. Click OK to carry out the sort.

 **SHORTCUTS**

Select the range you want to sort; then within the range, activate a cell in the row or column that will serve as the key to the sort. Then click the Sort Ascending or the Sort Descending tool on the Utility toolbar.

 **NOTES**

To sort by a text key, click Ascending for alphabetical order or Descending for reverse alphabetical order. To sort by a key that contains date or time values, click Ascending for chronological order or Descending for reverse chronological order.

To sort a range by more than three keys, sort first by the least significant keys, and then by the most significant keys. See the example below for details.

You can undo a sort by choosing Edit ➤ Undo Sort (or pressing ⌘-Z) immediately after the sort operation. When you design a large database that you intend to work with in a variety of sorted orders, consider including a record number field, where the values represent the original unsorted record order. You can then restore the original order by using this number field as a key.

EXAMPLE

The following worksheet shows a short employee database containing fields for each employee's office location, department, last name, and first name:

	A	B	C	D	E
1	No.	Office	Department	Last	First
2	0	NY	Production	Greene	Candy
3	1	LA	Accounting	Brown	Art
4	2	SF	Production	Smith	Jill
5	3	NY	Production	Hines	Gail
6	4	SF	Accounting	Weinberg	Doug
7	5	LA	Clerical	Granville	Ellen
8	6	SF	Production	Smith	Jack
9	7	SF	Clerical	Maxwell	Ben

Suppose you want to sort this database by the four field keys: Office, Department, Last, and First. Here are the general steps:

1. Select the range A2:E9. (Note that the field names are not included in the sort range.)

2. Choose Data ➤ Sort and sort by the First field (column E).

3. Choose Data ➤ Sort and sort by the remaining fields: Office (column B) as the first key, Department (column C) as the second key, and Last (column D) as the third key.

Here is the resulting sorted database:

	A	B	C	D	E
1	No.	Office	Department	Last	First
2	1	LA	Accounting	Brown	Art
3	5	LA	Clerical	Granville	Ellen
4	0	NY	Production	Greene	Candy
5	3	NY	Production	Hines	Gail
6	4	SF	Accounting	Weinberg	Doug
7	7	SF	Clerical	Maxwell	Ben
8	6	SF	Production	Smith	Jack
9	2	SF	Production	Smith	Jill

SEE ALSO

Databases SnapGuide, Undo.

Spelling Checks

The Options ➤ Spelling command checks and corrects the spelling of words in a worksheet or a macro sheet. The Chart ➤ Spelling command performs the same operation for the text in a chart window.

To Check the Spelling in a Document

1. Activate a worksheet or macro sheet and choose Options ➤Spelling, or activate a chart window and choose Chart ➤ Spelling. If Excel finds a misspelled word in the document, the Spelling dialog box appears. The message "Not in Dictionary" appears at the top of the dialog box, and a suggestion for the correct spelling appears in the Change To box.

2. Click one of the following buttons in the Spelling dialog box:

   ▲ Change replaces the word with the Change To suggestion.

   ▲ Change All replaces all occurrences of the word in the current document.

   ▲ Ignore or Ignore All leaves the word as it appears in the document.

   ▲ Add inserts the word in the current dictionary file. (You can also enter the name for a new dictionary file in the Add Words To box.)

   ▲ Cancel stops the spelling check.

3. Repeat step 2 for each misspelled word that Excel finds.

NOTES

To check the spelling in a range of text entries, select the range before you choose Options ➤ Spelling. Otherwise, if a single cell is selected on the active worksheet, Excel checks the spelling in all text entries, notes, and text boxes on the worksheet. (The Spelling command also checks the spelling of headers and footers if you have added them to your worksheet; see PAGE SETUP for details.)

Excel does not check the spelling of cells that contain formulas. Also, you can check Ignore Words in the UPPERCASE option to omit all-uppercase text from the spelling check.

SEE ALSO

Text Box, Text Operations.

Statistical Functions

Excel's library of statistical functions includes commonly used tools—such as average, count, minimum, and maximum functions—along with a large collection of technical tools used by statisticians.

To Enter a Statistical Function into a Worksheet

1. Select the cell or range where you want to enter the function.

2. Choose Formula ➤ Paste Function, and select the Statistical category. The Paste Function box shows the entire list of statistical functions.

3. Select the name of a function and click OK.

4. Enter arguments for the function in the active formula bar, and press Enter.

 **SHORTCUTS**

From the keyboard, enter an equal sign followed by the function's name, and then press Control-A to display names for the function's arguments in the formula bar.

 **NOTES**

Here is a grouped list of the functions available in this category:

▲ Average, median, and mode functions (AVERAGE, CONFIDENCE, GEOMEAN, HARMEAN, MEDIAN, MODE, TRIMMEAN).

▲ Correlation coefficient functions (CORREL, FISHER, FISHERINV, PEARSON).

▲ Counting functions (COUNT, COUNTA).

▲ Deviation and variance functions (AVEDEV, COVAR, DEVSQ, STDEV, STDEVP, VAR, VARP).

▲ Distribution functions (BETADIST, BETAINV, BINOMDIST, CHIDIST, CHIINV, CHITEST, CRITBINOM, EXPONDIST, FDIST, FINV, FREQUENCY, FTEST, GAMMADIST, GAMMAINV, HYPGEOMDIST, KURT, LOGINV, LOGNORMDIST, NEGBINOMDIST, NORMDIST, NORMINV, NORMSDIST, NORMSINV, POISSON, PROB, SKEW, STANDARDIZE, TDIST, TINV, TTEST, WEIBULL, ZTEST.)

▲ Gamma function (GAMMALN).

▲ Linear regression functions (INTERCEPT, RSQ, SLOPE, STEYX).

▲ Maximum and minimum functions (MAX, MIN).

▲ Percentile, rank, and standing functions (LARGE, PERCENTILE, PERCENTRANK, QUARTILE, RANK, SMALL)

▲ Permutations (PERMUT).

▲ Trend functions (FORECAST, GROWTH, LINEST, LOGEST, TREND).

SEE ALSO

Analysis Tools, Mathematical Functions.

Styles

A style is a combination of formatting attributes that you define for use in a particular worksheet or macro sheet. The categories you can include in a style are represented by the first six commands in the Format menu: Number, Alignment, Font, Border, Patterns, and Cell Protection. You can create a style by example or by definition. After creating a style and assigning it a name, you can easily apply the style's entire set of format definitions to any range of cells. The Style box on the Standard toolbar lists all the styles defined for the active worksheet. You can copy the styles in this list from one document to another. Excel's Normal style represents the default formatting characteristics for a document.

To Create a Style by Example

1. Select a range of cells and apply any combination of formats to the range.

2. While the range is still selected, activate the Style box in the Standard toolbar.

3. Type a name for the style and press Enter.

NOTES

A style name can include letters, digits, spaces, and special characters.

To Apply a Style to a Range

Select the range, and then select the style name from the Style box in the Standard toolbar.

SHORTCUTS

Press ⌘–Shift-L to activate the Style box.

To Create a Style by Definition

1. Choose Format ➤ Style. The Style dialog box initially contains a Style Name box that shows the name of the current style, a Description box that lists the formatting attributes belonging to the current style, and a column of command buttons.

2. In the Style Name box, enter a name for the style you are about to define. Then click the Define button.

3. In the Style Includes group, select the format categories that you want to include in this new style. An X appears in the check box next to each included category.

4. Click one of the six format category buttons in the Change group: Number, Font, Alignment, Border, Patterns, or Protection. The corresponding dialog box appears on the screen. Select the formatting attributes you want to include in the style, and click OK. The Style dialog box remains on the screen.

5. Repeat step 4 for all the formatting categories you want to include in the Style. Then click OK.

NOTES

By selecting a combination of categories in the Style Includes group, you define the exact set of formats that the style will affect. Categories that are not checked will not be changed when you apply the style to a range. For example, suppose you uncheck the Number category for a particular style definition; when you apply that style to a worksheet range, the current number format in the range will remain as it is.

To delete a style definition, select the style name in the Style dialog box, and click Define to expand the dialog box. Then click the Delete button. You cannot delete the Normal style, although you can change the combination of formats that it represents.

To Change the Normal Style for a Document

In the Style dialog box, select the Normal style; then follow the steps (outlined earlier in this entry) for defining the format attributes of a style. Click OK. Excel applies the new Normal style to all unformatted cells.

To Copy Style Definitions from One Document to Another

1. Open both documents, and activate the document to which you want to copy styles.

2. Choose Format ➤ Style. Click the Define button to expand the Style dialog box, and then click Merge.

3. In the Merge Styles dialog box, select the name of the document from which you want to copy styles. Click OK.

4. Click the Close button on the Style dialog box.

NOTES

After the Merge Styles operation, the Styles box for the destination document contains all the style names from the source document.

SEE ALSO

Alignment, AutoFormat, Borders, Copying Formats, Custom Number Formats, Fonts, Formatting Worksheet Cells, Number Formats, Patterns, Point Size, Protecting Cells, Template.

Summation

Summation is one of the most common arithmetic operations in a worksheet. The SUM function calculates the sum of all the values in a range or list of ranges. Because you frequently need to find the total of all the values in a row or column, Excel supplies a special AutoSum tool that automatically enters a SUM function in the cell beneath a column of numbers or to the right of a row of numbers. The AutoSum tool is on the Standard toolbar.

To Use the AutoSum Tool

1. Select the cell just beneath a column of numbers, or just to the right of a row of numbers.

2. Click the AutoSum tool. Excel enters a SUM function into the formula bar. The function's argument is the numeric range just above or just to the left of the current cell.

3. If necessary, adjust the argument of the SUM function, either by pointing to a new range on the worksheet, or by editing the reference directly in the formula bar.

4. Press Enter to enter the function into the selected cell.

SHORTCUTS

Select a cell beneath or to the right of a range of numbers, and double-click the AutoSum tool. Excel determines an appropriate range argument for the SUM function, and enters the function into the current cell.

NOTES

To enter totals for several columns or rows of a table, select the row immediately beneath the table or the column just to the right of the table, and double-click the AutoSum tool.

EXAMPLE

The following illustration shows a monthly expense worksheet:

	A	B	C	D	E
1		January	February	March	
2	Rent	$550.00	$550.00	$550.00	$1,650.00
3	Telephone	$68.23	$98.12	$47.81	$214.16
4	Utilities	$105.23	$112.34	$78.31	$295.88
5	Supplies	$89.32	$119.34	$69.45	$278.11
6	Postage	$265.37	$123.44	$97.33	$486.14
7	Repairs	$68.43	$543.23	$78.33	$689.99
8		$1,146.58	$1,546.47	$921.23	$3,614.28
9					

To enter the monthly totals into row 8 and the expense category totals into column E of this worksheet, follow these steps:

1. Select B8:E8 and double-click the AutoSum tool.

2. Select E2:E8 and double-click the AutoSum tool again.

SEE ALSO

AutoFill, Formula Bar, Formulas SnapGuide, Functions SnapGuide, Mathematical Functions.

Template

A template is a model document that you design for the convenience of opening other new documents. In a template you can strore formats and styles, along with text, numbers, and formula entries. When you open a new document based on a template, Excel copies all the formats and other contents of the template to the new document. You can create templates from worksheets, macro sheets, charts, and workbooks.

To Create a Template

1. Create a document that contains all the formats, styles, and entries that you want to save in the template.

2. Choose File ➤ Save As. Enter a name for the template file in the Save as box, and optionally select a folder for storing the file.

3. Click the Options button. In the File Format list, select Template. Then click OK.

4. Click Save to save the template. Then choose File ➤ Close to close the template file.

NOTES

For maximum convenience, you can save a template file in the Excel Startup Folder. (This folder is located in the Preferences folder, which in turn is stored in the System Folder on the Macintosh hard disk.) When you do so, Excel adds your template's name to the list of document types in the File ➤ New dialog box.

A template can also contain graphic objects. In a chart template, you can save any general elements of a chart, including formats, attached and unattached text, arrows, a legend, and a chart type. Excel does not save a SERIES formula in a chart template; rather, the chart itself is created when you select a range of worksheet data and open a new chart document based on the template.

To Open a New Document Based on a Template

If you have stored the template file in the Excel Startup Folder, choose File ➤ New, select the template name in the New list, and click OK.

If the template file is stored elsewhere, choose File ➤ Open, select or enter the name of the template file, and click Open.

NOTES

You can open multiple new documents based on the same template. Excel gives each new document a temporary name. For example, suppose your template file is named Invoice. The documents you open from this template will be named Invoice1, Invoice2, Invoice3, and so on.

To open a template file for editing, choose File ➤ Open, select the template file name, and hold down the Shift key while you click Open. In this case, Excel opens the template file itself, not a new document based on the template. You can make changes to the template, and then choose File ➤ Save to save the changes.

SEE ALSO

Charting SnapGuide, Formatting Worksheet Cells, Folders, Formulas SnapGuide, Graphic Objects, Macros SnapGuide, Styles, Workbooks.

Text Box

A text box is an object that you can use for displaying a block of text at any location within a worksheet or macro sheet. Like other graphic objects, a text box can be moved and resized to meet the requirements of a particular document. You can apply patterns to the interior and border of a text box, and you can apply fonts, styles, and point sizes selectively to the text within the box. (You can also assign a macro to a text box in a worksheet. See GRAPHIC OBJECTS for details.) In a chart window, an item similar to a text box is known as unattached text.

To Add a Text Box to a Worksheet or Macro Sheet

1. Activate the document in which you want to add the text box. Open the Utility toolbar if it is not already displayed.

2. Click the Text Box tool in the Utility toolbar. When you now point to the active document, the mouse pointer appears in a cross-hair shape.

3. Hold down the mouse button and drag the mouse over the area where you want to display the text box. Release

the mouse button to complete the box. Excel activates the box and displays a flashing insertion point at the upper-left corner.

4. Type the text that you want to display inside the box. Then click elsewhere on the active document to deselect the box.

NOTES

The Text Box tool also appears in the Drawing and Chart toolbars.

To move a text box to a new location, drag its border with the mouse. To change the size and shape of the text box, click the object's border, then drag any one of the sizing handles displayed around the perimeter of the box.

To edit the contents of a text box, click the box once to select the object and then click inside the box to place the insertion point at any location in the text.

To change the border style or fill pattern of a text box, double-click the object's border to view the Patterns dialog box (or choose Format ➤ Patterns), and select options from the Border and Fill groups. Other object-related commands also apply to text boxes, including Format ➤ Object Properties and Macro ➤ Assign to Object. See GRAPHIC OBJECTS for details.

If a macro is assigned to a text box, the mouse pointer appears as a pointing hand when positioned over the object. To run the macro, click the object. To select the object, hold down the ⌘ key while you click.

You can use a text box along with an arrow object to draw attention to a particular entry in a worksheet. The Arrow tool is in the Drawing toolbar. See GRAPHIC OBJECTS for an example.

To delete a text box from a document, select the object and choose Edit ➤ Clear or press the Del key.

To Change the Alignment or Orientation of Text in a Text Box

1. Select the box and choose Format ➤ Text.

2. Select an option in the Horizontal alignment group. Text can be left-aligned, centered, right-aligned, or justified horizontally.

3. Select an option in the Vertical alignment group. Text can be top-aligned, centered, bottom-aligned, or justified vertically.

4. Select an option in the Orientation group. You can display text horizontally or vertically inside the text box.

5. Click OK to apply the new alignment and orientation options.

SHORTCUTS

Select the text box and click the Left Align, Center Align, or Right Align tool on the Standard toolbar.

NOTES

If you select a vertical orientation for the text in a text box, Excel temporarily switches to the default horizontal orientation whenever

you edit the contents of the box. The vertical orientation is res-
tored when you deselect the box.

To Change the Font, Style,
or Size of Text in a Text Box

I. Select the entire text box, or select only the portion of the
text that you want to reformat.

2. Choose Format ➤ Font. Make selections in the Font, Size,
and Style boxes, and click OK.

SHORTCUTS

Select the text box or a portion of the text, and click any of the formatting tools on the Standard or Formatting toolbars; for example,
click the Bold, Italic, Increase Font Size, Decrease Font Size, or Underline tool. In the Formatting toolbar, you can also select a font
name from the Font box, or a point size from the Size box.

NOTES

You can apply different text formatting options to selections of
text within the text box. For example, you can display more than
one font or point size within a box, and you can apply bold, italics,
and underlining to selected words within the box.

The Font dialog box also has a Color list from which you can
select colors for the text. You can display text in multiple colors
within a text box.

To Add Unattached Text to a Chart

Activate the chart window, and click the Text Box tool on the
Chart toolbar. Excel initially displays the word "Text" as the contents of the new unattached text item. While the item is

selected, type a text entry into the formula bar and then press Enter to replace the unattached text.

SHORTCUTS

Press Esc to deselect any chart item, and simply begin typing the unattached text.

NOTES

Unattached text in a chart window has many of the same characteristics of a text box in a worksheet. You can move and resize the unattached text by dragging it with the mouse. Choose Format ➤ Font and Format ➤ Text to change the appearance of the text, as described in earlier sections of this entry. By default an unattached text item in a chart window has no border. Choose Format ➤ Patterns to apply a border and fill pattern.

You cannot assign a macro to unattached text in a chart window. (However, you can assign a macro to an embedded chart in a worksheet.)

SEE ALSO

Attached Text, Charting SnapGuide, Colors, Graphic Objects, Macros SnapGuide, Patterns.

Text Functions

Excel has a collection of over twenty text functions that perform various operations on text entries in a worksheet or other document. These functions appear most commonly in macros that perform special text processing operations, but they can also be used directly in worksheets.

To Enter a Text Function into a Worksheet

1. Select the cell or range where you want to enter the function.

2. Choose Formula ➤ Paste Function, and select the Text category. The Paste Function box shows the entire list of text functions.

3. Select the name of a function and click OK.

4. Enter arguments for the function in the active formula bar, and press Enter.

SHORTCUTS

From the keyboard, enter an equal sign followed by the function's name, and then press Control-A to display names for the function's arguments in the formula bar.

NOTES

Here is a grouped list of the functions available in this category:

▲ Alphabetic-case conversion functions (LOWER, PROPER, UPPER).

▲ ANSI code conversion functions (CHAR, CODE).

▲ Character removal functions (CLEAN, TRIM).

▲ Comparison function (EXACT).

▲ Length function (LEN).

▲ Numeric and text conversion functions (DOLLAR, FIXED, T, TEXT, VALUE).

▲ Repetition function (REPT).

▲ Replacement functions (REPLACE, SUBSTITUTE).

▲ Search functions (FIND, SEARCH)

▲ Substring functions (LEFT, MID, RIGHT).

TEXT FUNCTIONS

EXAMPLE

The following worksheet illustrates the use of a selection of text functions. Each of the functions displayed in column A of this worksheet uses the text entry in cell A1 as an argument. Column B shows the result of each function:

	A	B
1	text functions in Microsoft Excel	
2		
3	Function	Result
4		
5	= FIND("Microsoft",$A$1)	19
6	= SEARCH("microsoft",$A$1)	19
7		
8	= LEFT($A$1,15)	text functions
9	= MID($A$1,19,9)	Microsoft
10	= RIGHT($A$1, 15)	Microsoft Excel
11		
12	= LEN($A$1)	33
13		
14	= LOWER($A$1)	text functions in microsoft excel
15	= PROPER($A$1)	Text Functions In Microsoft Excel
16	= UPPER($A$1)	TEXT FUNCTIONS IN MICROSOFT EXCEL
17		
18	= REPLACE($A$1,6,10,"operations ")	text operations in Microsoft Excel
19	= SUBSTITUTE($A$1,"functions","operations")	text operations in Microsoft Excel
20		
21	= REPT(RIGHT($A$1,5),5)	ExcelExcelExcelExcelExcel
22		

Here are brief explanations of the functions illustrated in this worksheet:

▲ The FIND function performs a case-sensitive search for one text value within another. If the search is successful, FIND returns an integer representing the position where the text was found. The SEARCH function performs a search without regard for alphabetic case.

▲ The LEFT, MID, and RIGHT functions return substrings from the beginning, interior, or end of a text entry.

▲ The LEN function gives the length of a text entry in characters.

▲ The LOWER, PROPER, and UPPER functions revise the alphabetic case of a text entry. PROPER capitalizes the first letter of each word in the text.

▲ The REPLACE and SUBSTITUTE functions both replace a portion of a text entry with another text value. REPLACE operates on the substring at a specified position, whereas SUBSTITUTE searches for the substring that is to be replaced.

▲ The REPT function returns an entry consisting of repeated text.

SEE ALSO

Functions SnapGuide, Text Operations.

Text Operations

The process of combining two or more text values is known as concatenation. In Excel, the ampersand character (&) represents this text operation.

To Concatenate Two or More Text Values

Use the & operator in a formula to join the text values and display the result in a cell.

EXAMPLE

The following two formulas use concatenation to produce messages giving the date and the time:

```
="Today is "&TEXT(TODAY(),"ddd, mmm dd, yyyy")&"."
="The time is "&TEXT(NOW(),"hh:mm AM/PM")&"."
```

If you enter these formulas into cells in a worksheet, the result will be text entries such as the following:

Today is Sat, Jun 27, 1992.
The time is 11:26 AM.

SEE ALSO

Macros SnapGuide, Text Functions.

Time Entries

You can enter time values into worksheet cells in any of several time formats that Excel recognizes. In response, Excel applies a time format to the cell, but stores the time itself as a special type of numeric value known as a serial number. The serial number format allows you to perform time arithmetic operations in a worksheet.

To Enter a Time into a Worksheet Cell

Select the cell and type the time in a recognizable format.

EXAMPLES

Here are some examples of time entry formats that Excel recognizes:

    6:00

    6 AM

    6:00 AM

    6:00:00 AM

In response to any of these entries, Excel applies one of its built-in time formats to the cell—displaying the time as 6:00 or 6:00 AM or 6:00:00 AM. Excel stores the time internally as the serial number 0.25, which represents the fraction of the day that is over at 6:00 AM.

NOTES

A full serial number contains digits both before and after the decimal point. The integer portion before the decimal point represents the date, and the fractional value after the decimal point represents the time. For example, 32580.25 represents the date/time value March 14, 1993, 6:00 AM. See DATE ENTRIES for more information.

To Find the Difference between Two Time Entries

Enter a formula that subtracts one time from the other.

EXAMPLE

Suppose you have entered the following values in cells B1 and C1:

    B1   6:00 AM
    C1   8:24 AM

The following formula gives the difference between the two times:

    =C1–B1

Internally, Excel subtracts one entry's serial number from the other, resulting in the difference between the two times. In this case, 6:00 AM is represented by the serial value 0.25 and 8:24 AM is represented by 0.35. The difference between them is therefore 0.1.

In the following worksheet, time arithmetic formulas are used in column D to display the amount of time spent on a series of jobs:

	A	B	C	D
1			Time Sheet	
2			7/22/92	
3				
4	Job	Start	Finish	Time
5	1	6:00 AM	8:24 AM	2 hr. 24 min.
6	2	8:30 AM	9:45 AM	1 hr. 15 min.
7	3	10:00 AM	12:30 PM	2 hr. 30 min.
8	4	1:30 PM	3:15 PM	1 hr. 45 min.
9	5	3:30 PM	4:10 PM	0 hr. 40 min.
10	6	4:10 PM	5:45 PM	1 hr. 35 min.
11				

For example, the formula in cell D5 is =C5−B5. To display the result of this formula in an hr./min. format, the following custom number format has been applied to the range D5:D10:

h "hr." mm "min."

See CUSTOM NUMBER FORMATS for details.

NOTES

To include a time value in a formula, enclose the time in double quotation marks and use a time format that Excel recognizes. For example, the formula

="6:00 AM"+.5

adds half a day to the time 6:00 AM. The result is 0.75, the serial number equivalent of 6:00 PM.

To View the Serial Number for a Time Entry

1. Select the cell that contains the entry displayed in a time format.

2. Choose Format ➤ Number. The Number Format dialog box appears.

3. Select All in the Value Type box, and then select General in the Format Codes box. Click OK.

SHORTCUTS

Select the cell and press Control-Shift-~ to apply the General format, or Control-Shift-@ to apply a time format.

SEE ALSO

Copying Formats, Custom Number Formats, Date and Time Functions, Date Entries, Formatting Worksheet Data.

Toolbars

Excel has seven major built-in toolbars, each of which you can display or hide at any time. They are named the Standard, Formatting, Utility, Chart, Drawing, Microsoft Excel 3.0, and Macro toolbars. They provide dozens of different tools that you can use to streamline your activities in Excel. Initially, only the Standard toolbar appears on the screen, but the other toolbars are just a mouse-click away. In addition, Excel has a collection of extra tools that are not initially assigned to any toolbar. To use one of these tools, you can assign it to an existing toolbar, or you can create new toolbars of your own. Finally, there are over 30 "custom" tools to which you can assign your own macros.

To Display a Toolbar

Point to any toolbar with the mouse, and press ⌘-Option while you click the mouse button. On the resulting shortcut menu, select the toolbar you want to display. (Alternatively, choose Options ➤ Toolbars, select a toolbar from the Show Toolbars list, and click Show.)

 **NOTES**

Once a toolbar is displayed on the screen, you can move it to a new position or change its shape. Some of Excel's built-in toolbars appear initially as floating toolbars, and others are located in toolbar docks.

A floating toolbar is displayed as a window with its own title bar. To move a floating toolbar to a new place on the screen, drag its title bar with the mouse. To change its shape, position the mouse pointer over the window's size box, and then drag the window into a new shape. To hide a floating toolbar, click the close box at the upper-left corner of the toolbar window.

The toolbar docks are fixed locations at the top, bottom, left, or right sides of the desktop. Three built-in toolbars are docked by default: Standard, Chart, and Excel 3.0; the rest appear initially as floating toolbars. You can change a docked toolbar to a floating toolbar by dragging it away from the dock. Conversely, you can dock a floating toolbar by dragging it toward the top, bottom, or side of the desktop. To hide a docked toolbar, press ⌘-Option and click any toolbar, and select the name of the checked toolbar that you want to hide.

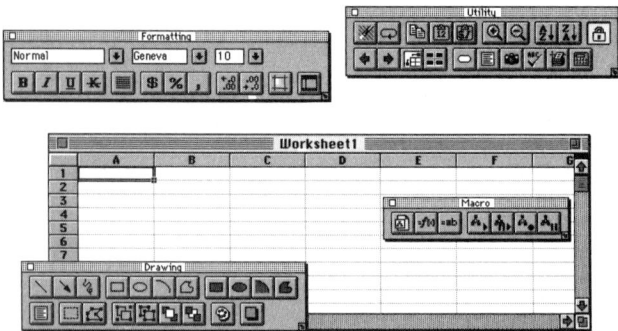

To Add Tools to a Toolbar

I. Display the toolbar to which you want to add one or more tools.

2. Press ⌘–Option and click any toolbar; then choose the Customize command from the resulting shortcut menu. (Alternatively, choose Options ➤ Toolbars and click the Customize button on the Toolbars dialog box.) The Customize dialog box displays a list of tool categories and a group of tools corresponding to the current category.

3. Select a name from the Categories list. Then drag a tool from the Tools group to the toolbar where you want to display the tool. Excel adds the tool to the toolbar.

4. Repeat step 3 for each tool that you want to display in a toolbar.

5. Click Close to close the Customize dialog box.

 **NOTES**

When you drag a tool to a toolbar, a copy of the tool remains in the Customize dialog box. Excel allows you to add a given tool to as many different toolbars as you like.

You can remove tools from a built-in toolbar. To do so, display the toolbar and then open the Customize dialog box. Drag any number of tools from the toolbar to the Customize dialog box, and then click Close. To restore a built-in toolbar to its default status, choose Options ➤ Toolbars, select the name of the toolbar you want to restore, and click the Reset button.

To Create a Custom Toolbar

1. Press ⌘–Option and click any toolbar, and then choose the Toolbars command from the resulting shortcut menu. (Alternatively, choose Options ➤ Toolbars.) The Toolbars dialog box appears on the screen.

2. In the Toolbar Name box, enter a new name for the custom toolbar you are about to create. Click the Add button. Excel creates and displays the new toolbar (as a floating toolbar), and also opens the Customize dialog box.

3. Select a tool category from the Categories list, and then drag a tool from the Tools group to the new custom toolbar.

4. Repeat step 3 for all the tools that you want to add to the custom toolbar.

5. Click the Close button to close the Customize dialog box.

NOTES

As you add tools to the new custom toolbar, Excel increases the size and modifies the shape of the toolbar. After you close the Customize dialog box, you can move and resize the custom toolbar, or you can place it in one of the toolbar docks.

To delete a custom toolbar from the set of available toolbars, choose Options ➤ Toolbars, select the name of the toolbar you want to delete, and click the Delete button. Excel displays a dialog box asking you to confirm the deletion. Click OK to delete, or Cancel to retain the toolbar.

To Assign a Macro to a Custom Tool

1. Develop the macro that you will assign to a custom tool. For maximum convenience, store the macro in the global macro sheet, Global Macros. (See MACRO RECORDING for details.)

2. Display the toolbar to which you want to add the custom tool. You can use one of Excel's built-in toolbars or a custom toolbar of your own.

3. Press ⌘-Option and click any toolbar, and then choose the Customize command from the shortcut menu.

4. In the Categories list, choose the Custom option. The Tools group displays the custom tools to which you can assign macros.

5. Drag one of the custom tools from the Customize dialog box to the toolbar where you want to display the tool. When you do so, Excel automatically displays the Assign

To Tool dialog box. This box lists the names of the macros available in all macro sheets that are currently open, including the hidden global macro sheet.

6. Select a macro from the Assign Macro box and click OK.

7. Click Close on the Customize dialog box.

NOTES

After you assign a macro to a custom tool, you can click the tool to run the macro.

SEE ALSO

Customizing Excel, Macro Recording, Shortcut Menus.

Transposing Ranges

You can use the Edit ➤ Paste Special command to transpose a range of worksheet data—copying rows of data to columns and columns to rows.

To Transpose a Range of Data

I. Select the entire range that you want to transpose, and choose Edit ➤ Copy. Excel displays a moving border around the range.

2. Select the cell at the upper-right corner of the location where you want to copy the transposed data.

3. Choose Edit ➤ Paste Special. In the Paste Special dialog box, click the Transpose option. An X appears in the corresponding check box.

4. Click OK.

 **NOTES**

If the data you are transposing contains formulas, Excel adjusts ranges in the formulas appropriately.

 **EXAMPLE**

The following worksheet shows an expense table in the range A1:D6, and a transposed copy of the same table in the range A10:F13. The Paste Special command was used to transpose the data.

	A	B	C	D	E	F
1		January	February	March		
2	Rent	$550.00	$550.00	$550.00		
3	Telephone	$68.23	$98.12	$47.81		
4	Utilities	$105.23	$112.34	$78.31		
5	Supplies	$89.32	$119.34	$69.45		
6	Postage	$265.37	$123.44	$97.33		
7						
8						
9						
10		Rent	Telephone	Utilities	Supplies	Postage
11	January	$550.00	$68.23	$105.23	$89.32	$265.37
12	February	$550.00	$98.12	$112.34	$119.34	$123.44
13	March	$550.00	$47.81	$78.31	$69.45	$97.33
14						

 **SEE ALSO**

Charting SnapGuide, Copying Data.

Undo

The Edit ➤ Undo command undoes the effect of your most recent action. Undo is available for many—but not all—operations in Excel.

To Undo the Most Recent Action

Choose Edit ➤ Undo immediately after the action that you want to reverse.

SHORTCUTS

Press ⌘-Z or F1. Alternatively, click the Undo tool on the Utility toolbar.

NOTES

In the Edit menu, the Undo command identifies the action that will be reversed. For example, the command might be displayed as Undo Font or Undo Delete. If the command is dimmed or displayed as Can't Undo, the undo feature is not available for your last action.

After you choose Edit ➤ Undo, the first command in the Edit menu changes to Redo. Choose this command if you want to restore the effect of the action that you have just undone.

SEE ALSO

Repeating Commands.

Views

The View Manager is an add-in macro that you can use to define and save different views of a worksheet. A view consists of a variety of settings that affect the information you see on the screen and the format of the document you send to the printer. These include column width and row height, settings you select in the Options ➤ Display and File ➤ Page Setup commands, and a variety of window settings—size, position, selection, panes, and frozen titles. You use the Window ➤ View command both to create views and to switch to a particular view you have created.

The View Manager works along with the Scenario Manager (Formula ➤ Scenario Manager) and the Report Manager (File ➤ Print Report) to give you detailed control over the content and appear-ance of reports you create from a worksheet. See REPORTS and SCENARIOS for further information.

To Create Views of a Worksheet

I. Activate the worksheet on which you want to create the views, and prepare the worksheet in any combination of the following ways:

 ▲ Select the portion of the worksheet that you want to see in the view, and adjust column widths and row heights as needed.

 ▲ Adjust the size and position of the worksheet window on the screen.

 ▲ Add panes and frozen titles if appropriate.

 ▲ Select display settings from the Options ➤ Display command.

 ▲ Select print settings from the File ➤ Page Setup command.

2. Choose Window ➤ View. The Views dialog box contains a list box for displaying the names of defined views, and a column of command buttons.

3. Click the Add button. The Add View dialog box appears on the screen. Enter a name for the current view in the Name box, and select any combination of the View Includes op-tions. Then Click OK.

4. Repeat steps 1 to 3 for any additional views you want to create for the active worksheet.

NOTES

When you next save your worksheet, the views you have defined are saved with it.

To Show a View of a Worksheet

1. Activate a worksheet on which you have defined views, and choose Window ➤ View.

2. In the Views dialog box, select a name from the list of views, and click Show.

NOTES

If your view includes specific print settings, you can now print the worksheet without having to choose the File ➤ Page Setup command.

To delete a view from the view list, choose Window ➤ View, select the name of the view you want to delete, and click the Delete button. Excel deletes the view immediately, without asking for confirmation. (You cannot undo this deletion.)

SEE ALSO

Column Widths, Page Setup, Panes, Reports, Row Heights, Scenarios, Window Operations.

*W*indow Operations

You can use familiar mouse techniques to adjust the size and position of document windows within Excel. In addition, several commands in the Window menu and the Options menu give you control over the appearance and organization of windows.

To Change the Size and Position of a Document Window

Drag the window's size box (at the lower-right corner of the border) to change the size and shape of the window. Drag the title bar to move the window to a new position on the screen. Click the zoom box (upper-right corner) to expand a window's size to the entire available screen space. Click the zoom box again to restore the window's previous size and position.

To Activate the Window for an Open Document

Pull down the Window menu and choose the name of the document you want to activate.

To Open Multiple Windows for Viewing the Active Document

Choose Window ➤ New Window.

NOTES

Multiple windows allow you to view different parts of a document at one time. When you open more than one window for a document, the title bar of each window displays the document's name, followed by a colon and the window number—for example, Worksheet1:1 and Worksheet1:2.

The New Window command is not available for a chart window.

To Rearrange Two or More Open Windows

1. Choose Window ➤ Arrange.

2. Click one of the options in the Arrange group: Tiled, Horizontal, Vertical, or None.

3. If you want to arrange only the multiple windows of the active document, click the Windows of Active Document option. An X appears in the corresponding check box.

4. Click OK.

NOTES

The Tiled, Horizontal, and Vertical arrangement options allow you to view multiple documents side-by-side or one above another.

The Window menu has several other commands that affect the appearance of windows. These include Hide and Unhide for displaying or hiding windows, Split and Freeze Panes for dividing windows into panes, and Zoom for changing the viewing scale of windows. See HIDING, PANES, and ZOOMING for details.

To Close a Window

Activate the window and choose File ➤ Close, press ⌘-W or click the window's close box. If you have made changes in the document since the last save, Excel asks you if you want to save the document.

To Change the Display Options of an Active Sheet

Choose Options ➤ Display and select the settings that you want to apply to the active worksheet:

▲ The Formulas option determines whether the sheet displays formulas or their resulting values. Worksheets display values by default, but macro sheets display formulas by default.

▲ The Gridlines and Row & Column Headings options are for displaying or hiding a sheet's gridlines and headings. Both of these settings are checked by default. In addition, you can select a color for gridlines and headings by pulling down the Gridline & Heading Color list.

▲ The Zero Values setting specifies whether Excel displays a zero or a blank cell when an entry is equal to zero.

▲ The Outline Symbols setting is for switching the display of outlining symbols on or off in a worksheet that contains an outline.

▲ The Automatic Page Breaks option allows you to display or hide the page breaks that Excel determines for printing your document.

▲ The three option buttons in the Objects group determine how Excel displays graphic objects in the active worksheet. The default is Show All, but you can also choose to represent embedded objects with blank placeholders (Show Placeholders), or to hide all objects (Hide All).

 **SHORTCUTS**

Press ⌘-' or Control-' (left quotation mark) to toggle between formula-display and value-display on the active worksheet or macro sheet.

 **NOTES**

You can use the Window ➤ View command to define and save different sets of Options ➤ Display selections as views. You assign a name to each view that you define. Then, when you want to look at your worksheet in a different way, you can simply choose Window ➤ View and select a view. See VIEWS for details.

 **SEE ALSO**

Colors, Graphic Objects, Hiding, Opening Files, Outlines, Panes, Views, Zooming.

Workbooks

A workbook is a file in which you store a group of related worksheets, charts, and macro sheets. You can use a workbook effectively to manage information that is located in more than one document. When you open a workbook, you have access to all the documents that the worksheet contains.

Documents in a workbook can be bound or unbound. A bound document is stored as part of the workbook file. An unbound document is stored in its own separate file, and can be opened independently or stored in more than one workbook. Your choice between the bound and unbound options will depend on the way you plan to use the documents in your workbook.

To Create a Workbook and Add Documents

1. Choose File ➤ New. In the New dialog box, select Workbook and click OK. Excel opens a new workbook window with a temporary name like "Workbook1." What you see initially is called the Workbook Contents window; this is where Excel will list the documents that you add to the workbook. At the lower-left corner of the window are three command buttons labeled Add, Remove, and Options. At the lower-right corner are three paging icons.

2. Click the Add button. The Add To Workbook dialog box appears on the screen.

3. Perform any of the following steps to add a document to the workbook:

   ▲ In the Select Documents to Add list, highlight the name of an open document and click Add to move the document into the workbook.

   ▲ Click the New button, select a document type from the New dialog box, and click OK. Excel creates the new document and adds it to the workbook.

   ▲ Click the Open button to open a document from disk and add it to the workbook. Select a file from the Open dialog box and click Open.

4. Repeat step 3 for each document you want to add to the workbook. Then click Close to close the Add To Workbook dialog box. The Workbook Contents window displays a list of all the documents you have added. All documents are initially bound to the workbook file.

5. If you want to change the status of a document from bound to unbound, select the document's name in the Workbook Contents window, and then click the Options button. In the Document Options dialog box, click the Separate file (Unbound) option, and then click OK.

6. Repeat step 5 for each document whose bound/unbound status you want to change.

7. Choose File ➤ Save Workbook. In the resulting dialog box, enter a file name for the workbook, and click Save. Excel also displays a dialog box for saving any new unbound documents you have added to the workbook. Enter a file name for each such document and click Save.

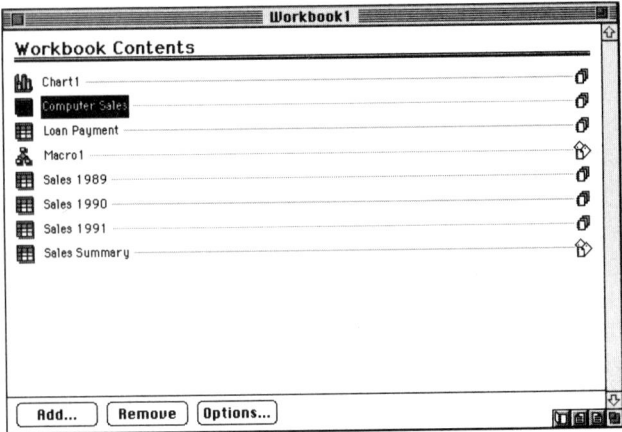

```
┌──────────────────── Workbook1 ────────────────────┐
│ Workbook Contents                                   │
│  Chart1                                         ⟠   │
│  Computer Sales                                 ⟠   │
│  Loan Payment                                   ⟠   │
│  Macro1                                         ⟠   │
│  Sales 1989                                     ⟠   │
│  Sales 1990                                     ⟠   │
│  Sales 1991                                     ⟠   │
│  Sales Summary                                  ⟠   │
│                                                     │
│  [ Add... ]  [ Remove ]  [ Options... ]             │
└─────────────────────────────────────────────────────┘
```

SHORTCUTS

Click the New Workbook tool to open a new workbook. (This tool is not initially part of any toolbar; see TOOLBARS for instructions on adding it to a toolbar.) To change the status of a document in the workbook, click the document's bound/unbound icon displayed at the right side of the Workbook Contents window. Alternatively, press ⌘-Shift-O to view the Document Options dialog box. Press ⌘-Shift-A to view the Add To Workbook dialog box.

NOTES

The Workbook Contents window is the central point from which you access the documents stored in the workbook. To activate and view a document, double-click its name in the Workbook Contents list. To return to the Workbook Contents window, click the first of the three paging icons located at the lower-right corner of the workbook window. To page backward or forward to other documents, click the second or third paging icon.

You can also activate a document in the workbook by holding down ⌘-Option and clicking any of the three paging icons. The resulting shortcut menu contains a list of all the documents stored in the workbook. Select a name to activate the document. The shortcut menu also contains a New command for opening the New dialog box and a Group Edit command for initiating a group editing session of the documents in the workbook. See GROUP EDIT-ING for details.

To Remove a Document from a Workbook

Select the document's name in the Workbook Contents window, and click the Remove button. The document remains open but moves out of the workbook to a separate window of its own.

SHORTCUTS

Press ⌘-Shift-R to remove the current document from the Worksheet Contents list. Alternatively, use the mouse to drag the document's name and icon out of the Workbook Contents window.

NOTES

You can also use the dragging technique to drag a document from the Workbook Contents window of one open workbook to another.

SEE ALSO

Group Editing, Opening Files, Window Operations.

*W*rapping Text

When you enter a long text value into a worksheet cell, Excel initially displays the entry across adjacent cells to the right. You can use the wrapping option to display the entire text entry in a single cell.

To Wrap a Long Text Entry in a Cell

1. Select the cell that contains the long text entry.

2. Optionally, adjust the column to the width you want for the wrapped text.

3. Choose Format ➤ Alignment. In the Alignment dialog box, click the Wrap Text option. An X appears in the corresponding check box.

4. Click OK to wrap the text.

NOTES

Excel adjusts the height of the row in order to display the entire entry of wrapped text.

EXAMPLE

The following two worksheets show a long text entry before and
after the wrapping option has been applied:

	A	B	C	D	E	F	G
1							
2		The following information is confidential; please keep it to yourself.					
3							

	A	B	C
1			
2		The following information is confidential; please keep it to yourself.	
3			

SEE ALSO

Alignment.

Zooming

The Window ➤ Zoom command allows you to enlarge or reduce
the viewing scale of a worksheet window.

To Change the Scale of a Worksheet

1. Activate the worksheet and choose Window ➤ Zoom. The
   Zoom dialog box contains a group of Magnification option
   buttons.

2. Click one of the preset magnification or reduction options.
   Alternatively, click the Custom option, and enter a value
   from 10 to 400 in the % text box.

3. Click OK to apply the zoom scale.

SHORTCUTS

Click the Zoom In or Zoom Out tool on the Utility toolbar. You can click these tools repeatedly to step through the available zoom scales. Excel beeps when you have reached the largest or smallest scale.

NOTES

The Zoom command affects only the active worksheet or macro sheet. Other open documents retain their current scale setting.

Zoom is not available for an active chart window. However, you can zoom a worksheet that contains an embedded chart; in this case, the chart is displayed at the same scale setting as the worksheet.

To Find the Best Scale for Displaying a Range Selection

1. Activate the worksheet and select the range that you want to display.

2. Choose Window ➤ Zoom. In the Magnification group, click the Fit Selection option, then click OK.

NOTES

When you select the Fit Selection option, Excel calculates the best scale for displaying the selection. For a small range of cells, this may mean increasing the scale; for a large range, Excel will reduce the scale.

SEE ALSO

Page Setup, Window Operations.

INDEX

$ (dollar sign), for reference
    designation, 236–237
& (ampersand)
    in label, 71
    for text concatenation, 287
* (asterisk) wildcard character
    in comparison criteria, 84
    in Consolidate dialog box, 51
    in searches, 70, 118, 242
? (question mark) icon, 142
? (question mark) wildcard
    character
    in comparison criteria, 84
    in Consolidate dialog box, 51
    in searches, 70, 118, 242
    ⌘ key, designating character
    for, 71

a

A1 reference style, 236–237
Absolute Record (Macro menu),
    166
absolute references, 56, 57–58,
    236, 238
absolute value function, 177
active documents and color
    palette changes, 46

active windows, 231, 300
add-in macros, 1–5, 245
    in Analysis ToolPak, 10
    installing in startup list, 3–4
    library of, 164–165
    Macro Debugger, 164
    opening, 2, 3
    removing from startup list, 4
    Solver as, 263
    View Manager as, 297–299
Add-ins (Options menu), 1, 3, 174
addition, 13–14
alignment, 5–10
    of attached text, 19
    of buttons, 9
    copying, 55
    default settings for, 6
    in text box, 9, 282
    of titles, 10
Alignment (Format menu), 5,
    121, 123
alphabetic-case conversion
    functions, 285
ampersand (&)
    in label, 71
    for text concatenation, 287
Analysis ToolPak, 3, 10–13, 108
Analysis Tools (Options
    menu), 10

installing, macros in startup
list, 3–4
integers
functions, 178
series entries as, 260
interest, functions to calculate,
116
internal rate of return functions,
116
inverse trigonometric functions,
178
ISNUMBER function, 148
italic fonts, 119, 120, 283
Item menu, 99
➤ Edit Box, 71
➤ Text, 71
iteration, 151–153, 267

j

justification, of text within
cell, 7
Justify (Format menu), 7

k

keys, for sorting, 268–269

l

labels
for charts, 18, 27, 30
for consolidation
categories, 49

for data form fields, 71
landscape icon, 205
LEFT function, 286
left margins, 206
legends for charts, 28, 38
LEN function, 286
length function, 285
library of macros, 4, 164–165
Light Shading tool, 261
Limits report, from Solver, 268
linear formulas, series from, 256
linear regression, 12, 273
linear series, 257, 258
lines, multiple
in cell, 123
in headers or footers, 142
links
dynamic, 101–108
between worksheet data and
chart, 38
between worksheets,
153–156
Links (File menu), 104–105
list boxes, in custom dialog
box, 99
lists, function to read value
from, 160
loan payment calculation
functions, 116
Lock Cell tool (Utility toolbar),
228
"Locked cells cannot be
changed" message, 229
Locked option (Cell Protection
dialog box), 227
locking cells, 228–229
logical functions, 156–159
lookup functions, 159–161

point size, 215–217
polygons, drawing, 134
portrait icon, 205
position, consolidating by, 48, 49
precedent cell, 125
Preferences Folder, 2
Preferred Chart tool, 35
present value functions, 116
previewing, 217–219
previous command, repeating, 239
Previous tool (Print Preview), 217
Print (File menu), 34, 146, 191, 192, 224
print area, deleting settings, 226
Print Preview (File menu), 139, 217
Print Preview tool, 219
Print Report (File menu), 243
print titles, deleting settings, 226
Print Topic (File menu), 143
printer setup, 219
printing
  charts, 206, 220–223
  gridlines, 206
  grouped document, 139
  headings, 206
  help topics, 143
  Info window, 146
  notes, 190–192
  preview of, 217–219
  reports, 243–244
  scenarios, 252
  settings in view, 299
  worksheets, 224–227

worksheets without notes, 192
products functions, 50, 178
Promote tool (Utility toolbar), 203
PROPER function, 286
properties
  of graphic objects, 136
  of multiple objects, 135
Protect Document (Options menu), 227, 228, 229, 230
protecting cells, 227–229
protecting documents, 230–232
Protection Password box, 211
publisher, source document as, 102
publisher-subscriber links, 101
  creating, 106

q

quarter labels, creating series, 21
queries, on external databases, 233–234
Query Assistant (Data menu), 234
question mark (?) wildcard character
  in comparison criteria, 84
  in Consolidate dialog box, 51
  in searches, 70, 118, 242
Quit (File menu), 110
quotients functions, 178

macros in Global Macros
sheet, 174
scenario definitions, 251
worksheets, 244
Scale to Fit Page (Chart Size),
220, 221
Scenario Manager (Formula
menu), 3, 243, 249
scenarios, 249–254
scientific notation, 194
scroll bars, displaying or
hiding, 110
scrolling, and panes, 208
Search button (Help), 143
searches
case sensitivity in, 241
functions, 285, 286
for records in data form,
70–71
SECOND() function, 93
security functions, 116
Select Chart (Chart menu), 35
Select Dialog (Edit menu), 72,
100
Select Special (Formula menu),
17, 53, 125–126, 204
Select Visible Cells tool (Utility
toolbar), 203
selecting
cells, 255, 262
columns, 256, 262
data markers, 30
embedded objects, 197
entire worksheets, 256
graphic objects, 134, 135
ranges, 255–256, 262
records from database, 81
rows, 256, 262
series in charts, 30

selection criteria
for finding records, 88
for record deletion, 90–91
for record extraction, 89
selection handles, 30
Sensitivity report, from Solver,
268
serial numbers, 93–96, 288, 289
default starting date for, 94
viewing, 95–96, 290–291
series, 256–260
in charts, 30, 31–33
creating, 20–21
Series (Data menu), 256, 257
SERIES formulas, 31–32, 155,
279
SERIES function, 32, 33
Set Criteria (Data menu), 81,
83, 84, 87, 234
Set Database (Data menu), 59,
67, 80, 87, 112, 233
Set Extract (Data menu), 81, 89,
234
Set Page Break (Options menu),
226
Set Print Area (Options menu),
225
Set Print Titles (Options area),
225
Set Recorder (Macro menu), 165
Set Table Creation Options
button, 62
shading, 43, 213, 260–261
shadow style, 119
sharing data. See also Object linking and embedding
on networks, 233
with worksheet links, 153
shortcut keys, for macros, 165

INDEX

top margins, 206
totals, 201, 277–278
and outline levels, 201
transparencies, 205
transposing, ranges, 295–296
Treasury bill functions, 116
trend functions, 273
trend series, 257, 259–260
trial solutions, from Solver, 267
trigonometric functions, 178
TRUE logical operations, 158
t-Test tool, 12
two-input data table, 74, 76–78

U

unattached text, adding to
chart, 283–285
unbound documents, 303, 304
underlined style, 119, 120
in text box, 283
undisplayed fields, 68
undo, 296–297
deleting, 69–70, 97
sorts, 269
Undo (Edit menu), 40,
296–297
Undo Clear (Edit menu), 193
Undo Delete (Edit menu), 70, 97
Undo Insert (Edit menu), 150
Undo Parse (Edit menu), 210
Undo Paste (Edit menu), 52
Undo Sort (Edit menu), 269
Unhide (Window menu), 3,
144, 175
unhiding
columns or row, 145

macro sheets, 3
Unprotect Document (Chart
menu), 232
Unprotect Document (Options
menu), 229, 232
updating
automatic. *See also* Dynamic
Data Exchange
files, 248
manual, 104–105
UPPER function, 286
Use Full Page (Chart Size), 220,
221
Utility toolbar, 132–133,
203–204, 291
Button tool, 137
Lock Cell tool, 228
Text Box tool, 280

V

#VALUE!, 86
Value Type (Number Format
dialog box), 63
values
converting formulas to
fixed, 58
entering, 122
formatting, 193–196
as function argument, 129
pasting without format, 55
reading from worksheet, 160
replacing formula with, 125
VAR function, 50
variance, 86, 273
VARP function, 50

reading value from, 160
replacing data, 240–242
saving, 244, 247
saving as graphic, 41
scale of, 307
scenarios in, 249–252
selecting entire, 256
sorting data range on, 268
styles for, 274
text box in, 280
views of, 298
Workspace (Options menu),
    110, 146, 237
wrapping text, 246, 306–307

Y

y-axis, text for, 18, 38
YEAR( ) function, 93
YEARFRAC( ) function, 92

Z

zero values, display of, 301
Zoom (Window menu), 307
Zoom tool (Print Preview), 217
zooming, 307–309
z-Test tool, 12

X

x-axis, labels for, 18, 30, 38

Utility Toolbar

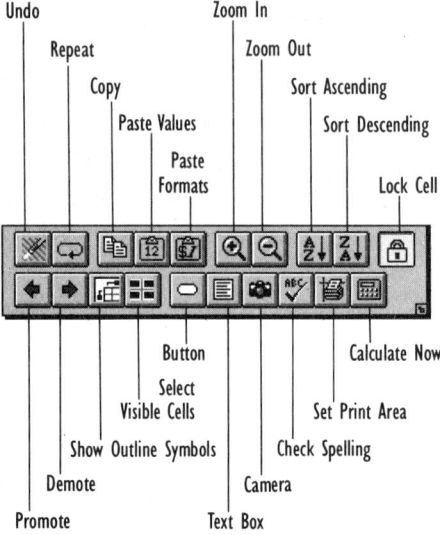

Undo

Repeat

Copy

Paste Values

Paste Formats

Zoom In

Zoom Out

Sort Ascending

Sort Descending

Lock Cell

Button

Select Visible Cells

Show Outline Symbols

Demote

Promote

Calculate Now

Set Print Area

Check Spelling

Camera

Text Box

Drawing Toolbar

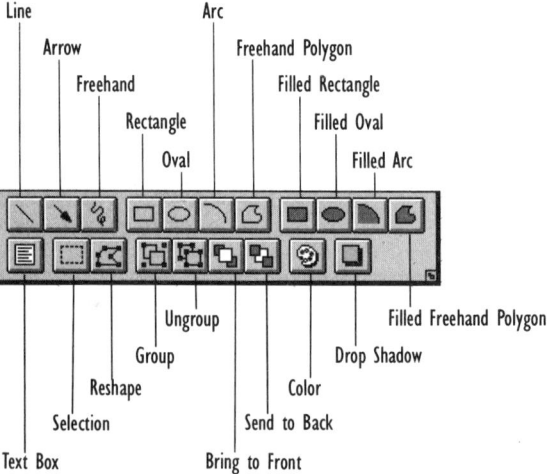

Line

Arrow

Freehand

Rectangle

Oval

Arc

Freehand Polygon

Filled Rectangle

Filled Oval

Filled Arc

Ungroup

Group

Reshape

Selection

Text Box

Filled Freehand Polygon

Drop Shadow

Color

Send to Back

Bring to Front